from Jerusalem to Gaza

an Old Testament Theology

B. DONALD KEYSER &

H. WAYNE BALLARD

SMYTH&HELWYS

PUBLISHING, INCORPORATED • MACON, GEORGIA

Smyth & Helwys Publishing, Inc.
6316 Peake Road
Macon, Georgia 31210-3960
1-800-747-3016
©2002, 2015 by Smyth & Helwys Publishing
All rights reserved.

Library of Congress Cataloging-in-Publication Data

Keyser, B. Donald, 1922–.
    From Jerusalem to Gaza: an old testment theology
  by B. Donald Keyser and H. Wayne Ballard.
    p. cm.
    Includes bibliographical references and indexes.
    ISBN 978-1-57312-377-8 (pbk.)
    1. Bible. O.T.–Theology. 2. Bible. O.T.
    –Textbooks. I. Ballard, Harold Wayne, 1963–
    II. Title.

    BS1192.5 .K47 2002
    230'.0411–dc21

                                        2001055128
                                          CIP

Contents

To Our Families

Preface

Everything has a history, including this publication. It is difficult to pinpoint exactly the first thought given to this project. In fact, during my lifetime I have had very little serious aspirations to write for publication. Rather, my desires have focused more on preaching and teaching. When I did contemplate taking pen to paper, as it used to be expressed before the days of the computer, my thoughts turned to church history, my doctoral field of study at The Southern Baptist Theological Seminary. From the seminary I went into the pastorate and then into college, teaching as a professor in Campbell University's Department of Religion and Philosophy (1959–1997).

During my tenure at Campbell, the Religion Department would periodically re-examine its curriculum. On one such occasion it was agreed that one of my duties would be the teaching of a new entry-level course in Old Testament theology. This was something of a challenging task because of the educational level of the students in the class (mostly sophomores) and the lack of a suitable text. When I sometimes vocally complained about a text we were using at a particular time, the students often suggested that I write one of my own. If I have to choose a point in time for the genesis of this publication, it was with those gracious student suggestions.

But year after year this book remained nothing more than an idea. Perhaps that was just as well, since the last quarter of the twentieth century was a time for rethinking what the content and shape of such a book should be. This is vividly reflected in a series of books published by Fortress Press titled "Overtures to Biblical Theology." The idea behind the series at its beginning about 25 years ago was that the time was ripe for the publishing of small books on new ideas, addressed in new ways. It was also agreed that it definitely was not a time for the publication of a massive Old Testament theology to replace those written by such giants as Walther Eichrodt or Gerhard von Rad. The first of the books in the series, titled *The Land*, was written by Walter Brueggemann, one of the series editors. In 1997, Brueggemann published his acclaimed *Theology of the Old Testament*, certainly a massive production (777 pages), based on what he considered the proper (or at least *a* proper) new way of doing Old Testament theology.

During the course of 25 years, I shared with my students the new ideas and methodologies that were presented in "Overtures to Biblical Theology" and many other similar sources. For instance, two of the chapters that appear in this book — "Thinking God's Thoughts," and "Tending God's World" — were not even treated during those early days. Further, older traditional topics, such as "humanity," began to reflect the writing of such people as noted feminist scholars.

The pen to paper stage of the book did not begin until my retirement in 1997. As the work began to take shape, Wayne Ballard, co-author, assumed a position with Campbell University's Department of Religion and Philosophy as a specialist in the Hebrew Bible and Language, and possessed knowledge in the efforts of publishing. During the course of my preparation of the rough draft, he assisted me as a consultant in matters of Old Testament interpretation and modern application. Eventually, at my request, he joined me in the authorship of the book. He has been particularly helpful in moving the book from that of rough draft to a finished product suitable for publishing. I am grateful for his encouraging Smyth & Helwys in the publication of our manuscript and his oversight in seeing it to completion.

Our individual strengths are reflected throughout the pages of the book. For instance, besides my general understanding of the Old Testament and organizational abilities, my working knowledge of history is evident in the excursus in Chapter 7, "Thinking God's Thoughts." The excursus includes an examination of Daniel J. Boorstin's trilogy (*The Discoverers*, *The Creators*, and *The Seekers*) related to humanity's grand achievements.

Dr. Ballard's strengths are reflected in his overall understanding of the Old Testament, his special technical understanding of the Hebrew language, and his passion for that language. For instance, his input can be detected in the meaning of the Old Testament words (*adam* for example) in their context. Specifically, the transliterations (the representations of appropriate English alphabetical letters for Hebrew alphabetical letters) that appear throughout the book are his. He has attempted to transliterate Hebrew words to an English equivalence using a phonetic rendering of each word rather than using a technical or standardized guide foreign to beginning readers of the English Old Testament. His input can further be detected in the presentation of such difficult subjects as God's names in chapter three. See especially his excursus in that chapter: "The Ineffable Name: YHWH."

This book on Old Testament theology has been written with two basic readers in mind: college students and church members. It is a small book when compared with the recent work of Walter Brueggemann. Further, the language has deliberately been kept simple, with a minimum of technical terms. It is hoped that my former students will feel that the wait has been worthwhile and that college teachers will consider the text useful for their purpose.

When writing the book I had in mind a readership beyond that of college students, including namely the great host of serious Bible students in the church. Too often many of those in the church have failed both to understand and appreciate the Old Testament. Since my retirement from the college classroom I have had the opportunity to present to fellow members of my local church some of the materials contained in this work. Now, through the kind efforts of Smyth & Helwys, this information is available for other church members as well. The uses of the book are potentially many. Pastors can refresh their memories of old truths and gain new insights. It can be used in leading congregations in a series of thematic studies based on all or selected portions of the text. It may prove useful for Sunday school teachers in lesson preparation. Individuals may also find it useful for their own private edification.

Words of thanks are in order for many people: to Donald Penny, my former student and colleague at Campbell University, for the foreword; to Phebie Smith, Stephen J. Hamilton, and Jonathan Parker for their assistance in manuscript preparation; to David Cassady, Mark McElroy, and Keith Gammons of Smyth & Helwys for their encouragement and support throughout the publication process; and finally to the members of Memorial Baptist Church of Buies Creek and Buies Creek First Baptist Church for the role they continuously play in the lives of myself and Dr. Ballard, respectively.

Unless otherwise noted, the biblical text used throughout the book is the New Revised Standard Version. The terms "Old Testament" and "Hebrew Bible" are used interchangeably throughout the manuscript. The Appendix demonstrates the differing order between the two, though the textual material is the same.

—B. Donald Keyser
Buies Creek, North Carolina
2001

Foreword

From the very beginning, the stories, songs, and other materials of the Old Testament have shaped the faith and imagination of Christian people. Yet the diversity and complexity of the Old Testament can make its pages seem inscrutable to the novice or the ordinary reader. Some guidance through the often rugged terrain of these ancient texts is not only welcome but often necessary. One would be hard-pressed to find more trustworthy guides through the Old Testament than the two authors of the present volume. I am proud to call both of them colleagues, friends, and brothers in Christ.

Don Keyser is an "amateur" student of the Old Testament in the truest sense of that term. Although his doctoral work was in the area of church history, his early teaching assignments were in biblical studies. He fell in love with Old Testament studies and read voraciously in that area for the rest of his career. Throughout his career his two passions have been the church and the classroom, which, in his mind, were never very far apart. Whether teaching a class of college students or a Sunday school class of adult men, his overriding aim has been to make the lesson intensely practical, to find lines of connection between the biblical text and the lives of God's people. I first witnessed Don's special teaching skills when I sat in his classes as an undergraduate student at Campbell. Later, I benefited from his gracious guidance when I joined the faculty. Both his teaching style and his lifestyle have been models worthy of greater emulation than I have been able to achieve.

Wayne Ballard is a highly trained student of the Hebrew Bible, with all the expertise that comes from earning a doctorate in Old Testament studies. Now in his fifth year of full-time teaching experience, he has published a growing number of studies and articles. He literally would rather teach Hebrew than eat lunch. He is known on campus as a caring professor who takes personal interest in individual students. Wayne also has the heart of a pastor. With a number of years of pastoral experience before joining the Campbell faculty, he remains a highly sought-after interim pastor and Bible study leader. One of his special gifts is the ability to interpret scholarly insights in ways appropriate for audiences or readers of varying levels of skill.

Both authors have demonstrated Christian faith that has been tested in the trials of life and found genuine. Both are committed to looking honestly at the biblical text and at life and are not afraid to ask hard questions about either. Neither is willing to settle for simplistic answers to complex issues. The present volume may be gauged for beginning students or lay readers, but it will not ask them to be unthinking or to refrain from asking unsettling questions.

Finally, one of Don Keyser's endearing quirks manifests itself during walks across campus. A consummate storyteller, he regales his companions as they briskly walk along—Don has always been a brisk walker. Then, when he comes to a part of the story he feels especially passionate about, he stops right in the middle of the sidewalk and stands perfectly still until he finishes. My wish for you, the reader, is for a delightful walk with our authors through the Old Testament. Keep alert, however, for those especially passionate passages, and be prepared to linger a while and ponder.

—**Donald N. Penny**
Buies Creek, North Carolina
September, 2001

1

Introduction

Then an angel of the LORD said to Philip, "Get up and go toward the south to the road that goes down from Jerusalem to Gaza." (This is a wilderness road.) So he got up and went. Now there was an Ethiopian eunuch, a court official of the Candace, queen of the Ethiopians, in charge of her entire treasury. He had come to Jerusalem to worship and was returning home; seated in his chariot, he was reading the prophet Isaiah. Then the Spirit said to Philip, "Go over to this chariot and join it." So Philip ran up to it and heard him reading the prophet Isaiah. He asked, "Do you understand what you are reading?" He replied, "How can I, unless someone guides me?" And he invited Philip to get in and sit beside him. Now the passage of the scripture that he was reading was this:

> "Like a sheep he was led to the
> slaughter,
> and like a lamb silent before
> its shearer,
> so he does not open his mouth.
> In his humiliation justice was denied
> him.
> Who can describe his generation?
> For his life is taken away from
> the earth."

The eunuch asked Philip, "About whom, may I ask you, does the prophet say this, about himself or about someone else?" Then Philip began to speak, and starting with this scripture, he proclaimed to him the good news about Jesus. As they were going along the road, they came to some water; and the eunuch said, "Look, here is water! What is to prevent me from being baptized?" He commanded the chariot to stop, and both of them, Philip and the eunuch, went down into the water, and Philip baptized him. (Acts 8:26-38)

Israel's History

The New Testament book of Acts records the story of the selection of seven men (seemingly all non-Palestinian Jews) to assist Jesus' twelve apostles in the work of the fledgling church to which they all belonged. As set forth in our paradigm passage, among the seven chosen was Philip, who helped an Ethiopian eunuch interpret a passage of scripture from the Old Testament book of Isaiah.

The story of Philip and the eunuch can generally be understood without a full knowledge of Israel's history. However, the passage takes on an added significance when it is studied within its original context and with study helps (for example, commentaries and biblical dictionaries) at our disposal. Understanding something of the long history of the Israelite (later Jewish) people from the time of Abraham to the coming of Jesus is essential to an understanding of both Philip's actions and the themes that appear in this book on Old Testament theology.

When we speak of a history of Israel, we must remember that the Israelites did not follow the accepted methodologies of the modern western historian. For instance, the biblical authors speak of what God did or said. No modern western historian would make such a remark. For instance, Sydney Ahlstrom, in his massive *A Religious History of the American People*, nowhere tells us how God felt about the American Civil War. Rather, he does what is acceptable; he quotes President Lincoln's opinion.[1]

If the Israelite "historians" did not follow modern western methodological procedures, how shall we approach their materials? To put it another way, how much historical trustworthiness shall we put in their accounts? Basically, three broad answers are currently being given to the question. First, at one extreme are those who maintain that the information concerning Israel, as told in Genesis through Kings, should be taken as historically accurate even in minor details. Typical of this approach is Walter Kaiser in his *History of Israel*.[2] Second, at the other extreme are those who question the historical value of most of the materials dealing with Israelite events prior to the kingdom under David or perhaps beyond David. Typical of this position is the one presented by Robert Coote, who declares: "The writers of the Hebrew Scriptures knew little or nothing about the origins of Israel, . . . [concerning such periods as] patriarchs, exodus, conquest, judges, [etc.]. These periods never existed."[3] Third, there are interpreters who espouse a mediating position accepting the broad outline of the accounts while examining the details with caution. Typical of this position is John Bright in his *A History of Israel*.[4] Bright's position is similar to the one held by the authors of this book.

How might proponents of these three views react to the statement in Exodus 12:37 of such an extremely large number of people (seemingly over two million) led by Moses into the Wilderness of Sinai? The question would be a non-issue for someone like Coote, who questions the existence of a "Mosaic" period. Kaiser simply accepts the various accounts of the extremely large number of persons without in any way explaining how Moses could have dealt with them in the wilderness.[5] Bright maintains that another interpretation is justified based on the story as recited in Exodus. He puts it this way:

> We see in the Bible itself a much smaller group, whose needs are cared for by two midwives (Exod 1:15-22), who cross the Reed Sea in a single night, and who cringe before a foe more numerous than they. The number that participated in the exodus was hardly more than a few thousand.[6]

The modern author of a history of Israel is faced with the same problem concerning the proper place to begin its history as is the author of a history of the United States. Since there was no entity known as the United States until after the Revolutionary War, shall a history include settlements at Jamestown and Plymouth and all that transpired before the Revolutionary War? Rather, should we call those early events "prehistory"? So it is with Israel before Abraham's descendants are settled in Palestine following the death of Moses. But if America's prehistory can be considered a part of the history of the United States, surely the same can be said of Israel's early story.

Thus we begin the story of Israel with Abraham and Sarah, Israel's first patriarch and matriarch. According to Genesis, Abraham moved from Mesopotamia to Palestine, led by God who promised him that someday his posterity would lay claim to that land. According to Israel's testimony, the day did come when the Israelites inherited that land, but not before suffering slavery in Egypt, followed by emancipation under Moses and a subsequent period of wandering in the Wilderness of Sinai.

Under the leadership of Joshua, following the death of Moses, the Israelites conquered certain strategic portions of Palestine, where they settled down. After Joshua's death, during the period of the Judges, the Israelites experienced great upheaval, including times of great sinfulness. According to Judges, except by God's grace, they more-than-likely would have lost their "Promised Land."

The period of the Judges was followed by the Kingdom period. In spite of his faults, King David became the standard by which all of the kings would be judged by God or by the people. Among the greatest and most pious of David's descendants was King Hezekiah, of whom the author of 2 Kings writes:

> He did what was right in the sight of the LORD just as his ancestor David had done . . . . He trusted the LORD the God of Israel; so that there was no one like him among all the kings of Judah after him, or among those who were before him. For he held fast to the LORD; he did not depart from following him but kept the commandments that the LORD commanded Moses. (2 Kgs 18:3, 5-6)

The day came when Abraham's descendants lost their Promised Land to such outsiders as Syria, Assyria, Babylonia, Persia, and Greece. With the latter period we come to the end of the biblical books that provide our materials for an Old Testament theology.

Before leaving this section on Israel's history, it is important to ask whether such a study is necessary to interpret properly Old Testament passages upon which an Old Testament theology is built. Such a study is absolutely essential for a passage like the Decalogue (Ten Commandments) with its foundation in Israel's emancipation from Egyptian bondage. On the other hand, much of the Wisdom literature and some passages from Psalms are not related to specific historical events.

Biblical Geography

Having looked briefly at Israel's history, we now look at that history in its geographical setting. In the Acts paradigm passage we read that the eunuch had been to Jerusalem to worship and that he was returning home by way of Gaza on the coast. While these are place names that give concreteness to the story, they are much more significant than that.

From the time of King David until the present, Jerusalem has been Israel's (and its successors) most important city. Rising some 2500 feet above sea level, Jerusalem, a Jebusite city, was captured by King David and made his capital. With roads running through it from north to south and east to west, the outside world had access to Jerusalem and her inhabitants had access to the outside world. At the same time, the city's rugged terrain provided a natural defense, breached only rarely. When it was breached, as it was by the Babylonians in 587 BC, the results could be devastating. Destroyed and rebuilt numerous times during the last 2500 years, Jerusalem stands today as a sacred place for Judaism, Christianity, and Islam. Ironically, it is a thorn in the flesh for any peaceful settlement between modern Israelis and Palestinian Muslims.

Gaza, the other place named in our paradigm passage, was near the coast, some 50 miles southwest of Jerusalem. It was one of five Philistine city-states that contended with the Israelites during the days of the judges and early monarchy. Further, the word *Palestine* is a Greek word (by way of the Greek historians) for "land of the Philistines."

It is not necessary to know what has been related above about Jerusalem and Gaza to get the main drift of the paradigm story of Philip and the eunuch. Yet, such information adds a dimension to the story that aids in its fuller understanding. For one thing, we are reminded that we are dealing with real people living in a real land. The reader can gain more knowledge of that land by consulting biblical atlases. If the reader wishes a fuller treatment of such subjects as topography, climate, roads, plants, and animals, one may consult, among others, Denis Baly's *The Geography of the Bible*.[7]

The Origin, Formation, Transmission, and Translation of the Old Testament

In Acts 8:26-38, the eunuch is reading aloud from the Old Testament book of Isaiah, one of 39 in the Protestant collection/canon. While Isaiah is one of the most quoted Old Testament books in the New Testament, one needs to be generally familiar with the origin and contents of many, if not all, Old Testament books in order to understand Israel's theology. A good source for such information is a Bible dictionary such as the *Mercer Dictionary of the Bible*.[8]

When one moves beyond a knowledge of individual Old Testament books to an understanding of the formation of the entire Old Testament, along with its transmission and translation, there are many good books (some technical, others popular) to aid in our search for information. A popular book is Craig Koester, *A Beginner's Guide for Reading the Bible*.[9] A book fitting somewhere between the technical and the popular is David Ewert's *A General Introduction to the Bible: From Ancient Tablets to Modern Translations*.[10]

As individual Old Testament books were written and used by the Israelites, some of the books began to take on greater significance than others until they were recognized as sacred or religiously authoritative, a process we speak of as canonization. As time passed, individual books were placed in collections (e.g., the Pentateuch/Torah: Genesis through Deuteronomy), with canonical authority being bestowed on the entire collection. The first major collection to be canonized was the *Torah* (law or instruction), followed by the *Nevi'im* (prophets) and finally by the *Ketuvim* (writings).[11] The reader needs to be aware that while the books in the Hebrew Bible are the same as those in the Protestant Old Testament, the books in the Hebrew Bible are in a different order and are numbered differently, as can be seen in the chart in the Appendix . It should also be noted, as shown in the same chart, that the Roman Catholic Old Testament contains books not included in the Protestant collection.[12]

By the first century AD, the Jews had a more or less fixed Bible written mainly in Hebrew. Two situations arose that affect our study of the Old Testament to this day. First, as numerous copies of the individual scrolls, such as that of Isaiah, were made for synagogue use, variance began to appear in the Hebrew text in the different synagogues. Today, scholars known as textual critics, by a study of the available copies of the variant texts (such as those found among the Dead Sea Scrolls), have arrived at a reasonably trustworthy, if not exact, text of the original books.[13] As the need for numerous synagogue Bibles led to variant Hebrew copies, the need for translations also arose for the benefit of those Jews who no longer understood the ancestral Hebrew language. The most important was a Greek translation known as the Septuagint (or LXX) and Aramaic translations referred to as Targums.[14]

More than likely, the eunuch of Acts 8 read the Septuagint translation of the scroll of Isaiah. During the early days of the church — predominated by Gentile converts — the Septuagint served the needs of worship and instruction. However, as Latin gradually superceded Greek as the common language of the Roman Empire, the Old Testament, along with the New Testament, were translated into Latin. The most notable Latin translation was that of

Jerome (c. AD 400) known as the Vulgate, from the Latin meaning "common." For a thousand years this version served as the main Bible of the church, especially in the West, and is still the official Bible (in a revised form) of the Roman Catholic Church.[15]

The Vulgate served as the Bible of the English people until the appearance of John Wycliffe's English Bible in the late fourteenth century. This pioneer version was followed by other significant ones, including the King James Version. The best-selling edition of all time, the King James Version has now been replaced by the New International Version as the current bestseller.[16]

Biblical Interpretation

Earlier we noted that the eunuch was reading from the scroll of Isaiah, a scroll he considered important, maybe even sacred and authoritative. We soon discover that his own personal reading did not satisfy him. When Philip asked if he understood what he was reading, the eunuch replied that he needed an interpretative guide. What the eunuch needed, most readers still need today. Three helpful books are suggested: Fee and Stuart, *How to Read the Bible for all its Worth*;[17] Hayes and Holladay, *Biblical Exegesis: A Beginner's Handbook*;[18] Tate, *Biblical Interpretation: An Integrated Approach*.[19] According to Randolph Tate, the interpreter must integrate three approaches, namely: (1) *author-centered* (with attention directed to the world behind the text), (2) *text-centered* (with the focus on the world within the text, or the textual world), and (3) *reader-centered* (where the spotlight is trained upon the world in front of the text, or the reader's world).[20]

The diagram below may serve to illustrate the approach:

Author's world < — Text — > Reader's world

The World of the Text

We begin our study of interpretation with the world of the text. From a literary standpoint, this means that a text must be studied, among other things, in its entirety from the largest units to the smallest segments (words, sentences, etc.). Furthermore, its *genre* (kind of literature) and figures of speech must be observed. In the broadest sense, the text is made up of prose and/or poetry. We naturally expect a more flexible use of words and ideas in poetry than in prose, though this is not always the case. For instance, *hyperbole* (exaggeration) may be used in either. Rather than examine all kinds of genre found in Old Testament prose and poetry, our study shall be limited to four genres, namely: narrative, psalms, prophecy, and wisdom.

Narrative. Hebrew narrative, like all good narrative, did not just happen and was not thrown together in some haphazard way. Randolph Tate reminds us that Hebrew narrative shares with all good narrative "plot, setting, characterization, point of view, and style."[21] Three of these elements shall be examined by way of the story of David's sin with Bathsheba and the subsequent results as detailed in 2 Samuel 11.

The *plot* in this narrative deals with the story of David, a great king who abuses his power by taking Bathsheba, the wife of Uriah, a man whom David conveniently arranges to die on the battlefield. For these sins David will eventually experience the tragic death of three of his sons.

The *setting* of the beginning of the narrative is the top of the king's palace from which David sees Bathsheba bathing. The king's palace is also the setting of the end of the story, as David lies on his death bed while two of his sons maneuver for the right to the throne and while Bathsheba sides with one of the parties, namely Solomon, her son.

Concerning the *point of view*, the author of 2 Samuel maintains that (presumably) he and God agree that both are exceedingly disappointed with David.

Psalms. Based on the pioneer studies of scholars such as Hermann Gunkel (1862–1932), many modern interpreters, using Gunkel's Form-Critical approach, divide the Psalms into categories "according to genre that can be classified on the basis of their literary form and setting in worship."[22]Daniel Mynatt in "Poetry and Literature of the Psalms," following Gunkel's general approach, places the Psalms into the following categories: *Hymns* (general songs of praise to God), *Laments* (both individual and community songs of distress), *Songs of Trust, Thanksgivings, Sacred History, Royal Psalms, Wisdom Psalms*, and *Liturgies*.[23]

Concerning the poetry of the Psalms, a special word needs to be said about *rhyme* and *parallelism*. While Old Testament poetry did not have rhyme as we think of it, it did feature a kind of rhythm which can still be detected in oral recitation of the Psalms. One author puts it this way: "Those who have heard the recitation of the Psalms in the Hebrew language recognize rhythmic tones of a song as much as the quotation of the Scriptures."[24]

A feature of Hebrew poetry readily recognized in English translations is parallelism. In parallelism, the second part of a verse is related to the first part as either synonymous (similar in content as in Ps 24:1), antithetical (using disparate themes as in Ps 1:6), or complementary/developmental (sometimes referred to as synthetic or formal parallelism as seen in Ps 95:3):

> The earth is the LORD's and all
> > that is in it,
> the world, and those who live
> > in it; . . . (Ps 24:1)

> for the LORD watches over the
> > way of the righteous,
> but the way of the wicked will
> > perish. (Ps 1:6)

> For the LORD is a great God,
> and a great King above all gods. (Ps 95:3)

Prophecy. The book of Amos serves as an example for some of the kinds of literature often found in prophetic writings, namely: oracle from God, vision, irony, and lamentation. The following speech spoken to Amaziah, priest of Bethel, is one example of an *oracle from God*:

> Therefore thus says the LORD:
> "your wife shall become a
> > prostitute in the city,
> and your sons and your
> > daughters shall fall by
> > the sword." (Amos 7:17)

Concerning a *vision*, note the following:

> This is what the LORD God showed me: he was forming locusts at the time the latter growth began to sprout (it was the latter growth after the king's mowings). When they had finished eating the grass of the land, I said,
> "O LORD GOD, forgive, I beg you!
> > How can Jacob stand?
> > He is so small!"

The LORD relented concerning this;
   "It shall not be," said the LORD. (Amos 7:1)

Amos declares that it is *ironic* that Israel has sinned so greatly while ben-
efiting from God's manifold graciousness (Amos 2:10-11). Perhaps it is
equally ironic that Amos can speak words of lamentation while at the same
time pronouncing God's ultimate judgment on his people:

Hear this word that I take up over you in lamentation, O house of Israel:
Fallen no more to rise,
   is maiden Israel;
forsaken on her land,
   with no one to raise her up.
For thus says the Lord GOD:
The city that marched out
   a thousand
   shall have a hundred left,
and that which marched out
   a hundred
   shall have ten left. (Amos 5:1-3)

Wisdom. We close our discussion of the various Old Testament literary
genres with the so-called Wisdom literature (Proverbs, Job, and Ecclesiastes).
We begin with two assumptions. First, Old Testament wisdom sayings or
expressions are not limited to the above-mentioned books nor to a special
class of Israelite wise men. Second, a special class did exist, however, with its
"characteristic mode of discourse," as described by James Crenshaw.[25] While
there is no general agreement concerning the categories or forms that make
up Wisdom Literature, Leo Perdue's list can serve our purpose: "Sayings,
instruction, narrative, dialogue, and poems."[26]

Perdue breaks the sayings down into smaller units: "proverbs, compara-
tive sayings, better sayings (or beatitudes), numerical sayings, questions, and
riddles."[27] The most common form of saying is the proverb, usually composed of two lines expressing a conclusion based on experience:

   A soft answer turns away
         wrath,
      but a harsh word stirs up anger. (Prov 15:1)

Besides short sayings like the one quoted above, Proverbs includes lengthier sayings that may be designated "instructions." The specific instruction will usually be introduced with a call to listen and with a conclusion concerning the results (good or bad), based on the student's attitude and action. For instance, note the introduction and conclusion in the following verses where the son is admonished to listen to his father's plea to stay away from robbers and their ilk, for the end is tragic for the perpetrator as well as his victim:

> Hear, my child, your father's
>   instruction,
> and do not reject your mother's
>   teaching. (Prov 1:8)

> . . . yet they lie in wait — to kill
>   themselves!
> and set an ambush — for their
>   own lives!
> Such is the end of all who are
>   greedy for gain;
> it takes away the life of its
>   possessors. (Prov 1:18-19)

Rather than discuss further the other categories or forms of the Wisdom genre as listed by Perdue, his following remark succinctly summarize the importance of Wisdom literature: "Becoming wise is a way of life, a process that continues for a lifetime, as the wise person seeks to live in harmony with God, the cosmos, the social order, and a human nature which requires the discipline and structure of teaching [as set forth in the Wisdom literature]."[28]

Smallest Literary Segments: Words and Sentences. While genre studies are important in the examination of a text, a study of words and sentences is equally essential. Take for example a study of the various Hebrew words that are translated as "sin" or some equivalent such as "iniquity." When the writer declares in Psalms 32:1 that God has marvelously blessed him through forgiveness of sin, he emphasizes the magnitude of his sin by the use of four different Hebrew words. There follows the transliterated Hebrew words with English renditions in the NRSV: *Pesha* (transgression), *Avon* (iniquity),

[C]Hata (sin), and *Remiyah* (deceit). Are we to suppose the writer meant that each of the Hebrew words stood for some specific sin he had committed, or was it his way of saying that he had been exceedingly sinful? Probably the latter. Whatever meaning each of the four words might have in some other context, the context of Psalm 32 determines their meaning in this instance.

Not only did the writer pile one Hebrew word on the top of another to emphasize the enormity of his sin, the writer (again presumably) also used three expressions (one from the financial world and two from his own cultic/worship world) to picture the greatness of God's forgiveness. The author declares that such a sinful person experiencing forgiveness must truly be called blessed or happy.

The Author's World

Behind any given text, such as the book of Isaiah of our paradigm passage, is an author or authors and their world. While some current scholars maintain that our present book of Isaiah was written by Isaiah of Jerusalem c. 700 BC,[29] others maintain that the book consists of several sources composed at different times by different persons. In a broad sense, while the statement is oversimplified, it may be said that our present book can be divided into three parts with seams showing between chapters 39 and 40 and between 55 and 56. A helpful introduction to this kind of approach is Cecil Staton's "Introducing the Book of Isaiah."[30] Staton remarks:

> Contemporary biblical scholarship suggests that a thoughtful reading of Isaiah reveals important differences between 1–39, 40–55, and 55–66: differences of time, differences of location, difference of mood, and differences of language and themes. And these are readily apparent in the text of Isaiah itself.[31]

The prophetic ministry of Isaiah of Jerusalem, author of Isaiah 1–39, is often dated from 742 BC to 701 BC based on the list of kings in Isaiah 1:1. During this period Assyria destroyed Israel (Israelite northern kingdom) and made Judah (Israelite southern kingdom) a vassal. During these traumatic times, Isaiah of Jerusalem announced that the Holy One of Israel had already brought judgment on Judah's sister nation to the north and that Judah's judgment was imminent. However, with the threat of judgment, the prophet also spoke of hope.[32]

The prophetic ministry of "Second Isaiah" (the prophet of the exile), author of Isaiah 40–55, took place near the end of the Jewish exile period, c. 540 BC, in Babylonia where the prophet addressed his people. Whereas Isaiah of Jerusalem spoke in terms of future judgment, the anonymous prophet of the exile spoke of a judgment that had passed and of an imminent return to Jerusalem. All of this would take place, according to the prophet, by God's mercy through the instrumentality of Cyrus the Persian, God's anointed one, translated from the Hebrew word *messiah*. There was a dimension to the message that went beyond hope for Israel; it was to be a hope that embraces the Gentiles as well. It was said that the Israelites would be a "light to the Gentiles" (Isa 42:6), a promise reminiscent of the promise made to Abraham that his descendents would be a blessing to the "families of the earth" (Gen 12:3).[33]

The prophetic ministry of "Third Isaiah" (the prophet of the return)[34] took place in Jerusalem, where he addressed the returnees from Babylonia. For these Israelites it was a time of hardship and discouragement, a discouragement that sometimes led to immorality and especially disinterest in spiritual matters. The prophet, through both the use of threat and encouragement, sought to rouse the people to renewal. With the use of glowing pictures, he promised the people a renewed Jerusalem that would surpass that of the days of Solomon.[35]

While much can be gained by examining the three sections of Isaiah separately, the full message is to be found by reading the book as a whole, as Staton reminds us: "Through the images of judgment, exile, and homecoming the people of God are shown a portrait of the action of God in history in the lives of his people."[36]

The Reader's World

The modern reader of the Bible can find valuable information about the authorship of Old Testament books in such works as Bible commentaries and Bible dictionaries. This information provides proper perspectives about Old Testament teaching concerning such themes as God, creation, and humanity. The reader also needs to be aware that one's own ideas and those of the world one brings to the study may slant an understanding of the Old Testament. Verification of this can be seen in a comparison of the views of those called "liberation theologians" and those known as "pacifists "as they relate to the downtrodden people of the earth.

Many Latin American liberation theologians see the Old Testament exodus story as one depicting God on the side of the downtrodden, and, at the same time, one favoring human force in the overthrow of despotic governments. Anthony Ceresko, in his *Introduction to the Old Testament: A Liberation Perspective*, insists that such views were grasped by ordinary Latin American Christians before they were espoused by their theologically-trained leaders. Of these people (forming what he calls "base communities") he remarks:

> [U]neducated and unsophisticated as they might appear to be, [ordinary Latin American Christians] nevertheless needed little encouragement or direction to find so much of their own lives and experience reflected in the stories and songs and the men and women of the Scriptures . . . . It was evident to these groups that the people and stories and songs they found in the Bible were relevant to their own social, economic, and political situation. The Bible was proving to be a powerful tool in bringing them to an awareness of their condition as oppressed and exploited people, and for inspiring their initial attempts at organizing and working together for change and reform . . . . [Further] they came more and more to think about the God of the Bible as a God of the people, a God who stands by them when they are oppressed and exploited, a God of the poor who acts on behalf of the poor and powerless to liberate and free them from their slavery.
>
> A story such as that of the Exodus, the story that stands at the heart of the Old Testament, held great meaning for those who comprised these Base Communities. *Theologians in touch with what was happening in the Base Communities gained new insights and perspectives from the astonishing affinity with Scriptures which these simple "exegetes" possessed.* (Italics added)[37]

Thus there came to be a new way of interpreting scripture and doing Old Testament theology, which became known as "liberation theology." It came about as the scriptures were read in a special way by Latin American Christian communities.

The opposite of a liberation theology approach, as far as force is concerned, is a pacifistic one. For example, Mennonites and other pacifistic groups find certain exilic themes more appropriate for modern downtrodden people than the exodus theme. John Howard Yoder expresses it this way:

Over against the paradigm of leaving Egypt and destroying the Pharaoh on the way, we find in the Old Testament, more often, another model on how to live under a pagan oppressor. It is the way of the Diaspora [exile].[38]

Daniel L. Smith, who was greatly influenced by Yoder, adopts Yoder's position. Among the passages considered by Smith is Jeremiah's letter from Jerusalem to a group of citizens of Judah who had been transported to Babylonia during the siege of Palestine, a portion of which follows:

Thus says the LORD of hosts, the God of Israel, to all the exiles whom I have sent into exile from Jerusalem to Babylon: Build houses and live in them; plant gardens and eat what they produce. Take wives . . . and have sons, and give your daughters in marriage, that they may bear sons and daughters; multiply there, and do not decrease. But seek the welfare of the city where I have sent you into exile and pray to the LORD on its behalf, for in its welfare you will find your welfare . . . . For thus says the LORD: Only when Babylon's seventy years are completed will I visit you, and I will fulfill to you my promise and bring you back . . . to the place from which I sent you into exile. (Jer 29:4ff)

Commenting on the above passage, Smith says it recommends nonviolent resistance for the exiles. As to how this might be applied today, Smith remarks:

Exodus is the road to nationalism and power. But there is another Biblical paradigm. It is a warning against Exodus theology. In the place of Joshua the revolutionary conqueror, it points to Jeremiah the prophet of subversive righteousness.... In the place of David the emperor, it points to Daniel the wise. In the place of Solomon's great Temple, it points to the perseverance of singing the Lord's song in a foreign land. It is a religion of the landless, the faith of those who dwell in Babylon.[39]

What is the reader to do when faced with such contrasting positions? Of course, for those readers who choose one position without question while disdainfully dismissing the other, no problem exists. We are not ready to dismiss either, out of hand, but urge the reader to keep listening to both sides. When students of our college religion classes are asked how they would handle the differences of opinion, their answer, most often, is that they see truth in both positions, with their own position being somewhere between the two. Further, they reply with insight that changing situations could affect which stance they might take at a particular time. What neither the liberation theologians nor the pacifists make clear is that in God's economy of time either approach might be serviceable and useful.

The following words of Randolph Tate serve as a reminder that the reader must give due regard at all times to the three worlds we have discussed above: the reader's world, the author's world, and the world of the text:

> It is undeniable that interpreters bring assumptions to the text. During the process of interpretation, however, the text itself may legitimate, deny, clarify, or modify those assumptions. This textual influence upon the reader is possible because while the text as signifier is inexhaustible, it does place parameters around interpretation, making one interpretation more or less plausible than another.[40]

Theological Method

Once we have interpreted a sufficient number of Old Testament passages, we are ready to begin the process of putting them together in such a way as to form some organized whole, or what might be designated an Old Testament theology. It should be noted that there is no definitive definition of theology in general or Old Testament theology in particular.

As an example of the putting together of various passages of scripture, we may juxtapose Psalm 44 and Isaiah 40:27-31. Both of these passages deal with Israel at some point of national calamity and despondency. While Isaiah 40 surely refers to the period of the Babylonian exile, the time of calamity of the psalm is not as certain.[41] Psalm 44, a group lament, closes with a cry to God to arise and save his people from their troubles. What hope they have is based on the past activities of God on behalf of their ancestors, activities they believe are still valid. While the group (perhaps worshipping congregation) looked to God's salvific experience, the prophet of the exile (Second Isaiah) directed the attention of the suffering exiles to God's unchanging, ongoing, creative activity.

What we have done above is to examine two passages under the general theme of God's care and power. Since one passage was chosen from the Psalms and the other from Second Isaiah, we have used what is sometimes referred to as a "cross-sectional" method, a method we shall be using throughout the remainder of the book. Further, since one passage calls attention to God's historical salvific experience and the other to his dependable creative activity, we have brought together in one place diverse expressions about God's activities. Some theologians prefer that the many kinds of diversity mentioned in the Old Testament be left that way without any attempt to seek diversity within unity. Among those theologians who believe that an attempt to seek diversity within unity is both possible and legitimate is John Goldingay. However, in his discussion on creation and salvation/redemption, he makes it clear that he does not favor dissolving the polarities between the two. Rather, he states that he prefers to "tease out the various ways in which the two poles relate to each other, preserving the tension between them."[42] He states further:

> The two ideas, creation and redemption, correspond to two aspects of our understanding of our position in the world. Although the Old Testament sometimes relates these to each other as a chronological sequence (humanity was first created, then redeemed), even Genesis recognizes that the world does not cease to be God's ordered creation when humanity is in a state of rebellion and in need of redemption . . . . Creation is not only the preparation for redemption but its permanent horizon.[43]

Besides the pair of creation and salvation, Goldingay suggests other pairs such as: "judgment and grace, law and promise, . . . exodus and exile, word and event, praise and lament, structure and freedom, form and reform."[44]

When interpreters-turned-theologians have covered subjects such as those just listed above, whether alone or in pairs, it can be said that they have presented a theology of the Old Testament from the standpoint of descriptive theology. In other words, they have presented in systematic fashion a theology of the Israelite/Jewish people as contained in the Old Testament. However, one step needs to be taken beyond the descriptive, namely the constructive (explaining the relevance of the scripture for the modern generation). At this point, Brevard Childs' remarks are appropriate whether the theologian is following the canonical approach, as Childs does, or some other approach:

> [A] canonical approach envisions the discipline of Old Testament theology as combining both descriptive and constructive features. It recognizes the descriptive task of correctly interpreting an ancient text which bears testimony to historic Israel's faith. Yet it also understands that the theological enterprise involves a construal by the modern interpreter, whose stance to the text affects it meaning. For this reason Old Testament theology cannot be identified with describing an historical process in the past . . . , but

involves wrestling with the subject-matter to which scripture continues to bear testimony. In sum, Old Testament theology is a continuing enterprise in which each new generation must engage.[45]

The Old Testament theological approach used in this book is one that may be described as thematic, cross-sectional, diversity within unity, descriptive, and constructive. While it is not essential for the reader to be aware of the many other approaches that have been used during the last two hundred years — especially the last one hundred — three books are cited (none that can be considered "easy" reading) for the interested reader dealing with the history of such theologies: Hayes and Prussner, *Old Testament Theology: Its History and Development*[46]; Hasel, *Old Testament Theology: Basic Issues in the Current Debate*[47]; Perdue, *The Collapse of History: Reconstructing Old Testament Theology*.[48] If the reader wishes to delve deeper into what many consider to be the finest Old Testament theologies written in the twentieth century, one needs to obtain the works of Walther Eichrodt and Gerhard von Rad.[49] Concerning the books by these men, Walter Brueggemann remarks, "Old Testament Theology has been dominated in the twentieth century by the magisterial work of Walther Eichrodt and even more by the powerful model of Gerhard von Rad."[50]

Before closing, a word needs to be said about our chosen themes and the order of their appearance, especially the first theme. Typical of some other works, which use a thematic approach, is Edmund Jacob's *Theology of the Old Testament*.[51] After an introductory section, he follows with a section on God (his nature, names, etc.). On the other hand, H.H. Rowley, in his *Faith of Israel*,[52] follows his introduction with a chapter on revelation. Only then does he discuss the nature of God. A more recent study, using the thematic approach, is Brevard Child's *Old Testament Theology in a Canonical Approach*.[53] After his introduction, he also follows with a lengthy discussion of revelation. However, unlike the works of Jacob and Rowley, there is no chapter, as such, on God.

After this introductory chapter and before the chapter on "God," we will discuss "God's Chosen: Israelites and Gentiles." This is done since the content of the Old Testament (the source of an Old Testament theology) is based on the relationship of God to his chosen, both Israelites and Gentiles, and their relationship to each other. The chapters follow in order: "God's Chosen: Israelites and Gentiles," "God," "Creation," "Humanity," "Thinking God's Thoughts," "Tending God's World," "Living in

Community Before God, parts I and II," "Sin," "Living Life under Threat and with Distress," and "Living Life with Hope."

Notes

[1] Sydney E. Ahlstrom, *A Religious History of the American People* (New Haven: Yale University Press, 1972), 678.

[2] Walter C. Kaiser Jr., *A History of Israel* (Nashville: Broadman & Holman Publishers, 1998).

[3] Robert B. Coote, *Early Israel: A New Horizon* (Minneapolis: Fortress Press, 1990), 2-3.

[4] John Bright, *A History of Israel,* 3rd edition (Philadelphia: Westminster Press, 1981).

[5] Kaiser, 102.

[6] Bright, 134.

[7] Denis Baly, *The Geography of the Bible: A Study in Historical Geography* (New York: Harper and Row Publishers, 1957).

[8] Watson E. Mills et al., eds., *Mercer Dictionary of the Bible* (Macon: Mercer University Press, 1990).

[9] Craig R. Koester, *A Beginner's Guide to Reading the Bible* (Minneapolis: Augsburg, 1991).

[10] David Ewert, *A General Introduction to the Bible: From Ancient Tablets to Modern Translations* (Grand Rapids: Zondervan Publishing House, 1990).

[11] Koester, 55-60.

[12] Ibid., 55-61.

[13] Ewert, 85ff.

[14] Ibid., 99ff.

[15] Ibid., 174ff.

[16] Ibid., 183ff.

[17] Gordon Fee and Douglas Stuart, *How to Read the Bible for all its Worth* (Grand Rapids: Zondervan Publishing House, 1982).

[18] John H. Hayes and Carl R. Holladay, *Biblical Exegesis: A Beginner's Handbook,* Revised edition (Atlanta: John Knox Press, 1987).

[19] Randolph W. Tate, *Biblical Interpretation: An Integrated Approach* (Peabody: Hendrickson Publishers, 1991).

[20] Ibid., xvi.

[21] Ibid., 74.

[22] Bernhard Anderson, *Out of the Depths: The Psalms Speak for Today* (Philadelphia: Westminster Press, 1983), 10.

[23] Daniel S. Mynatt, "The Poetry and Literature of the Psalms," in *An Introduction to Wisdom Literature and the Psalms*, ed. H. Wayne Ballard & W. Dennis Tucker (Macon: Mercer University Press, 2000), 61-66.

[24] Rodney Reeves, "Reading the Genres of Scripture," in *Biblical Hermeneutics*, ed. Bruce Corley (Nashville: Broadman and Holman, 1996), 268.

[25] James L. Crenshaw, *Old Testament Wisdom: An Introduction* (Atlanta: John Knox Press, 1981), 36.

[26] Leo G. Perdue, *Wisdom and Creation: The Theology of Wisdom Literature* (Nashville: Abingdon Press, 1994), 64.

[27] Ibid., 64.

[28] Ibid., 74.

[29] Gleason L. Archer, *A Survey of Old Testament Introductions* (Chicago: Moody Press, 1994), 390.

[30] Cecil Staton, "Interpreting Isaiah For Preaching and Teaching" in *Interpreting Isaiah for Preaching and Teaching* (Greenville: Smyth and Helwys, 1989).

[31] Ibid., 9.

[32] Ibid., 9ff.

[33] Ibid., 14ff.

[34] Some scholars maintain that he is the same prophet as the prophet of the exile, now returned to Jerusalem.

[35] Staton, 17ff.

[36] Ibid, 22.

[37] Anthony R. Ceresko, *Introduction to the Old Testament: A Liberation Perspective* (New York: Orbis Books, 1992), 9-10.

[38] Quoted by Daniel L. Smith in *The Religion of the Landless: The Social Context of the Babylonian Exile* (Bloomington IN: Myer Stone, 1989), vii.

[39] Ibid., 205.

[40] Tate, 212.

[41] Durham, "Psalms," in *The Broadman Bible Commentary*, vol. IV (Nashville: Broadman Press, 1971), 153ff.

[42] John Goldingay, *Theological Diversity and the Authority of the Old Testament* (Grand Rapids: William B. Eerdmans Publishing Company, 1987), 216.

[43] Ibid., 217.

[44] Ibid., 191-92.

[45] Brevard S. Childs, *Old Testament Theology in a Canonical Context* (Philadelphia: Fortress Press, 1990), 12.

[46] John H. Hayes and Frederick Prussner, *Old Testament Theology: Its History and Development* (Atlanta: John Knox Press, 1984).

[47] Gerald Hasel, *Old Testament Theology: Basic Issues in the Current Debate* (Grand Rapids: William B. Eerdmans Publishing Company, 1991).

[48] Leo G. Perdue, *The Collapse of History: Reconstructing Old Testament Theology* (Minneapolis: Fortress Press, 1994).

[49] Walther Eichrodt, *Theology of the Old Testament*, vols. 1 & 2 (Philadelphia: Westminster Press, 1967); Gerhard von Rad, *Old Testament Theology*, vols. 1 & 2 (New York: Harper and Row, 1962, 1968).

[50] Walter Brueggemann, *Theology of the Old Testament* (Minneapolis: Fortress Press, 1997), xv.

[51] Edmund Jacob, *Theology of the Old Testament* (New York: Harper and Brothers Publishers, 1958).

[52] H. H. Rowley, *The Faith of Israel* (Philadelphia: The Westminster Press, 1956).

[53] Childs, *Old Testament Theology in a Canonical Context* (Philadelphia: Fortress Press, 1990).

2

God's Chosen: Israelites and Gentiles

Listen to me, O coastlands
pay attention, you peoples
        from far away!
The LORD called me before I
        was born,
        while I was in my mother's
        womb he named me.
He made my mouth like a sharp
        sword,
        in the shadow of his hand he
        hid me;
he made me a polished arrow,
        in his quiver he hid me away.
And he said to me, "You are my
        servant,
Israel, in whom I will be
        glorified." (Isa 49:1-3)

May God be gracious to us and
        bless us
        and make his face to shine upon
        us,   *Selah*
that your way may be known
        upon earth,
        your saving power among all
        nations.

Let the peoples praise you,
    O God;
        let all the peoples praise you.
Let the nations be glad and sing
    for joy,
        for you judge the peoples with
    equity
    and guide the nations upon
    earth.   *Selah*
Let the peoples praise you,
    O God;
        let all the peoples praise you.
The earth has yielded its increase;
    God, our God, has blessed us.
May God continue to bless us;
    let all the ends of the earth
    revere him. (Ps 67)

The Concept of God's People (Israel) and Peoples (Gentiles)

The theological ideas that follow in this book are based mainly on the canonical writings (39 books of the Protestant Old Testament) of those people called Israelites or Jews, a people often spoken of as God's chosen people. It would be more appropriate to say that the Old Testament regularly speaks of them as the LORD's (Yahweh's)[1] especially chosen while others (Gentiles) are on occasion and in some fashion depicted as the LORD's chosen.

Among the things we will be investigating in this chapter is the way the LORD's chosen interact with each other even to the point of affecting the *content of Israel's scripture, the source of our theology.* Thus it is important that we consider this matter before looking further into the Old Testament ideas of "God," "humanity," or other traditional Old Testament theological themes.

While the Old Testament mainly depicts Israel as the LORD's especially chosen, there are passages that, when taken alone, seem to recognize no difference between God's relationship to Israel and to the Gentiles. For instance, there are passages that speak of the LORD's planting certain Gentiles in their geographical habitat as surely as the LORD gave Palestine to the Israelites. There are expressions usually reserved for Israel that are bestowed upon Gentiles. Further, when discipline is advisable, the LORD sees to it that neither Israelites nor Gentiles are exempt. Moreover, the LORD uses each chosen community to mete out discipline on the other.

The Old Testament's testimony, based on Amos and Deuteronomy, is that God plants various peoples in the places of God's choice. Amos puts it thusly:

> Are you not like the Ethiopians
> to me,
> O people of Israel? says the
> LORD.
> Did I not bring Israel up from the
> land of Egypt,
> and the Philistines from Caphtor
> and the Arameans from
> Kir? (Amos 9:7)

Similar views are expressed in Deuteronomy. As the Israelites prepared to leave the wilderness of Sinai they were commanded not to take the land of the Edomites, Moabites, and the Ammonites because Israel's God, the LORD, has previously given the land to those who already dwelt in those places (Deut 2:4-5, 9, 19). Note, for example, the words that apply to Edom:

> You are about to pass through the territory of your kindred, the descen-
> dents of Esau, who live in Seir. They will be afraid of you, so, be very
> careful not to engage in battle with them, for I will not give you even so
> much as a foot's length of their land, since I [the LORD] have given Mount
> Seir to Esau as a possession. (Deut 2:4-5)

While the passages from Amos and those from Deuteronomy do not address the relationship of the LORD to all Gentiles, we might rightly extrapolate from these that what holds true for the named Gentiles also holds true for others as well.

However, Israel's testimony concerning the LORD's gift of land to the Gentiles was not always of one piece. For instance, while Deuteronomy bears witness to the viewpoint that Ammon received its land from the LORD (Deut 2:16-19), Jephthah, an Old Testament Judge, maintains that the land came from the hands of Chemosh, Ammon's god.[2] By use of diplomacy rather than warfare, Jephthah tried to convince the Ammonite king to cease the plunder of Israelite land. It is in this context that Jephthah puts the

following question to the Ammonite king: "Should you not possess what
your god Chemosh gives you to possess? And should we not be the ones to
possess everything that the LORD our God has conquered for our benefit?"
(Judg 11:24).

It is Israel's dominant testimony that the LORD bestows on Israel her
land, and on the various Gentile nations their land, and it is this testimony
that provides the materials for our theology. We modern readers, like the
ancient ones, have to decide for ourselves what to do with the testimony. The
answer to many of modern Israel's problems hinge on the response of all parties involved to the testimony of ancient Israel. Israel's testimony is that not
only has the LORD planted others than herself in specific geographical terri-
tories, but the LORD has even addressed others with words usually reserved
for Israel: "people of the LORD"[3] and "work of your [the LORD's] hand."[4]
Note these amazing words in the book of Isaiah:

> On that day Israel will be the third with Egypt and Assyria, a blessing in
> the midst of the earth, whom the LORD of hosts has blessed, saying
> "Blessed be *Egypt my people*, and *Assyria the work of my hands*, and Israel my
> heritage. (Isa 19:24-25. Italics added)

If, as the "author" of Proverbs says, "the LORD reproves the ones he
loves," then the LORD loves both Israelites and Gentiles, because the LORD
disciplines both. Again, we are reminded that it is Israel's testimony that the
LORD disciplines the various Gentile nations even if the Gentile testimony
might be otherwise.[5] Not only does Amos declare that the LORD punishes
the Gentiles as well as the Israelites, he even introduces the punishment of
each with the same judgment formula:

> Thus says the LORD:
> For three transgressions of Israel,
> and for four, I will not revoke
>   the punishment;
> because they sell the righteous
>   for silver,
> and the needy for a pair of
>   sandals . . . (Amos 2:6)
>
> Thus says the LORD:
> For three transgressions of

> Damascus [Gentile],
> and for four, I will not revoke
>   the punishment;
> because they have threshed Gilead
> with threshing sledges of iron . . . (Amos 1:3)

As noted above, in some cases the LORD uses the chosen to mete out punishment on others. Concerning Israel's punishment of the Gentiles, Numbers puts it this way:

> In the plains of Moab by the Jordan at Jericho, the LORD spoke to Moses, saying: Speak to the Israelites, and say to them: When you cross over the Jordan into the land of Canaan, you shall drive out all of the inhabitants of the land from before you, destroy all their figured stones, destroy all their cast images, and demolish all their high places. (Num 33:50-52)

On the other hand, a Gentile nation, such as Assyria, can become the LORD's chosen rod of discipline of Israel:

> Ah, Assyria, the rod of my
>   anger —
> the club in their hands is
>   my fury!
> Against a godless nation [Israel] I
>   send him,
> and against the people of my
>   wrath I command him,
> to take spoil and seize plunder,
> and to tread them down like the
>   mire of the streets. (Isa 10:5-6)

Even if one day the LORD can declare that a Gentile nation, such as Egypt, is the LORD's people, the dominant testimony of the Old Testament is that this term is reserved for Israel throughout her long history from Abraham onward. The LORD's involvement with Israel is always more intimate and personal than with various Gentile nations. For instance, even Amos, who so strongly insists that there is equality in geographical placement between Israelites and Gentiles, declares that among the chosen the LORD "knows" (a term of intimacy) only Israel. Amos, thusly, quotes the LORD:

You only have I known
of all the families of the earth;
therefore I will punish you
for all your iniquities. (Amos 3:2)

Election Expressions

Israel

As shown above, we saw that God, in some fashion, chose both Israelites and Gentiles. Walter Brueggemann, in *Theology of the Old Testament*, discusses this idea under the chapter headings: "Israel as Yahweh's Partner" (ch. 14), and "The Nations as Yahweh's Partner" (ch. 16).[6] While Brueggemann uses the word "chosen," he also uses the word "recruit," a very felicitous word in helping us to understand the LORD's relationship to both Israelites and Gentiles. As Brueggemann puts it: "Yahweh in freedom has the power and capacity to recruit nations for Yahweh's own purposes, even if those purposes are not the intention of the nations . . . ."[7] The latter part of the statement is significant in helping us to understand that the Gentiles did not show the same kind of awareness of the LORD's plans as did Israel. Further, Israel's relationship to the LORD is depicted in every sense as more intimate and personal, including the making of covenants, than that of the Gentiles.

One way theologians speak of God's special choice of Israel is to speak of it as God's *election* of Israel. Edmond Jacob defines such election as "the initial act by which Yahweh comes into relationship with his people and the permanent reality which assures the constancy of that bond."[8]

When Israel's writers wished to express the belief that the LORD has especially chosen Israel, they did so by a variety of means such as grammatical forms (nouns, adjectives, and verbs), images, and stories. They regularly used the singular with such words as people, family, and nation when addressing Israel, while using the plural for the same words when addressing the Gentiles. The reader needs to be aware, however, that the plural form may at times include both Gentiles and Israelites. For instance, in the following speech of Moses, the terms "nations" and "peoples" may be inclusive. However, they seem to refer only to the Gentiles, while the "people" is reserved for Israel:

When the Most High
    apportioned the nations.
When he divided humankind,

> he fixed the boundaries of the
>   peoples
> according to the number of the
>   gods;
> the LORD's own portion was his
>   people,
> Jacob his allotted share. (Deut 32:8-9)

Israel's fondness for addressing herself as the "people of the LORD" is highlighted in the accounts of two experiences that come to us from the period of the Judges and the early days of the Kingdom. In the days of the judges, Barak, with the aid of the prophetess, Deborah, won a significant battle. In the glow of victory, Israel is addressed in song as the "people of the LORD." The song, in part, reads as follows:

> "Tell of it, you who ride on white
>   donkeys,
> you who sit on rich carpets
> and you who walk by the way.
> To the sound of musicians at the
>   watering places,
> there they repeat the triumphs
>   of the LORD,
> the triumphs of his peasantry in
>   Israel.
> Then down to the gates marched
>   the people of the LORD." (Judg 5:10-11)

However, God's people are not always victorious, as is evident in the deaths of King Saul, Jonathan, and many noble Israelite warriors at the hands of the Philistines. Upon hearing of the slaughter, David, along with his troops, expressed deep outward sorrow, including David's composition of a funeral elegy. The author of 2 Samuel expressed it thusly:

> Then David took hold of his clothes and tore them; and all the men who were with him did the same. They mourned and wept, and fasted until the evening for Saul and for Jonathan and for the army ["people," RSV] of the LORD and for the house of Israel, because they had fallen by the sword. (2 Sam 1:11-12)

Besides hearing the LORD address Israel as the LORD's people, she is also described as the LORD's own special possession, holy nation, and priestly kingdom:

> Now therefore, if you obey my voice and keep my covenant, you shall be my treasured possession out of all the peoples. Indeed, the whole earth is mine, but you shall be for me a priestly kingdom and a holy nation. (Exod 19:5-6)

"Treasured possession" is another way of saying that Israel had a special relationship to the LORD. Dale Patrick says that the term translated "treasured possession" refers to

> the private wealth of a king, in distinction from wealth held in trust for the people . . . . From this we can infer that Israel is YHWH's [the LORD's] private treasure, in distinction from the peoples of the earth.[9]

"Holy nation" means that while of necessity Israel might have to live with the nations, she must religiously and morally separate herself from them. To be a priestly nation meant that she was to live in the midst of the nations in such a way that she brought the nations to the LORD and to God's ways for all humans.

Verbally, Israel understood she was called by the LORD, separated for the LORD, and thus she belonged to the LORD (Deut 7:1-6; Hos 11:1). Several years ago at a church, the senior author met a middle-aged couple who showed the signs of a life of debauchery before their marriage. The husband told the author his life's story in some detail. The author will never forget the husband's closing words that went something like this:

> I said to her, "Woman I know what kind of life we both used to live, but no more. We now *belong* to each other. I will be faithful to you and you to me."

Besides the use of nouns, modifiers, and verbs, Israel used a variety of images to express her special relationship to the LORD. Since these will be discussed in some length in the next chapter on "God," they shall only be listed at this time: God's wife (Isa 54:5), God's son (Hos 11:1), God's flock (Isa 40:11), God's vine (Isa 5:1-7), God's pottery (Jer 18:5-6).

Lastly, we look at Israel's use of story, contained in the accounts in Genesis through Nehemiah, to testify to her strong belief in her close relationship to the LORD. It is a story that begins with small clan movements as told in Genesis, proceeds with rudimentary and more developed tribal movements as presented in Exodus through Judges, blossoms into nationhood as told in Samuel through Kings, suffers great national loss — including exile — as told in Kings through Chronicles, and regains some sense of identity as presented in Ezra and Nehemiah.

The shape of the Old Testament people of the LORD varies across the centuries from that of a large family/small clan such as Abraham, to a theocratic system (governed by God) of tribes from Moses through Samuel, followed by an institutional state as governed by David and Solomon, and an exile and returning remnant under Assyria, Babylonia, and Persia. Each of these various modes/models are either caused by the LORD (Abraham – Gen 2:1-3) or have God's consent (Monarchy – 1 Sam 8:1-9).

Formally, God expressed the election of Israel with a series of covenants. Some of the more significant ones are those made with the Patriarchs (Gen 17:1-8; 26:23-25; 28:10-17), with the Israelites at Sinai (Exod 19:1-6), and with the Davidic dynasty (2 Sam 7:8-17). An unusual Israelite expression for making a covenant is "cutting a covenant."[10] Translators are not likely to translate the Hebrew word for "cutting" literally. The term may refer to the cutting of letters in a clay tablet, though it more than likely refers to the cutting of animals.[11] On one occasion, when God pledged Abraham numerous posterity, the covenant ceremony between God and Abraham involved the actual cutting of heifers, she-goats, and a ram. God, in the form of a smoking fire pot and flaming torch, met Abraham between the cut halves of the animals. The author of Genesis records:

> On that day the LORD made [cut] a covenant with Abram, saying, "To your descendants I give this land…" (Gen 15:18)

Gentiles

If the story of the Israelites appears on many pages, if not all, of the Old Testament, this is not true of the Gentiles. However, neither are Gentiles hidden away in some dark corner of the Scriptures where they are stumbled upon by the reader. One way of recognizing scriptural references to the Gentiles is to note such specific names as Canaanite, Egyptian, Philistine, Assyrian, and Babylonian. Beyond this, the reader needs to be aware of more general terms such as "islands," "coastlands," and "ends of the earth."[12] These terms appear quite frequently in that portion of Isaiah we have designated as Second Isaiah:

> Even the nations are like a drop
>   from a bucket,
> and are accounted as dust on
>   the scales;
> see, he takes up the isles like
>   fine dust. (Isa 40:15)
> Listen to me in silence,
>   O coastlands;
> let the peoples renew their
>   strength;
> let them approach, then let
>   them speak;
> let us together draw near for
>   judgment. (Isa 41:1)

God's Blessing of Israelites and Gentiles

Blessing

According to Genesis 12, it is God's plan to bless Abraham with the understanding that Abraham will share the blessing with the Gentiles:

> Now the LORD said to Abram, "Go from your country and your kindred and your father's house to the land that I will show you. I will make of you a great nation, and I will bless you, and make your name great, so that you will be a blessing. I will bless those who bless you, and the one who curses you I will curse; and in you all the families of the earth shall be blessed." (Gen 12:1-3)

There are a number of ideas that are not made clear in this passage. For instance, is the blessing of the Gentiles to be accomplished by Abraham alone or with his posterity, what exactly is the nature of the blessing, does God have other ways to bless the Gentiles, and will God use the Gentiles to bless Abraham and his posterity? The answer to some of these questions is addressed, or at least suggested, in other Old Testament scripture. Concerning God's means for blessing the Gentiles, Walter Brueggemann remarks:

> Israel had to articulate how the nations were related to Yahweh, a relation
> that in part was mediated through Israel but in part stood independent of
> Israel. The tension of "through Israel" and "independent of Israel" . . . is a
> complicated matter, and one that admitted of no obvious or simple articu-
> lation. It is true that the Old Testament is pervasively preoccupied with
> Israel; and therefore it comes as a surprise to notice the richness of the
> material . . . beyond Israel . . . . [13]

Concerning whether God will use the Gentiles to bless Israel, Donald Senior
and Carol Stuhlmueller, in *The Biblical Foundations for Missions*, maintain
that we should not be surprised — in fact we should expect — that the
nations would "have something positive to contribute to Israel's understanding of God."[14]

In such areas as culture, technology, commerce, and government, the
Old Testament provides ample information that God blessed both the
LORD's people and peoples. Concerning the Israelites, it may be noted that
they were adept in such enterprises as shepherding, commerce, well digging,
and military prowess (Gen 14:13-16; 24:34; 26:12-22). Joseph, son of Jacob,
was so learned in matters of agriculture (production and preservation) and
commerce that he was placed in charge of these things in the land of Egypt
(Gen 41:39-45). Even in the wilderness of Sinai, the Israelites could fashion
a golden calf and a tabernacle with its furnishings (Exod 25–40).[15]
Additional examples could be traced through the periods of Conquest,
Judges, and Monarchy.

While God was blessing the Israelites in such matters as agriculture and
technology, God was blessing the Gentiles in even greater ways. And even if
we suppose that God stood aside and let the Gentiles develop their own
native intellect, it would still be of God as the Old Testament understood it.
For the Old Testament makes no sharp distinction between what God deliberately causes or permits. A few examples of Gentile intelligence and
accomplishment may be cited: the great store cities and military expertise of
the Egyptians (Exod 1:12; 14:5-7), the seafaring skill of the Phoenicians
(1 Kgs 9:26-28; Ezek 26-28), the military prowess of the Assyrians (Isa 10:5-
19), and the great literary and cultural achievements of the Babylonians (Isa
47:10; Dan 1:1-4).

Shared Blessings

To what extent the Gentiles and Israelites shared knowledge and technology is not always clearly stated in the Old Testament. We are informed that Isaac kept digging wells after each well was taken away from him by some neighboring clan until there finally was a well for everyone (Gen 26:19-22). Joseph, using his God-given agricultural and commercial acumen, was able to provide grain during a time of famine to the Egyptians and all who came from a distance seeking it (Gen 41:39-57). More than likely, the knowledge the Israelites used for fashioning a wilderness tabernacle with its furnishings had been learned, at least in part, from the Egyptians.

Solomon's relationship with his Gentile neighbors can help instruct us in the way of God's people with God's peoples. For instance, Hiram, king of Tyre, provided Solomon with cedar and cypress timbers for the erection of the Israelite temple (1 Kgs 5:7-9). Further, Hiram sent craftsmen to fashion bronze objects for the temple (1 Kgs 7:13-45). Besides the provisions for the temple, Hiram supplied Solomon with ships, along with trained sailors, for Solomon's Red Sea fleet (1 Kgs 9:25-28). Through the Red Sea commerce, augmented by overland trade, Solomon entered into trade agreements with many of the Gentile nations of the Near East. For instance, we read:

> A chariot could be imported from Egypt for six hundred shekels of silver, and a horse for one hundred fifty; so through the king's traders they were exported to all the kings of the Hittites and the kings of Aram. (1 Kgs 10:29)

The most interesting of all of Solomon's commercial activities were his transactions with the Queen of Sheba. The author of Kings concludes the visit of the queen as follows:

> Then she gave the king one hundred twenty talents of gold, a great quantity of spices, and precious stones; . . . . Meanwhile King Solomon gave to the Queen of Sheba every desire that she expressed, as well as what he gave her out of Solomon's royal bounty. (1 Kgs 10:10, 13)

When we turn from matters of technology and commerce to those of religion, Israel's dominant testimony is that she is religiously superior to her Gentile neighbors and is expected to share this superior insight with them.

In fact, she insists that at the proper time there will be Gentiles who will agree with this position. Zechariah puts it this way:

> Thus says the LORD of hosts: Peoples shall yet come, the inhabitants of many cities; the inhabitants of one city shall go to another, saying, "Come, let us go to entreat the favor of the LORD, and to seek the LORD of hosts; I myself am going." Many peoples and strong nations shall come to seek the LORD of hosts in Jerusalem, and to entreat the favor of the LORD. Thus says the LORD of hosts: In those days ten men from nations of every language shall take hold of a Jew, grasping his garment and saying, "Let us go with you, for we have heard that God is with you." (Zech 8:20-23)

The above passage reflects one of the positions of Israel concerning her mission to the Gentiles, namely, that it would be a centripetal or attracting mission. Along with the above quotation, other passages, such as the following from Isaiah, may be cited:

> In the days to come
> the mountain of the LORD's
>   house
> shall be established as the highest
>   of the mountains,
> and shall be raised above
>   the hills;
> all nations shall stream to it.
> Many peoples shall come and
>   say,
> "Come, let us go up to the
>   mountain of the LORD,
> to the house of the God of
>   Jacob;
> that he may teach us his ways
> and that we may walk in his
> paths." (Isa 2:2-3)

One passage speaks of Gentiles flowing into Jerusalem, bringing with them exiled Jews as an offering to Israel's God and now their God:

> For I [the LORD] know their works and their thoughts, and I am coming to gather all nations and tongues; and they shall come and see my glory, . .

> . . . They shall bring all your kindred from all the nations as an offering to the LORD, on horses, and in chariots, and in litters, and on mules, and on dromedaries, to my holy mountain Jerusalem, says the LORD, just as the Israelites bring a grain offering in a clean vessel to the house of the LORD. (Isa 66:18-20)

While the Old Testament evidence is sparse, it is clear that even in religious matters God hasn't totally left the Gentiles alone while giving complete attention to the Israelites. For instance, in order to shame the immoral and careless post-exilic Jewish priests of Jerusalem, Malachi compares unfavorably such priests with honest and true Gentile worshippers. While the passage may refer to Diaspora (exiled) Jews since the offering is said to be made in the name of the LORD, the reference to the worshippers being "from the rising of the sun to its setting" seems to argue against that position. Perhaps the passage can be interpreted to mean that true worship is in the name of the LORD whether one recognizes it or not. It certainly doesn't follow of necessity that such Gentile worship is superior to true Jewish worship. In any case, let the passage speak for itself:

> For from the rising of the sun to its setting my name is great among the nations, . . . says the LORD of hosts. But you [priest] profane it when you . . . bring what . . . is lame or sick . . . as your offering! . . . Cursed be the cheat who has a male in the flock and vows to give it yet sacrifices to the LORD what is blemished; for I am a great King, says the LORD of hosts, and my name is reverenced among the nations. (Mal 1:11-14)

There are also passages that reflect the occasional superior ethical insight of the Gentiles to that of the Israelites. For instance, sometime after Abraham entered Palestine he migrated to Egypt during a time of famine. There he allowed the Pharaoh to think that Sarah, his wife, was in reality his sister. Pharaoh placed her in his harem only to be subject to all sorts of problems. Pharaoh called in Abraham and "dressed him down," as we would say today, for the deception. It seems fair to conclude that it was out of a sense of morality that Pharaoh acted rather than just as a reaction to his sufferings (Gen 12:10-20). Clyde Francisco expresses it as follows: "It was most embarrassing for the father of the Jews to be deported from Egypt by a Pharaoh whose sense of right was higher than his own."[16]

Perhaps of greater significance concerning the relationship of Gentiles and Israelites in religious matters is the story of Abraham's encounter with

Melchizedek, the priest-king of Salem. Abraham graciously and humbly accepted Melchizedek's blessing in the name of Melchizedek's god, El Elyon (God Most High), and also paid Melchizedek a tithe. The Genesis text reads:

> And King Melchizedek of Salem brought out bread and wine; he was priest
> of God Most High [El Elyon]. He blessed him and said,
> "Blessed be Abram by God Most
> High,
> maker of heaven and earth;
> and blessed be God Most High,
> Who has delivered your enemies
> into your hand!"
> And Abraham gave him one tenth of everything. (Gen 14:19-20)

While Melchizedek blessed Abraham and received Abraham's tithe in the name of Melchizedek's God, Abraham also saw the hand of his God in all this.[17] Even though a review of the commentaries on Genesis sets forth many problems involved in the account, the story does seem to support the idea that the Israelites were aware that their God, the LORD, continued to influence the lives of the Gentiles even after the choosing of Israel, in the person of Abraham.

A study of the authorship of Proverbs can be very instructive concerning Israel's use of specifically non-Israelite materials in its writings, writings which eventually would be canonized. There are three sections/collections that bear the stamp of non-Israelite wisdom: "The Words of the Wise" (22:17-24; 34), "The Words of Agur" (30:1-33), and "The Words of King Lemuel" (31:1-9). There is a striking similarity between "The Words of the Wise" and the instruction of Amenemope, an Egyptian wise man.[18] Leo Perdue states:

> The material in 22:17–24:22 is an instruction based on a well-known
> Egyptian text, "The Teachings of Amen-em-ope," dating from the thir-
> teenth century BCE This is one clear example of the international
> character of the Israelite wisdom tradition.[19]

In the New Revised Standard Version of the Old Testament, "The Words of Agur" in chapter 30 and "The Words of King Lemuel" in chapter 31 are followed by the word "oracle" (God speech). In the original Revised Standard Version, as well as the Revised English Version and the New

Jerusalem Bible, the word "oracle" is rendered "from Massa." James
Crenshaw refers to Agur as "the Massaite" and to Lemuel as the "king of
Massa."[20] Assuming the reasonable correctness of the words "Massaite" and
"Massa," the reference could be to an Arabian tribe, tracing its origins to a
certain Massa, son of Ishmael (Abraham's and Hagar's son in Gen 25:12-14
and 1 Chron 1:29-30).[21] Leo Perdue states that the proverbial collections in
chapters 30 and 31 are derived "from the wisdom of Arabia."[22]

Israel's Special Mission to the Gentiles

Mission Consciousness

Throughout her history Israel was aware — however vague — that she had a
mission to the Gentiles. The first biblical reference, in its present canonized
form, is found in Genesis 12:

> Now the LORD said to Abraham, "Go from your country and your kin-
> dred and your father's house to the land I will show you. I will make of you
> a great nation, and I will bless you and make your name great, so that you
> will be a blessing. I will bless those who bless you, and the one who curses
> you I will curse; and in you all the families of the earth will be blessed.
> (Gen 12:1-3)

Abraham moved out of Haran with whatever knowledge he had to do
the bidding of the LORD. We can certainly praise him for such faith without
giving him credit for a full measure of understanding that would only gradually be revealed to Israel over a span of hundreds of years. Surely Henry
Cornell Goerner goes much too far when he remarks:

> If the plan was to work, God must take Abraham into his confidence.
> Abraham must understand the plan and the ultimate purpose. For he must
> become a willing, conscious co-worker with God in the effort to win men
> to voluntary obedience and co-operation by means of persuasion, educa-
> tion, and regeneration.[23]

Continuing expressions of Israel's consciousness of a mission to the
Gentiles are found in the Old Testament, especially in the Psalms and
prophetical books. At this point, one marvelous mission psalm, Psalm 67,
will suffice. The psalm begins with the worshippers praying for God's blessing, probably reflective of the Aaronic prayer of Numbers 6. The prayer is no

selfish prayer, however, for its ultimate intent is that the Gentiles may experience God's justice and saving power. The complete psalm is presented earlier as one of the paradigm passages.

Ideas Related to the Implementation of Israelite Mission to the Gentiles

The Genesis 12 account of Israel's testimony of an awareness of a mission to the Gentiles spells out neither the rationale nor the methodology/mechanics for such a mission. In fact, at no specific place in the Old Testament do we find a statement of such a plan. However, this does not mean that the Old Testament offers nothing by way of Israel's understanding of implementation of a Gentile mission. What follows, by way of organized selected passages, are some of the ideas related to the implementation of such a mission.

In the first place, Israel did not develop some master plan — in fact, the Jews to this day do not have such a plan — for carrying out her mission to the Gentiles. Rather, the contact would take place when the Gentiles flowed into Palestine — especially Jerusalem — seeking religious instruction from the Israelites/Jews. There were exceptions, of course. For instance, the book of Jonah tells the story of a reluctant prophet going to the Gentile city of Nineveh. Moreover, the exiled Israelites or Jews had the opportunity to minister to the Gentiles, if they chose.

If Israel was to carry out her mission to the Gentiles it meant, above all else, that she must be faithful to the LORD. When she went running after other gods, such as Baal, the mission was put in jeopardy. Prophets, such as Elijah, were adamant about Israel's exclusive commitment to the LORD. Concerning Elijah, the author of Kings states:

> Elijah then came near to all the people, and said, "How long will you go limping with two different opinions? If the LORD is God, follow him; but if Baal, then follow him." (1 Kgs 18:21)

Faithfulness to the LORD did not guarantee a successful mission unless Israel exhibited certain attitudes toward the Gentiles. For instance, Israel was instructed to show kindness to strangers in her midst who wanted nothing to do with her god. Note the command concerning nonconverted strangers as set forth in Leviticus:

> When an alien resides with you in your land, you shall not oppress the alien. The alien who resides with you shall be to you as the citizen among

you; you shall love the alien as yourself, for you were aliens in the land of
Egypt: I am the LORD your God. (Lev 19:33-34)

If there was the danger that Israel would treat aliens/resident
strangers/sojourners in a despicable way, there was equal danger that she
would refuse to embrace such strangers as converts, and this would be even
more devastating. God spoke to this probability through a postexilic
prophet. Faithful Israelites, faithful proselytes/converts, and future faithful
proselytes must all be treated alike. God will accept the worship of every
such person. Consider carefully the following:

> Thus says the LORD:
> Maintain justice, and do what
>   is right,
> for soon my salvation will come,
> and my deliverance be revealed.
> Happy is the mortal who does
>   this,
> the one who holds it fast
> who keeps the sabbath, not
>   profaning it,
> and refrains from doing any
>   evil.
> Do not let the foreigner joined to
>   the LORD say,
> "The LORD will surely separate
>   me from his people;…"
>
> And the foreigners who join
>   themselves to the LORD,
> to minister to him, to love the
>   name of the LORD,
> and to be his servants,
> all who keep the sabbath, and do
>   not profane it,
> and hold fast my covenant —
> these I will bring to my holy
>   mountain,
> and make them joyful in my
>   house of prayer;

their burnt offerings and their
    sacrifices
will be accepted on my altar;
for my house shall be called a
    house of prayer
for all peoples. (Isa 56:1-3, 6-7)

It is easy to assume that for Israel to attract the Gentiles to herself, and thus to her god, she must be attractive in our usual way of understanding it. However, one prophet, known as the prophet of the exile or Second Isaiah, expressed the unheard of idea that God's Servant,[24] who may be described as Israel as a whole, or as a righteous remnant, or individual representative, might actually attract the Gentiles through undeserved suffering. This is poignantly set forth in Isaiah 52:13ff. Reflecting on this passage, Walter Harrelson declares that Israel "serves to display before the nations such fidelity to God in the midst of suffering that the nations are caused to marvel, recognizing that Israel suffers in their stead, faithful to God despite the mistreatment endured at the hands of these nations."[25] And so these nations declare:

Surely he has borne our infirmities
and carried our diseases;
yet we accounted him stricken,
struck down by God, and
    afflicted.
But he was wounded for our
    transgressions,
crushed for our iniquities;
upon him was the punishment that
    made us whole,
and by his bruises we are
    healed. (Isa 53:4-5)[26]

Conclusion

Much of what Israel has learned about the LORD, and about creation in general and humankind in particular, she learned by way of her God-given observation and her intimate relationship with her Creator. However, it should be noted that Israel absorbed into her own culture institutions and belief systems that were part of larger humanity. John Walton and Victor Matthews state:

The issue is not a question of whether the Israelites "borrowed" from their neighbors or not. God's process of revelation required that he condescend to us, accommodate our humanity and express himself in familiar language and metaphors. It should be no surprise that many of the common elements of the culture of the day were adopted — at times adapted, at times totally converted — and used to accomplish God's purposes. Indeed we would be surprised if this were not the case.[27]

In any case, if the LORD is the source of all that is good and true, perhaps it matters not where one leaves off and the other begins. As we said at the beginning of this chapter, the theological ideas that follow are mainly based on those Israelite/Jewish scriptures that Christians speak of as the Old Testament.

The Church and Secular Learning

As Israel sought to relate to the gentiles, along with their culture, belief system, et cetera, so the early church had to come to grips with those people in whose midst she lived. One of the most difficult decisions—especially for the more intellectual—was the proper relationship to the philosophical ideas and writings of Greek and Latin authors. The various viewpoints may be summarized as negative, positive, and mixed.

Representative of the negative viewpoint are the off-quoted words of Tertullian in his *Prescriptions Against Heretics*:

> What is there in common between Athens and Jerusalem? What between the Academy and the Church? What between heretics and Christians? (Bettenson, 5-6).

Reflective of the positive view are the following words from Clement of Alexandria's *Miscellanies (Stromaties)*:

> Thus philosophy was necessary to the Greek's for righteousness, until the coming of the Lord. And now it assists towards true religion as a kind of preparatory training for those who arrive at faith by way of demonstration. For "Thy foot shall not stumble" if thou attribute to Providence all good, whether belonging to the Greeks or to us. For God is the source of all good things; of some primarily, as of the old and new testaments; of others by consequence, as of philosophy... For philosophy was a "schoolmaster" to bring the Greek mind to Christ, as the Law brought the Hebrews. Thus philosophy was a preparation, paving the way towards perfection in Christ. (Bettenson, 6)

Representative of those who struggled to come to a proper Christian attitude toward non-Christian writings were Jerome and Augustine. After his conversion to Christianity, Jerome (c. 400 A.D.) at first alternated between a revulsion to non-Christian writings and a continued attraction to them. He eventually made peace with the idea that such writings, rightly understood, could, serve Christianity. Harris Harbison puts it this way:

> Some twenty years after his Vision [In a vision Jerome promised never again to read a non-Christian book], he had found a solution of the conflict between his Christianity and his love of secular literature. To Magus, who reproached him of quoting so often from pagan authors, he gave a long list of Hebrew and Christian writers who had done the same, including Moses and Paul. Paul, he said, knew the command in Deuteronomy (21:10ff) that "when a captive woman had had her head shaved, her eyebrows and all her hair cut off, and her nails pared, she might then be taken to wife." So Jerome has taken secular learning to wife, he says, after "shaving off and cutting away all in her that is dead, whether this be idolatry, pleasure, error, or lust," in the confidence that his "so-called defilement with an alien" would increase the population of Christians. (11-12)

Augustine, a contemporary of Jerome, also had misgivings concerning non-Christian writing. Again we turn to Harbison:

> In the end, Augustine like Jerome came to terms with the pagan writers and wrote a classic defense of Christian Humanism in his book *On Christian Instruction*. But the two men thought of secular learning in characteristically different ways. To Jerome pagan learning was a captive woman who drew him by her charms and whom he would marry if the law allowed. To Augustine it was gold and silver, like the spoil which the children of Israel were commanded to take with them out of Egypt and turn to better use. (15)

Notes

Henry Bettenson, ed. *Documents of the Christian Church*, 2d ed. (London: Oxford University Press, 1963)

Harris E. Harbison, *The Christian Scholar in the Age of the Reformation* (New York: Charles Scribner's Sons, 1956).

Notes

[1] The word designated by the word "LORD" in small caps in English translations denotes the divine name in the Hebrew texts called the Tetragrammaton, or four letters represented by the English letters YHWH. A Jewish reader will always say, *adonai* ("the Lord") or *hashem* ("the name").

[2] It is probable that Chemosh was the god of the Moabites and Milcom the god of the Ammonites. See 1 Kgs 11:5, 7.

[3] For example see Judg 5:11.

[4] For example see Isa 64:8.

[5] The Mesha Stele/Moabite Stone depicts Chemosh, the Moabite god, as punishing Moab for her sins rather than the LORD as Amos declares (Amos 2:1). Joel F. Drinkard Jr., "Mesha Stele," *Mercer Dictionary of the Bible*, ed. Watson E. Mills et al. (Macon, Mercer University Press, 1990), 569.

[6] Walter Brueggemann, *Theology of the Old Testament: Testimony, Dispute, Advocacy* (Minneapolis: Fortress Press, 1997), 413 ff. and 492 ff.

[7] Brueggemann, 522.

[8] Edmund Jacob, *Theology of the Old Testament* (New York: Harper Brothers Publishers, 1958), 201.

[9] Dale Patrick, "Election," in *The Anchor Dictionary of the Bible*, vol. 2, ed. David Noel Freedman (New York: Doubleday, 1992), 438.

[10] The word "covenant" is translated from the Hebrew word *berit*. It can be defined as "a contract that establishes a new relationship between two parties." Common language used for entering into this new relationship in the Hebrew Bible includes "cutting, giving, establishing, entering, observing, breaking, transgressing, forgetting, and so forth."

[11] Jacob, 201.

[12] It should be noted that there are interpreters who understand these latter terms as referring to diaspora/dispersed Israelites rather than Gentiles. For instance, Stuhlmueller refers to them as "crypto [hidden] Israelites who were still believers at heart but had adopted Gentile patterns externally." See Donald Senior and Carroll Stuhlmueller, *The Biblical Foundation for Missions* (Mary Knoll, New York: Orbis Books, 1983), 94.

[13] Brueggemann, 492.

[14] Senior and Stuhlmueller, 11.

[15] See a more detailed description on the Tabernacle in chapter 6.

[16] Clyde Francisco, "Genesis," in *The Broadman Bible Commentary*, vol. 1 revised (Nashville, Broadman Press, 1969), 157-58.

[17] Gerhard von Rad, *Genesis*, trans. John H. Marks (Philadelphia: Westminster, 1972), 180.

[18] For the Egyptian text see Thomas D. Winton, ed. *Documents from Old Testament Times* (New York: Harper & Row Publishers, 1958), 175.

[19] Leo G. Perdue, "Proverbs, Book of" in *Mercer Dictionary of the Bible*, ed. Watson E. Mills et al. (Macon: Mercer University Press, 1990), 721.

[20] James L. Crenshaw, "Proverbs, Book of," in *The Anchor Bible Dictionary*, vol. 5, ed. David Noel Freedman (New York: Doubleday, 1992), 513.

[21] See the articles on "Massa (person)" and "Massa (place)" in the *The Anchor Bible Dictionary*, vol. 4, ed. David Noel Freedman (New York: Doubleday, 1992), 600.

[22] Perdue, "Proverbs, Book of" in *Mercer Dictionary of the Bible*, 721.

[23] Henry Cornell Goerner, *Thus It is Written* (Nashville: Broadman Press, 1944), 4.

[24] The Servant is mentioned in Isaiah 42:1ff; 49:1ff; 50:4ff; 52:13ff.

[25] Walter Harrelson, "Servant," in *Mercer Dictionary of the Bible*, ed. Watson E. Mills et al. (Macon: Mercer University Press, 1990), 812.

[26] It should be noted that some interpreters believe that the words are those of exilic Jews in reference to some unknown Jewish individual rather than the words of Gentiles to the Suffering Servant. For instance, see Page H. Kelley, "Isaiah" in *The Broadman Bible Commentary*, vol. 5 (Nashville: Broadman Press, 1971), 340ff.

[27] John H. Walton and Victor H. Matthews, *The Bible Background Commentary: Genesis-Deuteronomy* (Downer Grove IL: Intervarsity Press, 1997), 8.

3

GOD

The LORD said to Moses, "I will do the very thing that you have asked; for you have found favor in my sight, and I know you by name." Moses said, "Show me your glory, I pray." And he said, "I will make all my goodness pass before you, and will proclaim before you the name, 'The LORD'; and I will be gracious to whom I will be gracious, and will show mercy on whom I will show mercy. But," he said, "you cannot see my face; for no one can see me and live." And the LORD continued, "See there is a place by me where you shall stand on the rock; and while my glory passes by I will put you in the cleft of the rock, and I will cover you with my hand until I have passed by; then I will take away my hand, and you shall see my back; but my face shall not be seen." (Exod 33:17-23)

Where can I go from your spirit?
    Or where can I flee from your
    presence?
If I ascend to heaven, you are
    there;
if I make my bed in Sheol, you
    are there.
If I take the wings of the morning
    and settle at the farthest limits
    of the sea,
even there your hand shall
    lead me,
and your right hand shall hold
    me fast,

If I say, "Surely the darkness shall
    cover me,
and the light around me become
    night,"
even the darkness is not dark
    to you;
    the night is as night as bright as the day,
    for darkness is as light to you. (Ps 139:7-12)

These paradigm passages (along with other Old Testament passages) testify that God can be known, both in the sense of knowledge about God and in the sense of experience with God. Further, the passages teach us that the two ideas of knowledge are often so entwined that they cannot be separated. Again, it should be noted that there are limitations on our information about God and restrictions on our experiential relationship with God.

Many scholars have pointed out that the existence of God is taken for granted in the Old Testament.[1] Let the statement from Ludwig Koehler suffice:

> The assumption that God exists is the Old Testament's greatest gift to mankind. In the Old Testament God's existence is entirely a foregone conclusion, always presupposed; reference is continually being made to it; it is never denied or questioned. The fool says in his heart "there is no God," Psalm 14:1 . . . . But these are the words of people who are lacking in understanding . . . corrupt . . . They speak like that not in order to deny God but in order to evade His judgment . . . . They call in question His action as it affects their lives, but they do not call into question His existence. It is practical atheism, as the sinner practices it; not theological atheism. The latter is unknown in the Old Testament.[2]

How God is Known

How is God known? The present chapter shall organize the Old Testament answer to this question under the following categories: through creation/nature, through human experience, through teachings/pronouncements.

Through Creation/Nature

Throughout the Old Testament God is best known through direct experience (such as Moses at the burning bush) rather than through a more indirect encounter with God through nature. The latter, however, is not demeaned in the Old Testament. Today, an encounter with God through nature can be especially helpful to those persons not yet ready to experience the full knowledge that comes with a one-on-one human encounter with God.

A helpful book for understanding nature's contribution to humanity's understanding of God is James Barr's *Biblical Faith and Natural Theology.*[3] In chapter 5, Barr examines a number of Old Testament passages, including Psalm 19 and Psalm 104, that point to Israel's knowledge of God. Barr points out, however, that Karl Barth, the renowned European theologian, with his emphasis on special revelation as over against general revelation, does not think these Old Testament passages can bear the weight of an entranceway toward a knowledge of God. Echoing Barth's position are similar viewpoints held by Brevard Childs and Elizabeth Achtemeier, important American interpreters.[4]

Psalm 19 declares God can be known through nature, and Psalm 104 makes a statement about what certain Israelites knew about the character of God through their observation of nature.

> The heavens are telling the glory
>   of God;
> and the firmament proclaims
>   his handiwork . . . .
>
> The law of the LORD is perfect,
>   reviving the soul;
> The decrees of the LORD are sure,
>   making wise the simple; . . . (Ps 19:1,7)

Concerning this Psalm in its entirety James Barr remarks:

> God makes himself known in two complementary ways, first through the great works of creation which control the world, and secondly through his special communication exemplified here by his law. The two channels of natural and revealed theology are here very properly to be seen. It is not surprising that the Psalm was seen as a fine manifestation of their complementarity, as was traditional in the older Christianity.[5]

Psalm 104:27-28 states,

These [God's creatures] all look to you
to give them their food in due
    season;
when you give to them, they
    gather it up
when you open your hand, they
    are filled with good things.

The reader should read the entire Psalm to get its full flavor and to appreciate the following remarks of Barr: "No other biblical passage so strongly emphasizes that it was the *beneficent effects* of divine sustenance for animals and for humanity that signified the nature of God."[6]

Paul, Gentiles, Creation

In his mission tours it was Paul's practice to visit Jewish synagogues before moving on to Gentile audiences. At Lystra, on his first tour, he begins with Gentiles, leading us to believe that there was no synagogue there. Upon hearing that Paul had healed a crippled man, the local priest of Zeus made preparation to offer a sacrifice to Paul and Barnabas, Paul's companion, believing that they were gods incognito. In an effort to convince the people that he and Barnabas were really humans like themselves and to persuade them to become followers of his god, "the living God, who made the heavens and the earth," Paul tells them that his god had provided a witness: rain, fruitful seasons, and food. (Acts 14:8-18)

Commenting on this passage, F.F. Bruce remarks:

"God is one," they [Lystran Gentiles] are told, "and has not left Himself without witness; His works of creation and providence show Him to be the living God who supplies the needs of men; …for the way in which God ordered the seasons, so as to give food to all flesh, ought to have made men mindful of Him and of His claims upon their worship. (293)

At Lystra Paul appealed to the Gentiles through what Bruce calls "natural revelation" and James Barr speaks of as "natural theology" (293; 21ff). Was Paul's method successful? Seemingly so, based on the mention of disciples who tended to Paul's need at Lystra after he had been stoned.

Later Paul would tell an audience of philosophers at Athens that the God he, Paul, worshipped had already made himself known to them as the "God who made the world and everything in it." Paul may have had less success with the philosophers of Athens than he did with the more ordinary folk of Lystra, but it cannot be said that he was a

complete failure. In any case, seemingly the element in his address that upset the philosophers was not the mentioning of a creator god but the statement about the resurrection of
Christ (Acts 17:22-33). Barr remarks:

> Paul's Areopagus speech was, in St. Luke's [author of Acts] conception...a key
> statement of how the Christian faith must sound when stated for reception by
> an audience totally, or almost totally, Gentile, who had no background whatever
> in Hebrew scriptures. (31)

Notes

James Barr, *Biblical Faith and Natural Theology* (Oxford: Clarendon Press, 1993).
F. F. Bruce, *Commentary on the Book of Acts* (Grand Rapids: William B. Eerdmans
Publishing Co., 1954).

Through Human Experience

When we move from knowledge of God through creation/nature to knowledge that comes from human contact, we move into an entirely new,
dynamic dimension. For example, the proverbial alien from another planet
might learn something about humans by observing their various modes of
transportation from the unsophisticated wagon to the intricate spaceship.
However, such observation will tell him nothing about such things as human
body shape and size, color of skin, sex, age, ethical attitudes, etc. The fuller
knowledge will only come with contact with the human.

So it is with God: the more intimate the contact, the more we know. In
some cases, the knowledge will come from others who share their experiences
with us. Thus, we turn to the Old Testament to examine the personal and
corporate human experiences with God recorded there. On any given day, or
portion thereof, the presence of God might range all the way from unaware-
ness, to vague awareness, to an intense sense of awareness. Concerning
individuals, the Old Testament highlights certain persons as exceedingly
aware of God's presence, at least on special occasions. We will designate them
as extraordinary persons with extraordinary experiences. Along with these
there were numerous ordinary persons with ordinary experiences. It should
be noted it does not follow that God values the one more than the other.

Extraordinary Experiences of Extraordinary Persons

We shall focus our attention on the following extraordinary persons:
Abraham, Jacob, Moses, and Isaiah. Along with their various experiences we

will consider something of what each learned about the nature of God. We must also keep in mind, when examining these encounters, the words of God to Moses in the wilderness of Sinai: "You cannot see my face; for no one can see me and live" (Exod 33:20).

On one occasion, we are told, God appeared to Abraham at the Oak of Mamre, but Abraham saw only three men. It is difficult to tell from the unfolding story whether the author of Genesis wants us to believe all three men represent God, or only one with the others being attendants, or whether all three were attendants.[7] In any case, we are told that God addresses Abraham in a fashion that prevents Abraham's death and shares with Abraham God's intent to destroy the wicked cities of Sodom and Gomorrah. In the conversation that follows between God and Abraham, with Abraham interceding on behalf of the cities, Abraham comes to appreciate God's deep resolve that such terrible judgment will only be meted out after God is absolutely sure of the extreme wickedness of the cities. (Gen 18:1ff)

Abraham experienced God during broad daylight at the Oak of Mamre at God's initiative. On the other hand, Jacob took the initiative to wrestle all night in a deep gorge with some Being whom he desperately hoped could bless him in a time of deep distress. He was unaware until the breaking of the day that the Being with whom he wrestled was the one and same God worshiped by his grandfather Abraham, his father Isaac, and the one he had encountered at Bethel many years before. Upon the recognition, we are told that he "called the place Peniel, saying, `For I have seen God face to face, and yet my life is preserved'" (Gen 32:30). If the words of Jacob, "face to face," are to be taken literally in any sense, we can only suppose the darkness of the night within the deep gorge saved him from death. In any case, Jacob came to see that God is present, even if not always clearly, at those times of desperation. (Exod 32:22ff)

For Moses there would be no visiting strangers, as with Abraham, or deep, dark gorges, as with Jacob, to save him from sure death after the encounter with God's awesome, total presence. Rather, we are told that God provided a cleft in a rock where God could protect Moses with God's hand while passing by. Among the things Moses learned about God in this situation is that God goes to great lengths to fulfill humanity's desire for spiritual knowledge up to but not beyond the established safe barriers. For instance, God was willing for Moses to know the divine name, Yahweh, to experience God's goodness, but not to look upon God's face (Exod 33:12ff).

Before leaving Moses we must also deal with the following statement, which appears in the same chapter that informs us Moses cannot see God's face and live: "the LORD used to speak to Moses face to face, as one speaks to a friend" (Exod 33:11). Among the explanations for this seeming contradiction, the following statement by Roy Honeycutt will suffice: "*Face to face, as a man speaks to his friend* is a figurative way of expressing the reality and depth of communion between Moses and the Lord."[8]

Whatever claims Abraham, Jacob, and Moses made for themselves — or some other person made for them — about seeing God, Isaiah made a similar claim. The claim follows in detail.

> In the year that King Uzziah died, I saw the LORD sitting on a throne, high and lofty; and the hem of his robe filled the temple. Seraphs were in attendance above him; each had six wings; with two they covered their faces, and with two they covered their feet, and with two they flew. And one called to another and said:
> "Holy, holy, holy is the LORD of
>   hosts;
> the whole earth is full of his
>   glory."
> The pivots on the thresholds shook at the voices of those who called, and the house filled with smoke. And I said: "Woe is me! I am lost, for I am a man of unclean lips and I live among a people of unclean lips; yet my eyes have seen the King, the Lord of hosts!" Then one of the seraphs flew to me holding a live coal that had been taken from the altar with a pair of tongs. The seraph touched my mouth with it and said: "Now that this has touched your lips, your guilt has departed and your sin is blotted out." Then I heard the voice of the Lord saying, "Whom shall I send, and who will go for us?" And I said, "Here am I; send me!" (Isa 6:1-8)

If a modern reader experiences a sense of awe while reading Isaiah's words, think what the initial experience meant to him and the many times he reflected on it. Seemingly what began as a trip (a special one, of course) to the temple was transformed into a visionary transport to God's heavenly realm. Exactly what Isaiah means when he says, "I saw the LORD," we do not know. It can hardly be more than Moses was allowed to see. Was it just God's robe he saw? R.B.Y. Scott states:

It is only a glimpse, a sudden overpowering realization that he is in the presence of the Majesty on high; the <u>throne</u>, the royal robe, and the attendant beings are described, but not the appearance of the One upon the throne.[9]

As for the smoke, was it designed to hide God or something of his presence from Isaiah? Again, consider Scott's words:

> ...the <u>smoke</u> is the same as the "cloud" of glory which filled the tabernacle (Exodus 40:34)...both hiding and revealing the divine presence.[10]

Among the things that Isaiah learned about God during his temple experience were the following: God exposes humans to their deep sinfulness; God expresses gracious forgiveness and bestows spiritual healing; and God desires human cooperation in God's ministry of salvation.

Ordinary Experiences of Ordinary Persons

Where is the testimony of ordinary Israelites concerning the presence of God to be found in the Old Testament? Perhaps the testimony is to be found above all in the Psalms where the reciters have laid claim to the words for themselves, whether or not they were the actual composers. Such reciters may look upon God's presence with dread or great expectation. Typical of these two positions are the following:

Believing that God's staring eye has brought trouble on him, or has at least exacerbated the problem, one Israelite cries out to God as follows:

> Turn your gaze away from me,
>   that I may smile again,
> before I depart and am no
>   more. (Ps 39:13)

On the other hand, an Israelite who believes his distress has come from God's taking God's eye off of him might cry out:

> Answer me quickly, O LORD;
>   my spirit fails.
> Do not hide your face from me,
>   or I shall be like those who go
>   down to the Pit. (Ps 143:7)

Upon reflecting on such contrasting verses as those quoted above, Samuel Terrien remarks:

> Some of the psalmists were constantly begging for God's presence. Others tried to flee from it. The laments and supplications of the psalter include prayers of search and prayers of escape. Taken together . . . they point to the theological specificity of Hebraism, in which the relationship between God and man remains ambiguous.[11]

One psalmist discovered, as he believed, that whether "begging for God's presence," as Terrien puts it, or "flee[ing] from it," God's presence was a given fact. Of course, the sentiments of this particular psalmist, along with all reciters of the psalm who agree with him, go far beyond his own particular experience. They reach into the recesses of his hoped-for speculation:

> Where can I go from your spirit?
> Or where can I flee from your
>   presence?
> If I ascend to heaven, you
>   are there;
> if I make my bed in Sheol, you
>   are there. (Ps 139:7-8)

Instructions and Pronouncements

We close out this matter of how we know God by observing that the knowledge sometimes comes from the teachings or pronouncements of others. We will center our attention on the Mosaic, Prophetic, and Wisdom.

Mosaic Instruction. As for the Mosaic, we will give our primary attention to the Ten Commandments.

> Then God spoke all these words. I am the LORD your God, who brought you out of the land of Egypt, out of the house of slavery; You shall have no other gods before me. You shall not make for yourself an idol . . . . You shall not bow down to them or worship them; for I the LORD your God am a jealous God . . . . You shall not make wrongful use of the name of the LORD your God . . . . Remember the sabbath day, and keep it holy . . . . For in six days the LORD made heaven and earth, the sea, and all that is in them, but rested the seventh day; therefore the LORD blessed the sabbath

day and consecrated it. Honor your father and your mother, so that your
days may be long in the land . . . . You shall not murder. (Exod 20:1-13)

It is obvious to the reader of the above passage that God did not say, "I am
the LORD your God, let me tell you what kind of God I am," and then pro-
ceed to a self-description. There is a good deal, however, that we can learn
about God from the commands given. God begins by reminding them that
God is a Savior God who rescued them from Egyptian bondage. Further, in
the extended remarks of the sabbath commandment, God instructs them
that God is the Creator who "made heaven and earth, the seas and all that is
in them." Even if they agreed with God, based on their experience of God as
savior, they still needed to be instructed, or reminded, that this is the same
God who created the universe.

Further, God instructs them that God's Presence is not to be shared with
any other god or, for that matter, with some outward image of another god.
After all, God says, "I the LORD your God am a jealous God." Reflecting on
this passage, Brevard Childs remarks:

> The grounds for the commandment go beyond the authority provided in
> the prologue [concerning God's rescue of them from Egypt] and rest on
> the nature of God himself. Because he is a 'jealous God,' his passionate love
> for his people will not tolerate divided loyalty . . . . Idolatry is prohibited
> in order that true worship may flourish.[12]

The passage under consideration says nothing about the Lord being a
God who desires worship, nor does it spell out the nature of true worship.
However, other parts of the Old Testament do give such instruction.[13]

If God's nature is such that God cannot tolerate the misuse of God's
Presence by the inclusion of other gods or outward images, neither can God
tolerate the misuse of the divine name which is an integral part of God's
nature. We will have more to say below on the various names by which God
is known in the Old Testament.

In closing, we observe that the Israelites are informed that God's concern
for relationship includes that of humanity to itself. Among other things,
there is a God-approved relationship between parents and their offspring and
between one human and another beyond the parent-offspring relationship.

Prophetic Pronouncements. When we turn to the prophets to hear a
special word about the nature and ways of God, we turn to individual per-

sons who "claim to speak Yahweh's [the LORD's] revelatory word," according to Walter Brueggemann.[14] Yet, as Brueggemann points out, what they said was not exactly new, for "it is clear that [prophetic] oracles of judgment and oracles of hope correlate completely with the core themes of Mosaic faith."[15]

According to Hosea, God's "revelatory word" speaks of God's justice, including God's judgment, and compassion from which flows the prophet's hope for sinful Israel:

> Come, let us return to the LORD;
> for it is he who has torn, and he
>   will heal us;
> he has struck down, and he will
>   bind us up.
> After two days he will revive us;
> on the third day he will raise
>   us up,
> that we may live before him.
> Let us know, let us press on to
>   know the LORD;
> his appearing is as sure as
>   the dawn;
> he will come to us like the
>   showers,
> like the spring rains that water
>   the earth. (Hos 6:1-3)

Concerning the above passage, Paul Hanson profoundly remarks:

> In this remarkable confession, the prophet gave clear expression to the inseparability of God's tearing and healing. To have upheld a people in their apostasy and wantonness would have been the most cruel of acts, tantamount to sealing their covenant with death. But to rend and tear until in their brokenness their mesmerization with their idols would be ended and their attention would be redirected to the true God was an act of profound mercy. In it, the opportunity was renewed of "living before him" — that is, of foreswearing death and of entering into the covenant of life.[16]

There is a dimension of God's compassion that is sometimes overlooked, namely God's suffering or mourning. As the people of Judah approached the time of their exile in Babylonia, God called upon the professional women mourners to sing a funeral dirge in preparation for that event:

> Thus says the LORD of hosts:
> Consider, and call for the
>   mourning women to come;
> send for the skilled women
>   to come;
> let them quickly raise a dirge
>   over us,
> so that our eyes may run down
>   with tears,
> and our eyelids flow with
>   water. (Jer 9:17-18)

Do the eyes that "run down with tears" include the eyes of God? Abraham Heschel, among others, thinks they do:

> Does not the word of God mean: Cry for Israel and Me? The voice of God calling upon the people to weep, lament, and mourn, for the calamities are about to descend upon them, is itself a voice of grief, a voice of weeping.[17]

Terence Fretheim's agreement with Heschel is expressed this way:

> The use of the first person plural in this text clearly includes God. The professional mourners are to come and weep not only for Israel, but for God as well.[18]

An interesting thing about God's tears is that they are not limited to Israel. Note how, for instance, God mixes God's own tears with those of the Moabites in a time of calamity:

> I myself know his [Moab's] insolence, says
>   the LORD;
> his boasts are false,
> his deeds are false.
> Therefore I wail for Moab;
> I cry out for all Moab; . . .
> And I will bring to an end in Moab, says the LORD, those who offer sacrifice at a high place and make offerings to their gods . . . . On all the housetops of Moab and in the squares there is nothing but lamentation; for I have broken

> Moab like a vessel that no one wants, says the LORD. How it is broken! How
> they wail. (Jer 48:30-31, 35, 38-39)

Does the mourning and weeping spoken of above that seems to refer to God
really refer to the prophet instead? Fretheim thinks otherwise:

> To hear such mourning on the part of God for a non-Israelite people is
> striking indeed. Most of this language is also used to describe the weeping
> and wailing of the Moabites, so that the impression created is that of a God
> whose lamentation is as deep and broad as that of the people themselves.
> As with Israel, God is the one who has occasioned the judgment in the first
> place (Jer 48:38); but once the judgment has occurred, God joins those
> who mourn.[19]

Wisdom Instruction. We close out this section on knowing God with
an examination of the teachings of the sages as seen in the Old Testament
Wisdom literature (primarily Proverbs, Ecclesiastes, and Job). While some
scholars such as Claus Westermann claim that little, or nothing, can be
learned about God from this source,[20] other interpreters such as Walter
Brueggemann maintain that "this deposit of sustained reflection [as found in
Wisdom literature] is indeed revelatory; it reveals and discloses the God who
creates, orders, and sustains reality."[21]

There are indications within some wisdom traditions that there are certain orders of life that God has designed for humanity, a design that surely
says something about the designer. The author of Ecclesiastes declares:
"[God] has made everything suitable for its time" (Eccl 3:11). The author
elaborates, in part, as follows:

> For everything there is a season . . .
> a time to be born, and a time
>   to die; (Eccl 3:1-2)

While some wisdom traditions might come close to a deistic kind of relationship of creator to creation, there are wisdom sayings that indicate God's
close scrutiny of human creation. Note the following words from Proverbs:

> The eyes of the LORD are in every
>   place,
> keeping watch on the evil and
>   the good. (Prov 15:3)

All deeds are right in the sight of
    the doer,
but the LORD weighs the heart. (Prov 21:2)

Special Topics

We conclude our studies of an Old Testament theology of God with certain special topics: images of God and their value, God's names and titles, monotheism, and God's holiness.

Images of God and Their Value

Israelite images of God are drawn both from the natural world and the human sphere. God is described as a rock (a metaphor drawn from the inanimate natural world) or is said to be like an eagle (a simile drawn from the animate natural world).

You were unmindful of the Rock
    that bore you,
you forgot the God who gave
    you birth. (Deut 32:18)

As an eagle stirs up its nest
and hovers over its young...
the LORD alone guided him [Israel]. (Deut 32:11-12)

The dominant images of God in the Old Testament come from the human sphere. These are sometimes referred to as anthropomorphisms because they describe God as having human form or function (such as a mouth that speaks, eyes that see, ears that hear) and as having human feelings or emotions (such as joy, anger, or compassion):

God *heard* their groaning, and God *remembered* his covenant with Abraham, Isaac, and Jacob. God looked upon the Israelites, and God took notice of them. (Exod 2:24-25, italics added)

My heart recoils within me;
my compassion grows warm
    and tender.
I will not execute my fierce anger;
I will not again destroy
    Ephraim; . . . (Hos 11:8-9)

More important than human form and feelings is the Old Testament depiction of God exercising human roles (for example, spouse, king, shepherd, or craftsman):

> For your Maker is your husband,
> the LORD of hosts is his name . . . (Isa 54:5)

> The LORD is king forever and
> ever; . . . (Ps 10:16)

> He will feed his flock like a
> shepherd;
> he will gather the lambs in
> his arms, . . . (Isa 40:11)

> Yet, O LORD, you are our Father;
> we are the clay, and you are
> our potter; . . . (Isa 64:8)

Having examined some Old Testament images of God, we now inquire concerning their value. We note three. First, as one author has stated, anthropomorphic images serve as "accommodations to human speech."[22] Without them we could say very little about God. G.B. Caird observes:

> Comparison is one of our most valuable sources of knowledge, the main road leading from the known to the unknown. It comprises a large part of our daily speech and almost all the language of theology. God speaks to man in similitudes . . . , and man has no language but analogy for speaking about God, however inadequate it may be . . . . [23]

Not only do anthropomorphic images help us to say something meaningful about God, they help us in our understanding of God's accessibility. Ludwig Koehler puts it this way:

> One realizes at this point the function of anthropomorphisms. Their intention is not in the least to reduce God to a rank similar to that of man.... Rather the purpose . . . is to make God accessible to man . . . . They represent God as person.[24]

Finally, images help to determine what we think about God, and thus how we live. Consider the words of Terence Fretheim:

> It is not enough to say that one believes in God. What is important finally is the *kind* of God in whom one believes. Or, to use different language: metaphors matter. The images used to speak of God not only decisively determine the way one thinks about God, they have a powerful impact on the shape of the believer.... Witness any number of atrocities, from the Inquisition to Jonestown, committed in the name of God by those who believe in God.[25]

Concerning how we can use these Old Testament images of God in our lives, we turn to helpful suggestions by Fretheim in *The Suffering of God*. Fretheim looks upon the images as something less than purely literal and something more than purely figurative.[26] As he points out, we should not use the following passage to prove that God is an old man with white hair:

> As I watched,
> thrones were set in place,
> and an Ancient One took
>   his throne,
> his clothing was white as snow,
> and the hair of his head like
>   pure wool; . . . (Dan 7:9)

On the other hand, to dismiss all images as mere metaphors, as some interpreters do, is not helpful. Fretheim insists, for instance, that God does repent/relent; on occasion he does change his mind.[27] For example, note the following vision of Amos:

> This is what the LORD God showed me: he was forming locusts at the time the latter growth began to sprout (it was the latter growth after the time of the king's mowings). When they had finished eating the grass of the land, I said,
> "O Lord God, forgive I beg you!
> How can Jacob stand?
> He is so small!"
> The Lord relented concerning
>   this;
> "It shall not be," said the LORD. (Amos 7:1-3)

God's Names or Titles

The Israelites not only used a variety of images for God, they also addressed God by a number of names or titles. For them a name was more than a designation. It served also as a description. For instance, after Jacob, whose name means "heel holder" (with the implication of scoundrel), had stolen his brother's blessing, Esau asked his father, "Is he not rightly named Jacob?" (Gen 27:36). Many years later, after an all night wrestling match with God, God changed Jacob's name to Israel, remarking "you have striven with God and with humans" (Gen 32:28).

Elohim. The information that follows about God's names and titles is organized under three categories: generic names, personal names, and titles. We begin with the Hebrew generic word *Elohim* (a plural of the Hebrew word *El*) which is translated as God, god, gods, and angels. It is the Old Testament's second most used word for God, second only to Yahweh, a term derived from the tetragrammaton *YHWH*. *Elohim*, though plural in its form, often takes on a singular meaning when used with a singular verb.[28] The following passages in which the word *Elohim* appear are instructive:

> In the beginning when God [*Elohim*] created the heavens and the earth, ...(Gen 1:1)

> Then God [*Elohim*] spoke all these words: I am the LORD [Yahweh] your God [*Elohim*], who brought you out of the land of Egypt, out of the house of slavery, you shall have no other gods [*Elohim*] before me. (Exod 20:1-3)

> Yet you have made them [human beings] a little
>   lower than God [*Elohim*]. (Ps 8:5)[29]

YHWH. The Old Testament's most used word for God is the Hebrew word, *YHWH*, often designated in English as Yahweh, which may be looked upon as a personal or proper name. There is a question concerning the meaning of the name. There are interpreters who insist that it is impossible to know the meaning of the name.[30] On the other hand, other interpreters understand the word to mean God's eternal nature or eternal causation.

Robert Cate states, "The name focuses both upon the real existence of God and his creative power."[31]

There are a number of problems related to this word; we shall consider two. How should it be rendered in English? What is its meaning? An explanation of the English rendition follows in the excursus.

The Ineffable Name: YHWH

Yod – Y, *he* – H, *vav* – V (or W), and *he* – (H) are the four Hebrew characters commonly known as the *tetragrammaton* (lit. "four letters"). YHWH, YHVH, or JHVH are the transliterations frequently used for this name. This name is known in Jewish circles as the Ineffable Name because it was not to be spoken except at certain holy occasions and then only by the High Priest.

The Ineffable Name is used throughout the Hebrew Bible as the self-disclosed name for the God of Israel. Exodus 3:14 records God's self-revelation to Moses:

> And God spoke unto Moses, "I AM who I AM" and he continued, thus you shall say unto the children of Israel, "I AM has sent me unto you." (trans. Ballard)

Many scholars contend that the derivation of YHWH comes directly from a contraction of the phrase recorded here in Exodus 3:14, *Ehyeh Asher Ehyeh* or "I AM who I AM." The Ineffable Name is the most frequently used epithet for God in the Hebrew Bible. In addition to the over six thousand occurrences of this name in the Hebrew Bible, its shortened forms, *ya*, *yah*, or *yahu* are also found sprinkled mostly throughout the poetic passages, especially in the Psalms (Thompson). Exodus 6:2-3 is often used as a "proof text" to establish that the Ineffable Name was not known prior to the time period of Moses, though it appears on almost every page of the text of Genesis (Mettinger).

> God spoke unto Moses saying unto him, "I am the LORD (YHWH)." And I appeared unto Abraham, unto Isaac, and unto Jacob as God Almighty (*El Shaddai*), but my name "the LORD (YHWH)" I did not make known unto them. (trans. Ballard)

It is believed by many scholars that the Ineffable Name was once pronounced by the High Priest on certain religious festivals in Israel up until the destruction of the Solomon's Temple in 587 BC. The name, however, was not used by the time of the writing of the Septuagint (the Greek translations of the Hebrew Bible c. 250 BC) (Hartman).

During the codification of the writing and pronunciation of the Hebrew Bible by the work of the Masoretes (Jewish scribes) during the fifth to tenth centuries AD, the written form of the Ineffable Name also underwent another adaptation. The Masoretes began adding vowel points to the Hebrew texts that were previously only written with consonants. Due to the prohibition of pronouncing the Ineffable Name, the Masoretes recorded the familiar consonants of the Divine Name YHWH, but added the vowels "a, o, a" of the word most frequently substituted when reading the name, *Adonai* (which means "LORD"). This relationship worked well for those whose native tongue was Hebrew. They were reminded each time they saw the Ineffable Name to speak orally *Adonai*, or *HaShem* (lit. "the name"), another name sometimes substituted for YHWH. A problem arose, however, when Hebrew was eventually translated into German and into English. Christian scholars, not understanding the tradition and history behind the Ineffable Name, tried to pronounce the Ineffable Name with the results being the birth of a hybrid term, "Jehovah, or Yehovah."

In today's English-speaking world, the words Yahweh and Jehovah are known as words used to designate the God of Israel. General sensitivity calls for the responsible Christian reader to be conscious of the history and background of the English words assigned for the appropriation of the Ineffable Name of Israel's God, and to use these words only in a context that will not offend our Jewish colleagues and friends. With this general warning in mind, the authors of this book will frequently refer to Yahweh as an appropriation of the Ineffable Name.

Notes

Henry O. Thompson, "Yahweh," *The Anchor Bible Dictionary*, ed. David Noel Freedman, vol. 6 (New York: Doubleday, 1992), 1011-12.

Tryvvge Mettinger, *In Search of God: The Meaning and Message of the Everlasting Name* (Philadelphia: Fortress Press, 1987), 14ff.

Louis F. Hartman, "God, Names of," in *Encyclopedia Judaica*, vol. 7 (New York: The MacMillan Company, 1971), 674-683.

Other Titles. Along with the Old Testament words for God such as *Elohim* and Yahweh, certain others on occasion are used: *El Shaddai* (God Almighty — see Gen 17:1*); El Elyon* (God Most High – see Gen 14:22); *El Olam* (Everlasting God — see Gen 21:33).

Besides Old Testament generic and personal names for God, we also find the use of titles such as *Adonai*. The original RSV has translated *Adonai* as Lord, capitalizing only the first letter. The NRSV translates *Adonai* as Sovereign. An unusual confluence of the words Yahweh and *Adonai* appears in Isaiah:

> For, behold, the Lord [*Adonai*], the LORD [*Yahweh*] of hosts,
> is taking away from Jerusalem and from
>   Judah
> stay and staff,
> the whole stay of bread,
> and the whole stay of water. (Isa 3:1, RSV)

Monotheism

Someone has said that the greatest gift of Judaism to Christianity is the belief of monotheism. Whether or not the assessment is correct, the importance of the belief of monotheism cannot be overlooked. However, the full-blown idea is not clearly spelled out in Israel's earliest documents. For instance, in the Decalogue, God demands faithfulness without stipulating that God is the only God (Exod 20). Later, Jephthah, an Israelite judge, describes the land of the Ammonites as the land given to them by their god (Judg 11:24). Still later, Elijah insists that the Israelites show utter faithfulness to Yahweh without demanding their belief in monotheism. On the same occasion, however, he did demonstrate that for all practical purposes the god Baal did not exist (1 Kgs 18).

If, as someone has said, the Decalogue presents Incipient Monotheism and the story of Elijah presents Practical Monotheism, where do we look for a full, firm expression of monotheism? According to R.E. Clements, it is found in Second Isaiah. He remarks:

> Here with this exilic prophet the ultimate consequence is clearly drawn that Yahweh alone is God, and that other gods that men seek to worship do not in reality exist.[32]

> Thus says the LORD, the King
>   of Israel,
> and his Redeemer, the LORD
>   of hosts:
> I am the first and I am the last;
> besides me there is no god....
>
> Is there any god besides me?
> There is no other rock; I know
>   not one. (Isa 44:6, 8)

Holiness of God

We close our presentation on God with a brief discussion of God's holiness. As Robert Cate points out:

The word-picture behind the Old Testament concept of holiness appears to carry two basic images. It would appear that holiness meant to be burning, glowing, and radiant, yet at the same time it meant to be separate, set apart, different.[33]

Old Testament ideas concerning God's holiness range from the "primitive" (emphasizing the power of God without his compassion) to the "majestic" (emphasizing both God's power and compassionate redemption). The following accounts concerning Uzzah, Moses, and Isaiah are useful in illustrating this point. Each of the accounts refers to some holy object, each in its own way having a special relationship to the holy God. Again, as Gate points out:

> For Israel, only that was holy which belonged to God and had been separated for his use. In simplest terms, holiness was neither more nor less what God was.[34]

As David was transporting the Ark of the Covenant (a holy object of God not to be touched by human hands) to Jerusalem, Uzzah, one of the attendants, died while trying to steady the Ark which appeared to be falling off the wagon on which it was being carried:

> When they came to the threshing floor of Nacon, Uzzah reached out his hand to the ark and took hold of it, for the oxen shook it. The anger of the LORD was kindled against Uzzah and God struck him there because he reached out his hand to the ark; and he died there beside the ark of God. David was angry because the LORD had burst forth with an outburst upon Uzzah . . . . (2 Sam 6:6-8)

We look in vain in the passage for sorrow on God's part that Uzzah had died. Whatever sorrow, if any, that God felt is not recorded; the passage is silent.

If 2 Samuel is silent about any redemptive power that a holy object of God might possess, that is not true of the Exodus story of Moses. While it is true that the holy presence of God is depicted as dangerous in the Exodus story, and thus must be respected, God's self-revelation in the burning bush is that God is coming to redeem and save the people:

> When the LORD saw that he had turned aside to see, God called to him out of the bush, "Moses, Moses!" And he said, "Here I am." Then he said,

"Come no closer! Remove the sandals from off your feet, for the place on which you are standing is holy ground." He said further, "I am the God of your father, the God of Abraham, the God of Isaac, and the God of Jacob." And Moses hid his face, for he was afraid to look at God. Then the LORD said, "I have observed the misery of my people in Egypt, . . . I have come down to deliver them from the Egyptians, and to bring them up out of that land to a good and broad land . . . . " (Exod 3:4-8)

If God, through words and holy presence, made a promise to the Israelites in bondage, Isaiah actually experienced the redemptive power of God as the sacred coal from the altar cleansed his sinful lips:

And I said: "Woe is me! I am lost, for I am a man of unclean lips; yet my eyes have seen the King, the LORD of hosts!" Then one of the seraphs flew to me, holding a live coal that had been taken from the altar with a pair of tongs. The seraph touched my mouth with it and said: "Now that this has touched your lips, your guilt has departed and your sin is blotted out." (Isa 6:5-7)

Conclusion

How do we know God and what do we know about God? The answer to these two questions is at least partially answered by the above passage from Isaiah and more fully in the discussion in the chapter above.

Notes

[1] For example, see the works of Robert L. Cate, *Old Testament Roots for New Testament Faith* (Nashville: Broadman Press, 1982), 49; Brevard S. Childs, *Old Testament Theology in a Canonical Context* (Philadelphia: Fortress Press, 1985), 28; Ludwig Koehler, *Old Testament Theology* (London: Lutterworth Press, 1957), 19; Samuel Terrien, *The Elusive Presence* (New York: Harper & Row, 1978), xxvii.

[2] Koehler, 19.

[3] James Barr, *Biblical Faith and Natural Theology* (Oxford: Clarendon Press, 1993).

[4] See Childs, *Old Testament Theology in a Canonical Context*; and Elizabeth Achtemeir, *Nature, God, and Pulpit* (Grand Rapids: William B. Eerdmans Publishing Co., 1992).

[5] Barr, , 87.

[6] Ibid., 85.

[7] Terence E. Fretheim, "Genesis" in *New Interpreter's Bible*, vol. 1 (Nashville: Abingdon Press, 1994), 462ff.

[8] Roy L. Honeycutt, "Exodus," in *The Broadman Bible Commentary*, vol. 1, revised (Nashville: Broadman Press, 1969), 439.

[9] R. B. Y. Scott, "Isaiah," in *The Interpreter's Bible*, vol. 5 (New York: Abingdon Press, 1956), 207.

[10] Ibid., 209.

[11] Samuel Terrien, *The Elusive Presence* (New York: Harper and Row, 1978), 326.

[12] Childs, 65.

[13] See for example Amos 5:21-24; Micah 6:6-8.

[14] Walter Brueggemann, *Theology of the Old Testament* (Minneapolis: Fortress Press, 1997), 622.

[15] Ibid., 639.

[16] Paul D. Hanson, *The People Called* (New York: Harper and Row Publishers, 1986), 163.

[17] Abraham Heschel, *The Prophets*, vol. 1 (New York: Harper Torchbooks, 1969), 113.

[18] Terence E. Fretheim, *The Suffering God: An Old Testament Perspective* (Philadelphia: Fortress Press, 1984), 134.

[19] Ibid., 133.

[20] Claus Westermann, *Elements of Old Testament Theology* (Atlanta: John Knox Press, 1982), 11.

[21] Brueggemann, 681.

[22] H. H. Rowley, *The Faith of Israel* (Philadelphia: Westminster Press, 1956), 75.

[23] G. B. Caird, *The Language and Imagery of the Bible* (Grand Rapids: William B. Eerdmans Publishing Co., 1997), 144.

[24] Koehler, 24.

[25] Fretheim, 1.

[26] Ibid., 7ff.

[27] Ibid., 8.

[28] Cate, 65.

[29] The footnote in the NRSV indicates that the word *Elohim* might be translated in this context as "divine being" or "angel."

[30] Henry O. Thompson, "Yahweh," *The Anchor Bible Dictionary*, ed. David Noel Freedman, vol. 6 (New York: Doubleday, 1992), 1011.

[31] Cate, 56.

[32] R. E. Clements, *Old Testament Theology: A Fresh Approach* (Atlanta: John Knox Press, 1978), 73.

[33] Cate, 60.

[34] Ibid., 61.

Like Job of the paradigm passage above (and the larger passage from which it came), we stand on God's good earth, invited by God to view creation. In many ways we are better able to do that today than at any time in history. For one thing, we have better interpretive tools in Old Testament studies. We shall be making use of those in the following topics: selected Old Testament creation vocabulary; Old Testament creation models or motifs; creation according to Genesis and Job. Again, in recent years great strides have been made in the understanding of creation through such disciplines as biology, geology, and astronomy. We will have more to say about the latter in the excursus within this chapter.

Selected Old Testament Creation Vocabulary

In our presentation of Israel's creation vocabulary, we will do well to keep in mind the remarks of Walter Brueggemann that Israel "daringly made use of rich and diverse vocabulary in order to make its normative utterance about God's creation known."[1] For instance, there are passages where certain creation verbs are piled one upon another for effect. Take for example this passage from Isaiah:

> For thus says the LORD,
> who created [*bara*] the heavens
>   (he is God!)
> who formed [*yasar*] the earth and made [*asah*] it
>   (he established [*cun*] it;
> he did not create [*bara*] it a chaos,
>   he formed [*yasar*] it to be inhabited!) (Isa 45:18)

The first creation verb used in this passage is "*bara*," a word first used in the Old Testament in Genesis 1:1. According to John H. Steck, it is "the most distinctive" Hebrew word used in the Old Testament for Yahweh's creative activity.[2] However, as Steck further points out, other Hebrew words for create/make are often used synonymously with *bara*:

> The specific choice of words here [Genesis, ch. 1] may be deliberate, but it can be of little consequence that God is said to "make" [asah] rather than "create" [bara] the expanse that divides the waters above from the waters below (v. 7) and the heavenly bodies (v. 16), or that he is said on the one hand to "create" [bara] the forms of life that fill the waters and the air (v. 21) but on the other hand "make" [asah] the animals that live on the land.[3]

4

Creation

Then the LORD answered Job out
    of the whirlwind:
"Who is this that darkens counsel
    by words without
    knowledge?
Gird up your loins like a man,
    I will question you and you
    shall declare to me.
Where were you when I laid the
    foundation of the earth?
Tell me if you have
    understanding.
Who determined its
    measurements — surely you
    know!
Or who stretched the line upon
    it?
On what were its bases sunk,
    or who laid its cornerstone
when the morning stars sang
    together
    and all the heavenly beings
    shouted for joy?" (Job 38:1-7)

It should be also noted that the various words used for original creation are also used for the continuing creativity of God. For instance, both nonhuman life and human life continue generation after generation by God's continuing activity.[4]

> O LORD, how wonderful are your
>   works!
>   In wisdom you have made (*asah*)
>   them all...
> When you send forth your spirit,
>   they are created (*bara*); (Ps 104:24, 30)

> Your hands have made (*asah*) and
>   fashioned (*yasar*) me;... (Ps 119:73)

Beyond the individual human, God creates/makes those groups we know as Israelites and Gentiles.

> Know that the LORD is God.
>   It is he that made (*asah*) us [Israelites], and we
>   are his;
>   we are his people, and the sheep
>   of his pasture. (Ps 100:3)
> All the nations [Gentiles] you have made (*asah*)
>   shall come
>   and bow down before you,
>   O LORD,
>   and shall glorify your name. (Ps 86:9)

If the individual or groups go astray, God has made provision to create new hearts and new places to live:

> Create (*bara*) in me a clean heart,
>   O God (Ps 51:10)
> Be glad and rejoice forever
>   in what I am creating (*bara*);
>   for I am about to create (*bara*) Jerusalem
>   as a joy,
>   and its people as a delight. (Isa 65:18)

While numerous other examples could be given, we will summarize by observing that God has created in the past and continues to create/make. Some theologians would make a fine distinction between God's creation and God's providence. However, the above cited passages seem to indicate that the ancient Israelites made no such fine distinction.

Old Testament Creation Models/Motifs

While a study of individual Old Testament creation words can be instructive, we also need to examine larger literary units related to God's creation, especially the original creation. These literary units may be organized under such terms as models, motifs, and/or themes.

Among the Old Testament models for creation are the Divine Warrior (used in both poetic and prophetic passages), the Earthly King (used in Gen 1), and the Artisan (used in our paradigm passage).

Divine Warrior Model

We may speak of the Divine Warrior motif as a creation-by-battle theme. Such an approach was well-known by contemporaries of the ancient Israelites. Certainly it is a fair assumption that some of the Israelites knew these stories. One such story was the Babylonian story of creation known by the title *Enuma Elish*. Selections from that story follow:

He [Marduk] rested, the lord, examining her [original goddess] body:
Would divide up the monster, create a wonder of wonders!
He slit her in two like a fish of the drying yards,
The one half he positioned and secured as the sky...

(Therein) traced he lines for the mighty gods,
Stars, star-groups and constellations he appointed for them:
He determined the year, marked out its divisions,
For each of the twelve months appointed three rising stars . . .

He placed her head in position, heaped [the mountai]ns upon it . . .
Made the Euphr[ates] and the Tigris to flow through her eyes . . . [5]

The Old Testament contains similar battle themes. One psalmist expresses the theme thusly:

You divided the sea by your
    might;
you broke the heads of the
    dragons in the waters.
You crushed the heads of
    Leviathan;
you gave him as food for the
    creatures of the wilderness. (Ps 74:13-14)

Second Isaiah, writing in Babylon (the very territory where the story of Marduk's slaying of Tiamat the original goddess originated), says that it is Yahweh who has destroyed the water dragon:

Awake, awake, put on strength,
O arm of the LORD!
Awake, as in days of old,
the generations of long ago!
Was it not you who cut Rahab in
    pieces,
who pierced the dragon? (Isa 51:9)

Words reminiscent of those in the *Enuma Elish* are also recorded in the book of Job:

By his [God's] power he stilled the Sea;
    by his understanding he struck
    down Rahab.
By his wind the heavens were
    made fair;
his hand pierced the fleeing
    serpent. (Job 26:12-13)

We should not construe from the above-cited passage that the Israelites, in their *most developed* understanding, thought of Yahweh literally doing battle with other gods. For instance, Second Isaiah, who speaks of Yahweh cutting Rahab to pieces, quotes Yahweh as saying that there is no other God. (See Isa 44:6-8). Again, while the *Enuma Elish* depicts the god, Marduk, as being the son of Ea (a Babylonian god), one of the psalmists declares of Yahweh:

Lord, you have been our dwelling
 place
 in all generations.
Before the mountains were
 brought forth,
 or ever you had formed the
 earth and the world,
 from everlasting to everlasting
 you are God. (Ps 90:1-2)

Earthly King Model

If the above passages depict (metaphorically/figuratively) the creator bringing about creation by *battle*, other passages picture God doing it by *edict/command*. Note words of a psalmist:

By the word of the LORD the
 heavens were made,
and all their host by the breath
 of his mouth.
He gathered the waters of the sea
 as in a bottle;
he put the deeps in storehouses. (Ps 33:6-7)

Those familiar with the Old Testament will recognize that the author of Genesis 1 (referred to by some scholars as the Priestly Writer) has portrayed God (*Elohim*) as creating by *edict/command* in somewhat the same fashion as a powerful monarch might do. For instance, we read: "And God said, 'Let there be light'" (Gen 1:3). Similar words are said again and again in the ongoing account. We shall comment on this further below.

Artisan Model

Besides depicting creation in terms of *battle* with chaotic forces and by *edict*, the Old Testament pictures God as a great *artisan*. The paradigm passage from Job depicts God as using a measuring instrument while the author of Genesis 2 (sometimes referred to by some scholars as the Yahwistic writer) speaks of God molding Adam (from clay) and Eve (from Adam's side).

> Then the LORD God formed man from the dust of the ground.... And the
> rib that the LORD God had taken from the man he made into a woman
> and brought her to the man. (Gen 2:7, 22)

Furthermore, it is to Conrad Hyers' credit that he sees God's creative
activity in terms of a game, a game which he says "combines elements of
both work and play, discipline and enthusiasm, seriousness and laughter."[6]
Hyers remarks further:

> Is there no joy and delight in creating, no sense of creating for the sake of
> creating? Is this creative labor not also a marvelous form of play, a prodi-
> gious frolicking of whirling galaxies and whirling atoms and whirling
> whirligigs?[7]

A marvelous psalm that depicts something of what Hyers is saying is Psalm
104. Can you imagine, as did the psalmist, that a cloud is God's chariot or
that he rides the wind like a human would a mighty steed?

> you set the beams of your
>   chambers on the waters,
> you make the clouds your
>   chariot,
>   you ride on the wings
>   of the wind. (Ps 104:3)

Or can you imagine what kind of creative God it is who makes birds to sing
or one who provides for human enjoyment?

> By the streams the birds of the
>   air have their habitation;
>   they sing among the branches . . .
> You cause . . .
>   wine to gladden the human
>   heart,
> oil to make the face shine . . . (Ps 104:12, 14, 15)

Or, again, can you imagine what kind of creative God makes innumerable
creatures to sport in the vast seas of the world?

Yonder is the sea, great and wide,
creeping things innumerable are
     there,
living things both small and
     great.
There go the ships,
and Leviathan that you formed
     to sport in it. (Ps 104:25-26)

Creation According to Genesis

There are a number of ways theologically to approach the materials in
Genesis 1–2. (We shall consider the question of the relationship of science to
the Genesis creation account in the excursus at the end of the chapter.) One
way is to observe that chapter 1 depicts God as bringing forth creation by
both command and deed:

> And God said, "let there be a dome in the midst of the waters, and let it
> separate the waters from the waters." So God made the dome and sepa-
> rated the waters that were under the dome from the waters that were above
> the dome. And it was so. (Gen 1:6-7)

Another way to approach the materials theologically is to observe the
emphasis on order, not a stifling order but one with certain flexibility.
Genesis 1 begins by noting that the earth was formless [*tohu*] and void
[*vohu*]. First, God began dealing with such a "chaotic" (formless and
unshaped) condition by creating time:

> Then God said, "Let there be light," and there was light. And God saw
> that the light was good; and God separated the light from the darkness.
> God called the light Day, and the darkness he called Night. And there was
> evening and there was morning, the first day. (Gen 1:3-5)

Along with the creation of time on day one, God created places on days
two and three and various populations for those places on days four through
six. For instance, on day two God made the sky with a dome and in the
dome placed the planets on day four. On day three God provided for seas
and dry land, which on subsequent days were occupied by sea life, animals,
humanity, and birds flying overhead. Interestingly, plant life appeared on the
third day (not the fifth day as we would expect) along with the dry land.

Hyers likens the technique of the Genesis author, who first directs our attention to places and then to the various populations of the places, to that of a landscape painter:

> The procedure is not unlike that of a landscape painter, who first sketches in with broad strokes the structure and background of the painting: its regions of light and darkness, of sky and water, and of earth and vegetation. Then within this context are painted birds and fish, land animals and human figures. It would be quite inappropriate for anyone to try to defend the artistic merit and meaning of the painting by attempting to show that the order in which the painting was developed was geologically and biologically "correct." . . . The Genesis account is a painting of the totality, the design of which is to sketch in all the major regions and types of creatures . . . placed under the sovereignty of the Creator.[8]

Throughout chapter 1 we find at the end of every creative act the words, "And God saw that it was good" (vv. 10, 12, 18, 25). At the conclusion of those creative acts we read: "God saw everything that he had made, and indeed, it was very good" (v. 31). Whatever else the word good (*tov*) means, it means at least that God was satisfied with what had been accomplished. However, judging from the account of the creation of humanity in Genesis 2, God could express dissatisfaction with what God had done at some point in the creative process. For instance, after creating Adam. Genesis reports:

> Then the LORD God said, "It is not good that man should be alone; I will make him a helper as his partner." (Gen 2:18)

Therefore, God begins to make adjustments in creation that at first include the unsatisfactory animals and finally the satisfactory woman.

Thus we see that there is a kind of possible flexibility in creation as far as God's own creative activity is concerned. Over and above that, flexibility becomes inevitable when God determines that creation itself (plants, birds, sea creatures, land creatures, humans) shall participate in the creative process. However, we are not to look upon this ongoing process as one in which God is no longer involved, as some Deists may suppose. For instance, if God is unhappy with humanity's conduct, as in the time of Noah, God may consider eliminating humanity altogether. But that is not necessarily God's final decision. For it may be determined:

I will never again curse the ground because of humankind, for the inclination of the human heart is evil from youth; nor will I ever again destroy every living creature as I have done. (Gen 8:21)

As important as creation theology may be, we need to be reminded that God's creative activity preceded such a theology. Consider the following instructive words of Terence Fretheim:

God's actions in the world achieve priority of place over human knowledge of what God has done. When Israel does begin to articulate the place of creation in the divine economy, this amounts to Israel's "catching up" with what God has long been about. The development of a creation theology in Israel occurs secondary to God's actual engagement with the world.[9]

Creation According to Job

The words of Terence Fretheim remind us of a question that God put to Job, "Where were you when I laid the foundation of the earth?" (Job 38:4). This is the initial question in a series of questions during a speech often spoken of as God's whirlwind speech (so-called because God addressed Job out of a whirlwind) dealing with God's involvement in creation (Job 38–41).

Before examining in some detail the whirlwind speech, which contains the most extensive statement about creation in the book of Job, we need to note that Job has already demonstrated some knowledge of creation. We also need to inquire why God chose to use this medium to deal with Job's sufferings, especially Job's attitude toward the suffering and the resulting attitude toward God.

It is evident early in the book of Job that Job already knows something about creation. Much of what he knows is based on his attentive observation of the nature that has sustained him and given him wealth and health, until both were snatched away from him. Consider these words to his friends:

"But ask the animals, and they
     will teach you;
the birds of the air, and they
     will tell you;
ask the plants of the earth, and
     they will teach you;
and the fish of the sea will
     declare to you." (Job 12:7-8)

Further, Job's first public discourse (Job 3) bears witness to his knowledge of creation, in some ways akin to what is found in Genesis, except in reverse order. Whereas, according to Genesis, God appropriately deals with chaos (the shapeless stuff of creation) by, for instance, separating light from darkness, Job wishes for a return to chaos to snuff out his own life. He longs for perpetual darkness where no stars shine. Again, believing that his misery can be put to an end by the untamable beast, Leviathan, he begs those who have the power to arouse the beast to make themselves known.

Why did God decide to use the whirlwind speech to deal with Job's suffering? Was he trying to shame Job, to put him in his place? Consider William Brown's response to this question:

> [E]ntirely lacking in Yahweh's discourse is any hint of punishment leveled against Job. In addition to its caustic language, Yahweh's litany of nature bears a positive function, indeed, a pedagogical purpose. The evocative series of images drawn from the realms of cosmology and zoology plays a critical role in broadening Job's moral horizon, as well as in demonstrating his innocence before his detractors. Yahweh's discourse is as much a didactic treatise and source of resolution for Job as it is a deposition against him.[10]

In the passage quoted above, Brown speaks of the discourse as serving a "pedagogical purpose." He is not speaking of a speech designed simply to address the nature of God's creative activity. However, there is no reason to suppose that the speech cannot be used for that purpose. In any case, we have to keep in mind that this passage, along with other Old Testament passages, makes use of marvelous figures of speech. For instance, in this particular speech, thick darkness is said to be "the swaddling band" of the newly-born sea.

After the initial question in the whirlwind speech concerning Job's absence at the time God "laid the foundation of the earth," the speech proceeds to cover such cosmological elements as earth, seas, stars, and such meteorological elements as rain. God insists that Job understand and appreciate certain things such as the ultimate source of creation, the great care and precision (God's measuring, stretching, and laying) used by God in creation, and the orderly, built-in limits of this creation (the "prescribed bounds" for the sea). Further God informs Job that while the project proceeded, God's cheering squad (made up of stars and other heavenly creation) provided festive approval. "Where were you," God inquired of Job, "when the morning stars sang together and all the heavenly beings shouted for joy?" (Job 38:7).

By way of questions laced with strong verbs, God moves quickly from one creation truth to another. Note some of the verbs employed: have you *commanded... caused... changed ... entered into ... seen ... comprehended?* What God wants Job to understand is that creation is a continuous process (what some would describe as providence) as well as the initial act of creation itself. So, God continues the questions: can you *bind ... loose ... lead forth ... send forth?*

One of the interesting things about God's continuing creative activities (providence) in this speech is the emphasis that is placed on God's wild creatures, including God's involvement in their predatory activities. (See Job 38:39-40.) We will have more to say about this in the chapter titled, "Tending God's World." In the meantime, note that Brown, in assessing this speech, especially concerning God's original creation of and continuing care for God's wild creation, remarks:

> Predation is present, but does not ultimately define the contours of this wild community; rather freedom, vitality, fearlessness, and most of all wondrous difference define it.[11]

Genesis and Science

Above we approached the early chapters of Genesis from a theological point of view. Does this mean that these chapters contain no ancient "scientific" (in whatever sense) information or that they serve no useful scientific purpose in our own age? Presented below, in broad strokes, are some opinions about these matters, organized under two main points of view. First, we shall examine the view of those who maintain that Genesis presents timeless creation truths, over and above what might be generally called theological. Second, we shall look at the position of those who hold that whatever science there is in Genesis is the outdated science of the ancient Israelites.

Among those who posit the position of timeless truth (over and above theological) in the Genesis creation stories are those who prefer to think that language referring to things is observational/phenomenal (governed by the senses). For instance, it is permissible for those living 3000 years ago and those living today to speak of the sun rising and setting because it certainly appears to do that. John Calvin, a sixteenth century French/Swiss theologian, remarked that even though there are stars larger than the moon, it was appropriate for the author of Genesis to speak of the moon as a great light because that is the way it appeared to him (Hyers 29-30). This same view is picked up by such modern authors as Bernard Ramm in *The Christian View of Science and Scripture* and by Conrad Hyers in *The Meaning of Creation: Genesis and Modern Science*. Let the following quotation from Ramm suffice:

Consider the language of Genesis 1. Astronomically, it speaks of the earth, the sun, the moon and the stars. It does not mention asteroids, comets, nebulae or planets. The astronomical classification is phenomenal [as it appears to the sense of sight]. It is restricted to that which greets the eye as one gazes heavenward . . . . Genesis 1 is the classification of the unsophisticated common man. (67)

However, the above position is not satisfactory for a group of persons (made up of both theologians and scientists) who are known generally as Creation Scientists (partially so called because of their negative position of evolutionary science). They maintain that Genesis contains *true science* (their words) and that when Genesis 1 is properly interpreted (of course, they insist that their interpretation is the correct one) and when the raw data of modern science is properly evaluated and organized, Genesis and modern science both agree in such matters as the order of creation and the time involved (at the most 20,000 years). Their position is ably summarized by Raymond Eve and Francis Harrold:

Strict creationists follow a highly literal and straightforward reading of the first eleven chapters of Genesis. They believe that the entire universe was created in six twenty-four hour days . . . all kinds of life, mankind included, were created *ex nihilo* (from nothing) by God during creation week in essentially their present form . . . . Nearly all strict creationists also accept flood geology, which explains the geological record of sedimentary rocks and the fossil record of the past life as products of Noah's flood. (Gen. 6–8) (46)

Suppose there seems to be some discrepancy between the biblical account and the scientific understanding of the *Bible-believing* modern scientists? Since the problem cannot be in the Bible, it has to be in the methodology of the scientists. Again note the words of Eve and Harrold:

If science appears to show that the book of nature contradicts the book of scripture, then there must be a mistake somewhere. And since scripture is God's infallible word, it necessarily follows that the mistake is being made by scientists. The task of creation scientists, then, is to find and explain just where the mistakes are. "What I'm asserting," says biologist Kenneth Cumming of the Institute for Creation Research, "is that you will never find science proving scripture wrong." (50-51)

For those readers who would like to pursue more fully the modern Creation Science movement, it is suggested that the reader begin with the writings of Henry M. Morris, especially his work written in collaboration with John C. Whitcomb, titled *The Genesis Flood: The Biblical Record and its Scientific Implications*. Beyond this work, the following are recommended for the general understanding of the movement: Ratzsch, *The Battle of the Beginnings: Why Neither Side is Winning the Creation-Evolution Debate*; Eve and Harrold, *The Creationist Movement in Modern America*; Numbers, *The Creationists: The Evaluation of Scientific Creationism*.

Before leaving the view that there is such a thing as a true science that is the same throughout history and that such a true science can be correlated with the Old Testament, we need to consider the difficulties of such a view both for religion and science. Hyers expressed it well:

> Again and again in the history of modern science, efforts have been made to correlate the Bible with the newest scientific data and theory in geology, paleontology, biology, physics, chemistry, and astronomy. If Genesis, however, were to be harmonized with the prevailing science of any particular generation, it would be *out* of harmony with the prevailing science of every other generation . . . . To effect a "reconciliation" of science and Scripture at any point in history would be a dubious achievement. To try to discredit some prevailing scientific theory and discount scientific evidence on the grounds that they will eventually be proved wrong and the Bible proved right is to keep matters of faith in everlasting suspension. (30)

Finally, we consider the view of those who see timeless theological truth blended with outdated Israelite scientific theories in the Old Testament creation stories. For instance, Henry Jackson Flanders, Robert Wilson Crapps, and David Anthony Smith, in their *People of the Covenant*, depict the ancient Israelite worldview as follows, based on Genesis, other Old Testament passages, and compared with other ancient Near Eastern accounts:

> The flat, circular earth occupied the center of the world. Over it stretched a dome, the firmament of Genesis 1 (lit. "a beaten out place"), which rested on the mountains around the edge of the earth. Inside the dome the sun, moon, and stars moved in their proper courses, as if on tracks . . . . Beneath the earth was the great deep, a mighty ocean where all earthly waters, such as springs, or wells had their source. The earth rested securely on great pillars sunk deep in the subterranean waters. (109)

Without insisting that the above depiction is the only one that could be made based on the Old Testament data, it seems reasonable to understand that Israel shared with her neighbors their common cultural views about the operation of the universe. This being so, it seems proper today to blend our present scientific knowledge of the universe with both our and Israel's commonly agreed-on theological understanding, as recorded in the Old Testament, in the same way as Israel blended that theology with her scientific knowledge. Terence Fretheim expresses it well in the following words:

> The Genesis text remains both an indispensable theological resource and an important paradigm on the way in which to integrate theological and scientific realities in a common search for the truth about the world. (338)

In recent years a good number of Christian scholars have attempted to integrate, as Fretheim has suggested, the theological and modern scientific views. In some cases, these scholars have had formal training in both scientific and theological studies. Such an individual is John David Weaver who has studied and taught the sciences, especially geology. Further he has had formal theological training and has served as a practicing English Baptist minister. In his work, *In the Beginning God: Modern Science and the Christian Doctrine of Creation*, he seeks to erect a bridge between the scientific and religious ideas concerning creation. Among the ways he does this is to present various witnesses to creation. Besides "The Witness of Genesis," he has chapters on "The Witness of Physics and Cosmology," "The Witness of Biology," and "The Witness of Geology."

While Weaver's book is recommended as a good starting place to become acquainted with both the scientific and theological understanding of the universe, its Creator, and its inhabitants, there is no claim that the book will be easy reading for all readers. The following selection may serve as an introduction to the author's viewpoint:

> Both theology and science are seeking to make sense of the world that they experience . . . . Science is able to investigate the universe because human beings have a measure of transcendence over the world, and theology is able to bring a greater degree of understanding because it recognizes the transcendence of God, who reveals his purposes to humankind. (12)

Notes

Raymond A. Eve and Francis B. Harrold, *The Creationist Movement in Modern America* (Boston: T. Wayne Publishers, 1991).

Henry Jackson Flanders, Robert Wilson Crapps, and David Anthony Smith, *People of the Covenant: An Introduction to the Hebrew Bible* (New York: Oxford University Press, 1996).

Terence E. Fretheim, "The Book of Genesis," *The New Interpreter's Bible.*

Conrad Hyers, *The Meaning of Creation: Genesis and Modern Science* (Atlanta: John Knox Press, 1984).

Ronald L. Numbers, *The Creationists: The Evolution of Scientific Creationism* (Berkeley: University of California Press, 1992).

Bernard Ramm, *The Christian View of Science and Scripture* (Grand Rapids: Wm. B. Eerdmans Publishing Company, 1954).

Del Ratzsch, *The Battle of Beginnings: Why Neither Side is Winning the Creation-Evolution Debate* (Downers Grove IL: Intervarsity Press, 1996).

John David Weaver, *In the Beginning God: Modern Science and the Christian Doctrine of Creation* (Macon GA: Smith and Helwys Publishing, Inc., 1994).

John C. Whitcomb and Henry M. Morris, *The Genesis Flood: The Biblical Record and Its Scientific Implications* (Piladelphia: Presbyterian and Reformed Publishing Co., 1961).

Notes

[1] Walter Brueggemann, *Theology of the Old Testament* (Minneapolis: Fortress Press, 1997), 149.

[2] John H. Steck, "What says the Scripture?" in *Portraits of Creation: Biblical and Scientific Perspectives on the World's Formation*, ed. Howard J. van Till (Grand Rapids: William B. Eerdmans Publishing, 1990), 207.

[3] Ibid., 209.

[4] This certainly does not mean that the Israelites knew nothing of life being brought forth by the sexual union of male and female. For instance see Genesis 4:1 and 38:9.

[5] D. Winton Thomas, ed., *Documents From Old Testament Times* (New York: Harper and Row Publishing, 1958), 10-11.

[6] Conrad Hyers, *The Meaning of Creation: Genesis and Modern Science* (Atlanta: John Knox Press, 1984), 191.

[7] Ibid.

[8] Ibid., 70.

[9] Terence E. Fretheim, "The Book of Genesis," *The New Interpreter Bible*, vol. 1 (Nashville: Abingdon Press, 1994), 354-55.

[10] William P. Brown, *The Ethos of the Cosmos: The Genesis of Moral Imagination in the Bible* (Grand Rapids: William B. Eerdmans Publishing Co., 1999), 341.

[11] Ibid., 377.

5

Humanity

O LORD, our Sovereign,
    how majestic is your name in all
    the earth!
You have set your glory above the
    heavens . . .
When I look at your heavens, the
    work of your fingers,
    the moon and the stars that you
    have established;
what are human beings that you
    are mindful of them,
    mortals that you care for them?
Yet you have made them a little
    lower than God,
    and crowned them with glory
    and honor.
You have given them dominion
    over the works of your
    hands;
you have put all things under
    their feet,
all sheep and oxen,
    and also the beasts of the field,
    the birds of the air, and the fish of
    the sea,
whatever passes along the paths
    of the seas. (Ps 8:1, 3-8)

Introduction

Our paradigm passage above presents humans, as God intended them to be, exalted among the creation of God: "a little lower than God [*Elohim*]," "crowned with glory and honor," having dominion over God's other creation. In this chapter and others that follow, we shall examine the meaning of such an honor and humanity's propensity to stoop far below the intended ideal.

A theology of humanity can be found in some rudimentary form in the opening chapters of Genesis. For instance, Genesis declares that God (Yahweh *Elohim*) created man/humanity (*adam*) as living being/soul (*nephesh hayah*) composed from earth (*adamah*), animated by God. The declaration reads: "then the LORD God formed man from the dust of the ground, and breathed into his nostrils the breath of life; and the man became a living being" (Gen 2:7).

We have already observed in the previous chapter that God created space/place and time. While space/place and time are not limited to humanity, humanity is significantly involved. As for space/place, humans live on the earth and are related to the sky from whence comes needed water, and where the luminaries dwell, of equal importance for human existence. Also inhabiting the earth are other living things, including plants and animals. Humans have a special relationship to them that we shall consider more fully in chapter seven. Like space/place, time is of great importance to humanity. For instance, there is a time to work, a time to play, and a time to worship. Daily, there is a time to be awake and time to sleep; seasonally, there are special agricultural times and cultic times. In the time span of any one human being there is a time to be born and a time to die.

Within humanity itself there are important relationships. Among these are: husband and wife, parent and child, sibling and sibling, neighbor and neighbor.

A Theology of Human Physiology

While not having the modern knowledge of such things as DNA, the ancient Israelites were aware of such outward features as eyes, ears, faces, hands, and feet. In the Old Testament, the Israelites also refer to such inward parts as blood, hearts, livers, kidneys, and bones. In some cases, the parts are referred to in a literal way, while in others they are used as figures of speech. In some cases, a single part is used to depict the basic characteristics of a particular human. Concerning the latter use, even today we may say of a compassionate person that the person is "all heart." We are going to limit our discussion on human physiology to three important Hebrew words, namely: *basar*, *nephesh*, and *lev*.

Basar is usually translated flesh but is sometimes rendered as skin or body. For instance, *basar* has been translated in the NRSV in the same way we would say that a person is nothing but skin and bones. Listen to the Psalmist: "Because of my loud groaning my bones cling to my skin [*basar*]" (Ps 102:5). The most significant and deepest usage of *basar* (flesh) is the depiction of the total man as weak when compared to God.[1] This is clearly set forth in Second Isaiah:

> A voice says, "cry out!"
>   And I said, "What shall I cry?"
> All people [*basar*/flesh] are grass,
>   their constancy is like the flower
>   of the field . . .
> The grass withers, the flower
>   fades;
> but the word of our God will
>   stand forever. (Isa 40:6-8)

It does not follow that humans are to deprecate themselves. Such passages as Genesis 1:28, which depicts humankind as made in the image of God, and Psalm 8, which depicts humanity as a little lower than God/angels (*Elohim*), does not so treat humans.

One of the most intriguing words used of the human in the Old Testament is the word *nephesh*. The translations of this word in the NRSV range all the way from "throat/flesh" to "being" (meaning the entire person). One psalmist cries out:

> Save me, O God,
> for the waters have come up to
>   my neck [*nephesh*]. (Ps 69:1)

Before examining *nephesh* as a reference to the total human being rather than some part of him such as neck, it should be noted that the term *nephesh* is also used to denote a total fish, bird, animal, et cetera. This kind of Old Testament approach is first seen in Genesis 1:20:

And God said, "Let the waters bring forth swarms of living creatures
[*nephesh*], and let birds fly above the earth across the dome that moves the
sky." So God created the great sea monsters and every living creature, of
every kind, with which the waters swarm, and every winged bird of every
kind. And God saw that it was good…. And God said, "Let the earth bring
forth living creatures of every kind: cattle and creeping things and wild animals of the earth of every kind." And it was so. (Gen 1:20-21, 24)

This same terminology is again used to depict the nonhuman in the Genesis
Garden of Eden story and Genesis flood story:

So out of the ground the Lord God formed every animal of the field and every
bird of the air, and brought them to the man to see what he would call them;
and whatever the man called every living creature [nephesh], that was its name.
(Gen 2:19)

Then God said to Noah, and to his sons with him, "As for me, I am establishing
my covenant with you and your descendants after you, and with every living
creature [nephesh] that is with you, the birds, the domestic animals, and every
animal of the earth with you, as many as came out of the ark." (Gen 9:8-10)

The first Old Testament reference to a total human being as a *nephesh* is
found in Genesis 2:

then the LORD God formed man from the dust of the ground, and
breathed into his nostrils the breath of life; and the man became a living
being [*nephesh hayah*]. (Gen 2:7)

Readers familiar with the King James Version of the Bible will remember
that the translation of "*nephesh hayah*" there is "living soul" rather than "living being." Some of the other modern translations that render "*nephesh
hayah*" as "living being" are the Revised Standard Version, New American
Bible, New Jerusalem Bible, and New International Version. The New
English Bible and Revised English Bible render the term as "living creature,"
putting animals on a level with humans. The Contemporary English
Version, a highly paraphrased version published by the American Bible
Society, translates Genesis 2:7 as follows: "The LORD God took a handful of
soil and made a man. God breathed life into the man and the man started
breathing" (Gen 2:7).

If, in the Old Testament, the Hebrew word *basar* (flesh) presents humanity in its totality as inferior to God, how does the word *nephesh* present humankind? What follows can only be suggestive. Hans Walter Wolff suggests that we can think of a human, when spoken of as *nephesh*, as one with "ardent desire."[2] Otto Babb suggests "vitality,"[3] whereas Aubrey Johnson speaks of human "ebb and flow" rather than a constant state of vitality.[4] One way of expressing this is to say that an individual human, when compared with oneself, is sometimes up and sometimes down, as one of the spirituals puts it.

When we turn to our last word, namely *lev* (or *levev*) (usually translated "heart"), we come to what Wolff calls the "most important word in the vocabulary of Old Testament Anthropology."[5] One of the reasons for making this judgment is the frequency with which the word *lev* (along with *levev*) is used in the Old Testament. As Wolff points out, the word *lev* (along with *levev*) is used over 800 times in the Old Testament. Further, in contrast to *basar* (flesh), which is used often for animals, *lev* is used almost exclusively for humans.[6]

The Israelites did not seem to understand that the *lev* (heart) was an organ that pumped blood through the body. For them, like us, it was considered the seat of the emotions. However, *more importantly*, it was for them the seat of the rational and volitional. Consider the words of Wolff:

> It [*lev*] includes everything that we ascribe to the head and the brain — power of perception, reason, understanding, insight, consciousness, memory, knowledge, reflection, judgment, sense of direction, discernment. These things circumscribe the real meaning of the word [*lev*].[7]

The significant physiological terms (*basar, nephesh, lev*) we have examined should have prepared us for a more adequate and deeper meaning of the Old Testament theology of humanity. For instance, in his statement about God's requirements for Israel, Moses includes two of these words, namely *lev* (heart) and *nephesh* (soul or being depending on the translation):

> So now, O Israel, what does the LORD your God require of you? Only to fear the LORD your God, to walk in all his ways, to love him, to serve the LORD your God with all your heart [*lev*] and with all your soul [*nephesh*]. (Deut 10:12)

If we take our modern Christian understanding of heart to mean the emotional part of us and the soul to mean the permanent that remains after the body decays, we will miss completely the point of Moses' remarks. On the basis of what we learned above, we might paraphrase Moses' remarks as follows: "Serve the LORD your God with your total, vibrant being, especially your intellectual, willing self."

A Theology of Time

According to Genesis 1, the first act of creation was the creation of what we may speak of as the creation of time: the creation of light and the separation of light from darkness on day one. The same idea is expressed in the creation on the fourth day of the luminaries that govern time on the earth.

> And God said, "Let there be lights in the dome of the sky to separate the day from the night; and let them be for signs and for seasons, and for days and years, and let them be lights in the dome of the sky to give light upon the earth." And it was so. God made the two great lights — the greater light to rule the day and the lesser light to rule the night — and the stars. (Gen 1:14-16)

The author of Psalm 104 also contemplated God's marvelous provisions for daily time and yearly seasons. The author concluded that whatever claim humans might make on these provisions, non-human creation had a right to its own claim. The author further observed that certain wild animals prefer darkness as the best time to satisfy their needs while humans prefer daylight. With the capacity to turn darkness into daylight, even if artificial, humans today need to reflect if they have gained or lost in the process. In any case, hear the words of the psalmist:

> You [Yahweh] have made the moon to mark
>   the seasons;
> the sun knows its time for
>   setting.
> You make the darkness, and it is
>   night,
> when all the animals of the
>   forest come creeping out.
> The young lions roar for their
>   prey,

seeking their food from God.
When the sun rises, they withdraw
and lie down in their dens.
People go out to their work
and to their labor until the
    evening. (Ps 104:19-23)

Whereas the Psalmist spoke in a simple way of a daily time for human labor, *Qoheleth*, the author of Ecclesiastes, spoke of times for doing many things during one's lifetime. It is the most comprehensive statement to be found in one place in the Old Testament:

For everything there is a season, and a time for every matter under heaven:
a time to be born, and a time
    to die;
a time to plant, and a time to
    pluck up what is planted;
a time to kill, and a time to heal;
a time to break down, and a time
    to build up;
a time to weep, and a time
    to laugh;
a time to mourn, and a time
    to dance;
a time to throw away stones, and
    a time to gather stones
    together;
a time to embrace, and a time to
    refrain from embracing;
a time to seek, and a time to lose;
a time to keep, and time to
    throw away;...
a time to love, and a time to hate;
a time for war, and a time for
    peace. (Eccl 3:1-8)

While some interpreters insist that *Qoheleth* means for the reader to believe that all humans are predestined to live out their lives as set forth in the above statement, we believe that *Qoheleth* has left room for human freedom. If *Qoheleth* has not done so, at least other Israelites have. Consider Sibley Towner's words concerning this passage as it relates to freedom:

> Commentators and preachers alike have generally not wanted to consign the beautiful poem of 3:1-8 into the grim jaw of necessity [predestination], and they have warrant . . . . If one reads the poem with the understanding that the fixed orders provide structure rather than a calendar, then individual human moral decision making is possible. One can then hear in this poem a challenge to be wise, to be ethical, to discern when one's actions are in keeping with God's time and then to act decisively.[8]

In the life of each Israelite there was the inescapable movement from birth to death, the stages along the way, and the reflection on those stages. Take for example reflections on birth. As a sign of their great joy, Abraham and Sarah named their son Isaac (laughter). On the other hand, as a symbol of her deep sorrow and disgrace, the unnamed wife of Phineas, an Israelite priest, named her newly-born son Ichabod (no glory). She gave birth to a son whom her husband never saw because he died on the battlefield, along with many fellow Israelites, at the hands of the more powerful Philistines. Shortly after, she died believing that it would have been better if her son had never been born. Can we think of a sadder beginning for a child than to begin life without a father or mother in a country governed by an enemy?

As Ichabod grew into adulthood, assuming that he did, did he agree with his mother that it would have been better that he had not been born? Upon reflection, some adults did come to that conclusion. Such a person was the elderly Job, at a time when his body throbbed with pain, who reckoned that his birth was a terrible tragedy:

> After this Job opened his mouth and cursed the day of his birth. Job said:
> "Let the day perish in which I was
>   born;
> and the night that said,
> 'A man-child is conceived.'" (Job 3:1-3)

Without in any way judging Job's words in his time of great suffering, we put them along side the words of a psalmist who is glad of his birth:

> For it was you who formed my
>   inward parts;

you knit me together in my
    mother's womb.
I praise you, for I am fearfully and
    wonderfully made.
    Wonderful are your works;
that I know very well. (Ps 139:13-14)

Like today, we may suppose that there were many who neither spoke of regret nor happiness concerning their birth. They just lived out their days in a more-or-less humdrum fashion.

All of the mixed feelings we encountered above about birth, we also encounter about old age and death. For instance, in Genesis we have the story of the elderly Jacob, ill, blind, and near death. He speaks no word of sorrow about any of this. He only asks to be carried from Egypt to Palestine to be buried with his ancestors (Gen 49:29ff). On the other hand, the author of Genesis helps us to enter into the bereavement of Joseph, his son, over the death of his father: "Then Joseph threw himself on his father's face and wept over him and kissed him" (Gen 50:1).

If Jacob spoke nothing in an adverse way of his decrepit condition and his approaching death, other ancient Israelites did. For example, *Qoheleth's* metaphorical depiction of old age is one of the most disturbing to be recorded in the Old Testament.[9] Further, some of the psalmists look with horror upon their approaching death and their meager existence in Sheol, the place of the dead. We will have more to say about this in a later chapter.

Whatever the age span and the quality of life, all persons were expected to act their age and to respect the age of others. Among the many good qualities of youth was their strength and of the aged, their wisdom: "The glory of youths is their strength, but the beauty of the aged is their gray hair [wisdom]" (Prov 20:29). There was no guarantee, though, that the youth would properly use their strength or that the aged would act wisely. Concerning the latter, today there is a saying: "There is no fool like an old fool." There was no better example of such a fool than King Solomon, who at his inauguration asked God for wisdom but in his old age worshipped the gods of his wives (1 Kgs 3 & 11). So the writer of Proverbs reminds the aged that true wisdom has to be worked at continually and is closely related to the righteous life: "Gray hair is a crown of glory; it is gained in a righteous life" (Prov 16:31).

Such wisdom as is known by the elderly is to be sought out and acted upon by the young and those in the prime of life. Rehoboam, Solomon's successor, failed to do this upon his father's death. Because he listened to the advice of the friends his own age rather than that of his aged advisors, he lost most of his father's kingdom. As Hans Walter Wolff puts it:

> Rehoboam should have listened to the kindly and wise advice of the elders when they advised him to lighten the burden of the Israelites (1 Kgs 12:6ff), instead of letting himself be goaded on to severity by the young men with their crude vigor.[10]

One of the most beautiful examples for mutual respect between the young and the aged was that of the lad, Samuel, and the elderly priest, Eli. On a certain night, according to 1 Samuel, God spoke to Samuel (probably when he was about twelve). Thinking that Eli had called him, Samuel went to Eli's bed to be of assistance. On the third occasion that this happened, Eli said Samuel should address God if the voice spoke to him again. The voice did speak and Samuel replied. God had a very terrible message for Eli, a message to be delivered to him by Samuel. The message that Eli's sons would suffer greatly for their sins kept Samuel awake for the remainder of the night. It was only upon Eli's insistence that Samuel delivered the message the next morning. Deeply saddened, the old priest accepted the *words of Samuel as the very words of God himself.*

Like today, the lifetime of an ancient Israelite consisted of work and play, or the enjoyment of leisure time. For whatever reason, the Old Testament gives much more attention to work than it does to leisure. For instance, while the Garden of Eden story of Genesis 2 tells us that one of the tasks of Adam was to till the garden in which he lived, it says nothing about those times when he was not working. This is typical of most of the Old Testament.

It is in the Wisdom writings (especially Proverbs) where most attention is given to industriousness as over against sloth. (It does not follow that sloth and leisure are synonymous.) From his own personal observation, one of the authors of Proverbs declares:

> I passed by the field of one who
>   was lazy,
>   by the vineyard of a stupid person;
> and see, it was all overgrown with
>   thorns;
>   the ground was covered with nettles.

and its stone wall was broken
down.
Then I saw and considered it;
I looked and received
instruction.
A little sleep, a little slumber,
a little folding of the hands
to rest,
and poverty will come upon you
like a robber,
and want like an armed
warrior. (Prov 24:30-34)

It should be noted that Proverbs does not maintain that hard work necessarily equates with material wealth which, in turn, necessarily equates with happiness or God's favor.

If the Old Testament has less to say about leisure than work, one of the ways to begin an exploration of the concept of leisure is to examine some passages about sleep. Whereas sleep should be a time of rest, for some it is not because their fretful daytime activities are carried over into their sleep. *Qoheleth* noted that he had observed the following:

The lover of money will not be satisfied with money; nor the lover of wealth, with gain. This also is vanity.

When goods increase, those who eat them increase; and what gain has their owner but to see them with his eyes?

Sweet is the sleep of laborers, whether they eat little or much; but the surfeit of the rich will not let them sleep. (Eccl 5:10-12)

Another way to examine the concept of leisure is to look at the idea of rest. Of particular importance is God's sabbath commandment as recorded in Exodus 20:[11]

Remember the sabbath day, and keep it holy. Six days you shall labor and do all your work. But the seventh day is a sabbath to the LORD your God; you shall not do any work — you, your son or your daughter, your male or female slave, your livestock, or the alien resident in your towns. (Exod 20:8-10)

Among the things we can learn from the above command is that we are no more to become frantic toward leisure than we are toward work. Perhaps one of the most beloved of the Psalms can throw light on leisure and rest:

> The LORD is my shepherd, I shall
>   not want.
> He makes me lie down in green
>   pastures;
> he leads me besides still waters. (Ps 23:1)

Certainly it does not follow from what has been said above that leisure is a cessation from all activity. In fact, it may be difficult at times to distinguish between work and leisure.

Perhaps a brief mention of dance in the Old Testament can be instructive in our understanding of leisure. Frequently dances were recorded at weddings, agricultural harvests, and victories of various kinds. Concerning the latter, note the victory of the Israelites at the Reed (Red) Sea:

> Then the prophet Miriam, Aaron's sister, took a tambourine in her hand;
> and all the women went out after her with tambourines and with dancing.
> And Miriam sang to them:
> "Sing to the LORD, for he has
>   triumphed gloriously;
> horse and rider he has thrown into
>   the sea." (Exod 15: 20-21)

Alfred Sendry, a modern Jewish musicologist, has written a lengthy work titled *Music in Ancient Israel.*[12] In this work he includes a section on Israelite dance, both sacred and secular. He summarizes as follows:

> Should one put together these multifarious details into a composite picture, one would surely admit that dance played the same significant part in the life of Ancient Israel as music and singing. As a concurrent expression of any popular celebration, dance was always the most effective physical release of the psychic tension, especially when a common feeling of happiness pervaded the masses. Voice, instrument, and body, the natural media for singing, playing, and dancing, have been united in the music of Ancient Israel into an indivisible entity. In them, collectively, music in the broader sense became a reality.[13]

A Theology of Relationships

Whatever else defines humanity, a human is a relational being. The first —
and most important relationship — is with God. This relationship will be discussed later in this work. Humans are also related to the earth, plants, and
animals. This will be examined in the chapter titled "Tending God's World."
Human to human relationships fall under such categories as family, neighbors, et cetera. We shall cover this aspect in the two chapters on "Living in
Community before God." One of the most important, if not the most
important, human to human relationship is that of male and female.

Based on Israelite codes and narratives, "women are clearly subordinate
to the men of the household."[14] For instance, property was controlled by the
males except in some unusual situation such as that recorded in Numbers
concerning the daughters of Zelophehad who inherited their father's property (Num 27:1ff). Further, males had a great deal of control over female
sexuality. For instance, according to the Deuteronomic Code, a man who
could prove that his wife was not a virgin when he married her could have
her stoned to death. On the other hand, if his accusation against her was
proven to be a falsehood, he was simply fined (Deut 22:13-21).

However, there are some passages in the Old Testament that run counter
to what is said above about the inferior status of women. One such passage is
found in the Song of Solomon. According to Phyllis Trible: "In this erotic
poetry there is no tension between female and male, no male dominance, no
female subordination, and no stereotyping of either sex."[15]

Before taking a brief look at this work, we turn first to Genesis 2 and 3
that present a similar view, according to some modern interpreters. From the
entire passage, which the reader should consult, we have selected four
excerpts:

> [T]hen the LORD God formed man from the dust of the ground, and
> breathed into his nostrils the breath of life; and the man became a living
> being. (Gen 2:7)

> Then the LORD God said, "It is not good that the man should be alone; I
> will make him a helper as his partner." (Gen 2:18)

> So the LORD God caused a deep sleep to fall upon the man, and he slept;
> then he took one of his ribs and closed up its place with flesh. And the rib

that the LORD God had taken from the man he made into a woman and
brought her to the man. Then the man said,
> "This at last is bone of my bones
> > and flesh of my flesh;
> This one shall be called Woman,
> > for out of Man this one was taken" (Gen 2:21-23)

To the woman he [God] said,
"I will greatly increase your pangs
> in childbearing;
in pain you shall bring forth
> children,
yet your desire shall be for your
> husband,
and he shall rule over you." (Gen 3:16)

The choice of these Genesis passages to parallel the Song of Solomon
may seem rather strange since they are often used by interpreters to prove
God-ordained male dominance. For instance, many interpreters have
insisted that since male existence precedes that of female and she is created to
be his helper, the male is definitely ordained by God to be the superior one.
Besides, it is insisted by these same interpreters, it was her gullibility, when
tempted by the serpent, that not only got her in trouble but also Adam and
all humans since that time. Further, it is maintained that because of her inclination towards waywardness, the man was given rule over her to keep her in
line.

Many interpretative materials today, on the above passages, emphasize
that the passage teaches equality between the sexes rather than male superiority. In fact, some modern interpreters, such as Samuel Terrien and Paul
Jewett, go so far as to say that woman's superiority is taught. For instance,
Terrien titles one of his chapters, "Woman, Crown of Creation."[16]
Concerning the position that woman is supposedly inferior since woman is
made from man and after man, Jewett points out that since animals are
made before humans, according to Genesis 1, animals, by the same rationale,
must be superior to humans. Furthermore, by the same rationale, since man
(*adam*) was made from the ground (*adamah*), according to Genesis 2, the
ground must be superior to the man. Jewett remarks:

If one is to infer anything from the fact that the woman was created after the man, it should be, in the light of the first creation narrative, that the woman is superior to the man. But if men do not find this conclusion palatable, let them ask themselves why women should stomach the rabbinic conclusion that the woman is inferior because she is created after the man.[17]

If John Milton is correct, this understanding of the woman's superiority did not start with two twentieth century males but with Adam himself. In his *Paradise Lost*, Milton has Adam to say:

O fairest of creation, last and best
Of all God's works, creature in whom excelled
Whatever can to sight or thought be formed,
Holy, divine, good, amiable, or sweet![18]

But doesn't the fact that the woman is made to be Adam's helper (*ezer*) signify her inferiority? Not according to interpreters such as Trible and Terrien, who point out that God is often called man's helper/help (*ezer*).[19] Trible remarks that the Hebrew word "*ezer*" "often describes God as the superior who creates and saves Israel."[20] While that is enough to suggest female superiority to Terrien, Trible is willing to opt for an interpretation that puts male and female as equals. Trible expresses her opinion: "According to Yahweh God, what the earth creature [man] needs is a companion, one who is neither subordinate nor superior; one who alleviates isolation through identity."[21]

When we move from the story of creation in Genesis 2 to the story of disobedience in chapter three, the difference between man and woman and the relationship between the two continues to unfold. The woman is approached by a so-called serpent who suggests tremendous gains can come to her if she eats the fruit of the tree forbidden by God. Why did the serpent approach her rather than the man? According to those interpreters who have found her inferior according to creation, she is more likely to succumb to the serpent's wiles. Other interpreters, such as Trible and Terrien, believe the serpent chose her because of her superiority. For instance, Trible, whom we noted above was willing to see equality of man and woman in the creation narrative, definitely sees woman's superiority in the disobedience narrative. The serpent chose her because she was more intelligent than the man, and, as such, would carry on a better theological dialogue than the man. Trible summarizes as follows: "If the woman is intelligent, sensitive, and ingenious, the man is passive, brutish, and inept."[22] Much of what Trible says about the man is based on the man's eating of the fruit offered by the woman *without dialogue*. Surely too much emphasis is placed on *silence*. Why can't we say the passage depicts her as intelligent without, at the same time, saying that he is depicted as brutish?

Following the disobedience of the first couple, God begins to deal with the serpent, the man, and the woman. Concerning the latter, we read:

> To the woman he [God] said,
> "I will greatly increase your pangs
>   in childbearing;
> in pain you shall bring forth
>   children,
> yet your desire shall be for your
>   husband,
> and he shall rule over you." (Gen 3:16)

Concerning the above verse, Carol Myers, a Jewish Old Testament scholar, remarks: "Perhaps no single verse of scripture is more troublesome, from a feminist perspective, than is the divine oracle to the woman in Genesis 3:16."[23] Myers finds the answer to her problem by a different rendering/translation of the passage as we shall see below. On the other hand, Trible deals with the traditional translation with a different interpretation. Trible sees the words not so much as punishment but as a description of the alienation that God allows to happen because of their willful disobedience. She summarizes as follows:

> Hence, the woman is corrupted in becoming a slave, and the man is corrupted in becoming a master. His supremacy is neither a divine right nor a male prerogative. Her subordination is neither a divine decree nor the female destiny. Both their positions result from shared disobedience. God describes this consequence but does not prescribe it as punishment.[24]

On the basis of a very meticulous study of the original Hebrew, in the context of its times, Myers gives the following translation of Genesis 3:16:

> I will greatly increase your toil and your pregnancies;
> (Along) with the travail shall you beget children.

> For to your man is your desire,
> And he shall predominate over you.[25]

Myers's translation is based, in part, on her belief that the verse can be best understood in the context of Israelite agricultural life in the pre-monarchy period. The woman will share the toil with her agricultural husband (see Gen 3:17ff) and will bear many babies needed for her household. This will necessitate her sexual desire for her husband who will insist that pregnancies, no matter how burdensome they may be, are necessary for the maintenance of the household.[26]

Because of the traditional translation (NRSV and others) of Genesis 3:16, some interpreters insist God has *decreed* that women throughout the ages, because of Eve's disobedience, shall be *ruled by their husbands in all matters*. Other interpreters, such as Trible, maintain that God has *allowed* such rule. Still others, such as Myers, insist that the passage has nothing to do with man's rule over woman in all matters, whether by way of a prescribed curse by God or by way of God's allowance of sin taking its own deadly course. Rather, according to Myers, it describes life in an agricultural society in which both male and female, each in their own way, bare the toils of life. Thus, declares Myers, the "curse" (if that is what it is), is not some once-spoken, everlasting job description for either the man or the woman. If we can agree all men shall not be forever required to plow thorny fields, neither shall all women for all time be required to bear many babies.[27]

Whatever the Old Testament view (especially as expressed in Genesis 3 and following) on the relationship between man and woman, whether described by traditional interpreters or such non-traditional interpreters as Trible and Myers, woman's position was one of subordination. However, the Song of Solomon does present an ideal alternative view of equality, one already present in Genesis 2, according to Trible. The dominant voice in the Song of Solomon is that of the maiden, especially when augmented by the "daughters of Jerusalem." Trible expresses it this way: "Of the three speakers [the man, the woman, and the group of women], the woman is the most prominent. She opens and closes the entire Song, her voice dominant throughout."[28]

Trible would like to think of the Song of Solomon as an expression of the redemption of the lost Edenic relationship between male and female. However, she knows that neither life in ancient Israel nor life today will allow the Song of Solomon to bear that weight. Somewhere between the ideal lost in Eden and ideal yet to be redeemed there lies a present reality, which at least allows for the possibility of hope. Trible finds hope in such a book as Ruth where women (Naomi and Ruth), at great odds against them, take their rightful place in a man's world.[29]

Conclusion

According to the Old Testament, a human being is a creation of God living in space/place and time, one having a special relationship to oneself and others (God, other humans, and other created beings or things). As humans grow, they reflect on these relationships, adjusting themselves to them, and perhaps, where possible and worthwhile, adjusting them to themselves. To try to make impossible or ill-advised adjustments may play havoc to one's own being or to other persons or things. We'll have more to say about this later.

An individual, in one's totality, is *basar*/flesh (one who is weak when compared to God), *nephesh*/being (one with varying strengths and weaknesses), and *lev*/heart (one with the ability to feel, and, more importantly, with the ability to think and make decisions). According to Moses, a person owes it to God to serve God with the totality of one's being.

Time is one of humanity's most valuable commodities. We should spend it wisely for the glory of God and the well-being of ourselves and our significant others. We should make wise choices as they relate to hours of work, hours of leisure, and hours of worship.

Human relationships are exceedingly important. Except for the God-human relationship, none is more important than the male/female relationship. What the proper relationship is according to the Old Testament depends both on the biblical text selected and the perspective of its interpreter as we have seen above. The tendency today, at least among some interpreters, is to see womankind in the Old Testament in a more favorable light than she was seen by some previous interpreters. Whether this modern tendency is seen as good or bad will depend on the reader.

Notes

[1] Hans Walter Wolff, *Anthropology of the Old Testament* (Philadelphia: Fortress Press, 1974), 30.

[2] Ibid., 17.

[3] Otto J. Babb, *The Theology of the Old Testament* (New York: Abingdon-Cokesbury Press, 1949), 66.

[4] Aubrey Johnson, *The Vitality of the Individual in the Thoughts of Ancient Israel* (Cardiff: University of Wales Press, 1949), 14.

[5] Wolff, 40; see also Johnson, 77.

[6] Wolff, 40.

[7] Ibid., 51.

[8] Sibley W. Towner, "The Book of Ecclesiastes," *The New Interpreters Bible*, vol. 5, (Nashville: Abingdon Press, 199[?]), 308.

[9] See Ecclesiastes 12.

[10] Wolff, 124-25.

[11] See also: Exod 16:22ff, 31:12ff; Lev 26:1ff; Deut 5:12ff; Isa 56:4ff.

[12] Alfred Sendry, *Music in Ancient Israel* (New York: Philosophical Library, 1969).

[13] Ibid., 476.

[14] Tikva Frymer-Kensky, *In the Wake of the Goddess: Women, Culture, and the Biblical Transformation of Pagan Myth* (New York: Fawcett Press, 1992), 119.

[15] Phyllis Trible, "Women in the Old Testament," *Interpreters Dictionary of the Bible*, Supplement, 965.

[16] Samuel Terrien, *Till the Heart Sings: A Biblical Theology of Manhood and Womanhood* (Philadelphia: Fortress Press, 1985), 7.

[17] Paul K. Jewett, *Man as Male and Female: A Study of Sexual Relationships from a Theological Point of View* (Grand Rapids: William B. Eerdmans Publishing Co., 1975), 126-27.

[18] John Milton, *Paradise Lost*, Book 9, ed. William G. Madsen (New York: Random House, 1969), 251.

[19] See Exod 18:4; Deut 33:7; Pss 33:20, 115:9.

[20] Phyllis Trible, *God and the Rhetoric of Sexuality* (Philadelphia: Fortress Press, 1978), 90.

[21] Ibid., 90.

[22] Ibid., 113.

[23] Carol Myers, *Discovering Eve: Ancient Israelite Women in Context* (New York: Oxford University Press, 1988), 95.

[24] Trible, *God and the Rhetoric of Sexuality*, 128.

[25] Carol Myers, 118.

[26] Ibid., 99ff.

[27] Ibid., 120-21.

[28] Trible, *God and the Rhetoric of Sexuality*, 145.

[29] Ibid., 166ff.

6

Thinking God's Thoughts

Surely there is a mine for
    silver
    and a place for gold to be
    refined.
Iron is taken out of the earth,
    and copper is smelted from ore
Miners put an end to darkness,
    and search out to the farthest
    bound
the ore in gloom and deep
    darkness.
They open shafts in a valley away
    from human habitation;
    they are forgotten by travelers,
    they sway suspended, remote
    from people . . .

They put their hand to the flinty
    rock,
    and overturn mountains by the
    roots.
They cut out channels in the
    rocks,
    and their eyes see every precious
    thing. (Job 28:1-4, 9-10)

If humanity is to be responsible for caring for God's good earth, it must have the requisite knowledge for doing so. We'll have more to say about the tending of the earth in the next chapter. In this chapter we shall discuss more generally the source and use of knowledge at humanity's disposal.

God: Ultimate Source of Knowledge

Whence comes knowledge? It ultimately has its source in God.
For the Lord gives wisdom;
> from his mouth come
> knowledge and
> understanding. (Prov 2:6)

While there is a dimension of knowledge that is reserved for those who "fear the LORD" (Prov 2:5; Job 28:28), God has not withheld earthly knowledge from nonbelievers. Again observe the words of Proverbs:

> The poor and the oppressor have
> > this in common:
> > the LORD gives light to the eyes
> > of both. (Prov 29:13)

God has not withheld knowledge even from those who would use such knowledge to make idols or to elevate themselves to the status of God (Isa 44:9-13; Ezek 28:1ff).

Limitations of Knowledge

To say that God grants knowledge to humanity needs to be qualified by saying that God grants a measure of knowledge or by saying that God places limitations on that knowledge. There are limitations inherent in the very constitution of humanity and other limitations brought on by humanity's sin or willfulness. Perhaps no clear distinction can always be made between the two. In any case, we are not to suppose that every search for knowledge is based on sinful thoughts or for sinful purposes.

Humanity, by its very constitution, is limited when compared with God. We observed above that this distinction is made when man depicts himself as flesh, "*basar*." The book of Proverbs contrasts the limited knowledge of humanity with the unlimited knowledge of God:

> The human mind plans the way,
>   but the LORD directs the steps. (Prov 16:9)

> The human mind may devise
>   many plans,
>   but it is the purpose of the
>   LORD that will be
>   established. (Prov 19:21)

Certainly there is no sin in this constitutional limitation unless man forgets it or ignores it. Whereas the book of Proverbs, through pithy statements, contrasts humanity's limited and God's unlimited knowledge, Job 28 magnificently portrays the difference.

The book of Job tells the story of a wealthy man (shepherd, farmer, merchant) by the name of Job who tragically loses all his wealth, his children, and finally his health. His three closest friends try to convince him such a tragedy is a result of great sin and can only be rectified by repentance. Unconvinced that he is a great sinner, Job finds himself torn between his deep trust in the integrity of God and the nagging feeling that God is wrongfully responsible for his suffering. Exacerbating the problem is God's reply of silence to Job's plea for an audience. The conversation — with God doing most of the talking or overwhelming Job with questions about the creating and sustaining of the universe — is found in chapters 38 to 40. Job becomes convinced that there are many deep mysteries, including his own suffering, that only God is wise enough to know. This viewpoint is partially anticipated in chapter 28.

According to Job 28, humanity only thinks the thoughts of God after him, whereas the original thoughts (along with the resulting universe) are God's and God's alone (vv. 23-27). It should not be overlooked that in depicting God's knowledge as superior to that of humanity's, Job contrasts God's knowledge with the very best of humanity's knowledge as seen in humanity's technology and commerce. For example, Job observes humanity having great ingenuity in the extracting from the bowels of the earth raw ore that will be smelted into silver, gold, and copper. No proud lion has descended into the earth as has humanity and no falcon, from above the earth, has seen such treasure.

Job further declares that in order to extract the precious things of the earth, humans open up shafts in which they precariously sway back and forth. They rip mountains apart and cut "channels in the rocks." They even change the courses of the streams to get at the precious ore. The modern reader cannot help reflecting on the current mining practices of ripping the earth apart both beneath and on the surface of the earth. Earlier humans did the same thing, even if in a much less pronounced way, with the technology of their own time.

It is not enough, according to Job, for some humans to mine, smelt, and shape the treasures. Other humans must place such value on the treasures that they purchase them and thus provide for the commerce of a civilized society. Job specifically speaks of the "gold of Opir" and the "topaz of Ethiopia." Further, he speaks of commerce in such things as jewels and fine crystal. Gerald J. Janzen, in his commentary on Job, remarks:

> Humans can mine the earth for its hid treasures, and they can trade among themselves for the precious products of the earth; and in such activities they may be said to display a wisdom of sorts. The wisdom which Job seeks [concerning his problems] cannot be found or bought. God alone has access to such wisdom, for it is found and displayed only in the enactments by which creativity brings cosmos into existence.[1]

Of course, Janzen is right in insisting the best of humanity's wisdom is "wisdom of sorts." However, we must not so emphasize the superiority of God's wisdom that we utterly disparage that of humanity. To do so would denigrate the God who has deliberately made human beings in God's own image and has allowed them to think God's own thoughts even if in limited measure. As the author of Psalm 8 recognizes, it isn't just the heavens (moon and stars) reminding us of God's majesty — even more so does humanity remind us of God.

If it was only God's presence (Job 38–40) that gave Job any deep and abiding satisfaction in the face of his great suffering, both the days before and after his intense pain were enhanced by the earthly knowledge that brought him great wealth. Certainly earthly wisdom, with its accompanying wealth, was not accounted to him as sin. Before he lost his wealth it was said of Job that he "was blameless and upright, one who feared God and turned away from evil" (Job 1:1). After his health had been restored and he had double his previous wealth, it was said he "prayed for his friends" (Job 42:10).

If Job 28 points out that it is not part of God's design for man to search out the ultimate knowledge of God, the passage does not indicate what would happen to man if he did decide to push beyond his limits. The latter is set forth in some sense in the opening chapters of Genesis. According to Genesis, Adam, representing humanity, is provided with a garden that he may freely use, and the knowledge to "till it and keep it" (Gen 2:15). However, God prohibits Adam from eating from the "tree of the knowledge of good and evil" (Gen 2:17) without explaining why such eating is wrong. The words "good and evil" seem simple enough, but they have been interpreted in a great many ways. Claus Westermann, in his commentary on Genesis, has summarized many of them.[2] Some interpreters see them as having sexual connotations, others as referring to practical or moral discernment, and still others as referring to a knowledge of everything. At least, they refer to a kind of knowledge desired by, but not yet attained by, the human pair.

Seduced by a serpent, the woman and later the man eat of the tree, thus disobeying God. Soon after the disobedient act, the man and his female companion begin to experience, among other things, alienation: alienation from their bodies (they both express shame and the woman gives birth in pain), alienation from each other, alienation from the earth from which the man came (outside of the garden the man toils to bring forth crops), and alienation from God (the pair hide themselves from the presence of God).

Whatever helpful knowledge they attained from the tree, it was more than offset by a knowledge that upset the serene life they had been living. Were they like modern teenagers who discover certain facts of life long before they are mature enough to handle such facts? Perhaps the author of Proverbs expresses it well:

> Desire without knowledge is
>   not good,
> and one who moves too
>   hurriedly misses the way. (Prov 19:2)

Like the modern parent or society that seeks to work with the teenagers who have pressed forward too soon, God allowed early humanity, under certain restraints, such as Adam's refractory soil, to make progress in such knowledge as agriculture, technology, and the arts (Gen 4:17-22). Many years later, Augustine, the great early-church theologian, marveled at how much humanity had progressed in spite of humanity's sin and God's restraints. Writing c. AD 400, he remarks:

Just think of the progress and perfection which human skill has reached in
the astonishing achievements of cloth making, architecture, agriculture,
and navigation. Or think of the originality and range of what has been
done by experts in ceramics, by sculptors and by painters; of the dramas
and theatrical spectacles so stupendous that those who have not seen them
simply refuse to believe the accounts of those who have. Think even of the
contrivances and traps which have been devised for the capturing, killing,
or training of wild animals; or, again, of the number of drugs and appli-
ances that medical science has discovered in its zeal for the preservation and
restoration of men's health; or, again, of the poisons, weapons, and equipment used in wars, devised by military art for defense against enemy attack;
or even of the endless variety of condiments and sauces which culinary art
has discovered to minister to the pleasure of the palate.[3]

Use of Knowledge

The Old Testament not only deals with humanity's limited knowledge but
also with its use of such knowledge. In some cases, references are made to
that use without any critique. For instance, in brief and simple strokes, the
opening chapters of Genesis present, in a very elementary fashion, the beginnings of civilization as humanity exercises its knowledge. Adam, Cain, and
Jabel perform agricultural tasks.[4] As a "forger of all instruments of bronze
and iron," Tubal-Cain is the father of technology (Gen 4:22). Depending on
the interpretation, either Cain or his son, Enoch, founded the first city (Gen
4:17). Accompanying the development of agriculture and technology are the
arts as expressed in the statement that Jubal "was the ancestor of all those
who play the lyre and the pipe" (Gen 4:21).

At times the Old Testament critiques the proper and improper use of
man's knowledge and the resulting technological and artistic accomplishments. Among the improper use of such knowledge is man's aggrandizement
of self, even in some cases, of declaring oneself divine. The aggrandizement
of self is suggested in the Garden story of Adam and Eve we examined above.
We shall now give our attention to the Tower story, recorded in Genesis 11,
and the account of Tyre, recorded in Ezekiel 28.

In Genesis 4 we have the account of the origin of the first city, an ordinary one, begun by Cain or Enoch (Gen 4:17). Genesis 11 contains the
account of no ordinary city but a great one that will provide security for its
inhabitants (they will not be scattered abroad) and will bring them great
fame (they will make a name for themselves). God marvels at what they have

accomplished and considers where such accomplishments may lead. He opines, "nothing that they propose to do will now be impossible for them" (Gen 11:6). In order to prevent this, God confuses their language and scatters them far and wide.

Did God scatter them out of fear that humanity would usurp God's own power and prerogatives or out of concern for humanity's destruction of itself through the accumulation of unbridled knowledge and power? The answer is not given in the account in Genesis 11. Certainly, the tenor of the whole Old Testament reflects no fear on God's part. One of the psalmists puts it this way:

> Why do the nations conspire,
>> and the peoples plot vain?
> The kings of the earth set
>> themselves,
> and the rulers take counsel
>> together.
> Against the LORD and his
>> anointed . . .
> He who sits in the heavens laughs;
>> the LORD has them in derision.
> Then he will speak to them in his
>> wrath,
>> and terrify them in his fury,
>> saying,
> "I have set my king on Zion, my
>> holy hill." (Ps 2:1-2, 4-5)

If not fear on God's part, what purpose did the scattering serve? In the first place, it forced the descendants of Noah to populate the earth as God had commanded:[5] "God blessed Noah and his sons, and said to them, 'Be fruitful and multiply, and fill the earth'" (Gen 9:1).

Further, the scattering must have been designed to protect humanity from its own undoing. As Gerhard von Rad puts it, "Yahweh's interference has a preventative character."[6] Claus Westermann asserts that the improper use of knowledge and the overstepping of human boundaries are precisely what places "human existence in such great danger."[7]

If the citizens of Babel, in the story just examined, were in danger of destroying themselves by excessive power and the desire for fame, God

declares through Ezekiel that ancient Tyre shall be destroyed for the auda-
cious claim to be God, at least to be like God. Ezekiel depicts the marvelous
technological, artistic, and commercial achievements of Tyre (one of the city-
states of ancient Phoenicia and one of the seafaring queens of the
Mediterranean Sea) as a magnificent sailing ship (Ezek 28). The ship is con-
structed of the best woods, her "rails or gunwales"[8] are inlaid with ivory, and
her sails are made from the finest cloth from Egypt and exquisitely embroi-
dered. "Awnings, literally 'coverings,' of brilliant hue served as deck canopies
to shield the mariners from the sun."[9]

Following the description of Tyre as a magnificent sailing vessel, there is a
listing of Tyre's commercial allies along with exchanged wares (precious metal,
animals, jewelry, fine cloths, food, drink, and spices). Bunn states, "The listing in this section is a veritable catalogue of trade goods linked with the
primary sources of supply."[10] While Tyre had the right to feel proud of her
accomplishments — accomplishments even acknowledged by God — her
power and great splendor so went to her head that she, in the person of her
prince or king, boasted that she was God, or at least like God (Ezek 28:1, 6).

The wisdom of which the prince of Tyre boasts is practical wisdom
rather than spiritual, philosophical, or moral wisdom. Such wisdom is the
source of vast treasures in gold and silver and expertise in trade. We are
reminded of the words of 1 Kings concerning the Queen of Sheba and
Solomon:

> When the Queen of Sheba had observed all the wisdom of Solomon, the
> house that he had built, the food of his table, the seating of his officials,
> and the attendance of his servants, their clothing, his valets, and his burnt
> offering that he offered at the house of the LORD, there was no more spirit
> in her. (1 Kgs 10:4-5)

The Ezekiel passage contains an enigmatic reference to the prince of
Tyre being Adam of the Genesis story, or at least like Adam. However, unlike
Adam who was unclothed, the prince of Tyre was clothed with the most precious metals and jewels. Like Adam the prince of Tyre is also cast out of the
garden because of sin. However, unlike Adam who lives on, even though in
toilsome labor, the prince of Tyre is brought to a dreadful end to be no more
(Ezek 28:1-20). God's judgment is succinctly put: "you corrupted your wisdom" (Ezek 28:17).

If knowledge could be corrupted in the self-aggrandizement of some
men, even to the point of thinking of themselves as gods, the corruption

often came at the expense of others. Such was the case during Solomon's kingship. The books of Kings and Chronicles go into great detail concerning the tremendous growth of the kingdom during Solomon's reign. Building on the work of his father, David, Solomon added many elaborate buildings, including the temple. He maintained national security through key military cities with their hundreds of chariots. Further, he augmented his wealth and power through extensive trade, both by land and sea.

Surely a large number of Israelites shared in Solomon's wealth and power. As John Bright remarks:

> Solomon's projects, though state monopolies, must have given employment to thousands and stimulated others to private enterprise, thus raising the purchasing power of the entire nation and inducing a general prosperity. That many individuals grew rich either in Solomon's service or through personal efforts can hardly be doubted.[11]

But Solomon brought hardship to many and even slavery to some. He resorted to the hated *corvee*, an institution of forced labor. For instance, 1 Kings reports:

> King Solomon conscripted forced labor out of all Israel; the levy numbered thirty thousand men. He sent them to the Lebanon, ten thousand a month in shifts... (1 Kgs 5:13-14)

First Kings does not report that the people resented this during Solomon's lifetime. However, it is obvious they did because upon his death a group of citizens from the northern section of the kingdom informed his son, Rehoboam, that they would support Rehoboam's kingship only if he lightened the hard service placed on them by his father, Solomon (1 Kgs 12:3-4).

Certainly we would expect the misuse of Solomon's power to be resented by overburdened citizens. Further, through the canonical prophets, God spoke out in the strongest terms against the abuse of the use of God-given knowledge. Typical are the words of Jeremiah to King Josiah's sons who succeeded him as king. Josiah was one of the few Israelite kings who practiced justice. Concerning the corrupt sons who would abuse their powers, Jeremiah declares:

Woe to him who builds his house
    by unrighteousness,
    and his upper rooms by
    injustice;
who makes his neighbors work
    for nothing,
    and does not give them their
    wages;
who says, "I will build myself a
    spacious house
    with large upper rooms,"
and who cuts out windows for it,
    paneling it with cedar,
    and painting it with vermilion.
Are you a king
    because you compete in cedar?
Did not your father eat and drink
    and do justice and
    righteousness?
    Then it was well with him.
He judged the cause of the poor
    and needy;
    then it was well.
Is this not to know me?
    says the LORD. (Jer 22:13-17)

Though Solomon, the sons of Josiah, and other Israelites abused their God-given intellects, many humans, including Israelites, lived out their lives as good stewards of their talents.

It should be noted that while on occasion God used extraordinary measures, such as the provision of manna during the wilderness wanderings, to care for humankind, ordinarily the exercise of the human intellect in the tending of God's good earth was sufficient. Moses expressed it very well as the Israelites prepared to leave the wilderness to enter Palestine:

For the LORD your God is bringing you into a good land, a land with flowing streams, with springs and underground waters welling up in valleys and hills, a land of wheat and barley, of vines and fig trees and pomegranates, a land of olive trees and honey, a land where you may eat bread without scarcity, where you will lack nothing, a land whose stones are iron and from

whose hills you may mine copper. You shall eat your fill and bless the LORD
your God for the good land that he has given you. (Deut 8:7-10)

The Old Testament depicts countless men (along with their wives, children, and servants) who provide for the sustenance of their households in
God-approved ways. For instance, the book of Genesis recites the stories of
the Patriarchs, who tend their cattle and their sheep under the approving
gaze of God. Again, during the troubling days of the Judges the Israelites still
carry out such necessary tasks as planting and harvesting. For instance, the
book of Judges recounts the stories of Gideon threshing wheat in a wine
press away from the eyes of the enemy (Judg 6:11). The book of Ruth tells
the story of the harvesting and threshing activities of Boaz, the future husband of Ruth, in what was seemingly one of the quiet times during the
period of the Judges. First Samuel records the story of Saul, son of Kish and
future king of Israel, looking for Kish's mules that had strayed from home (1
Sam 9:3). Further, it recounts the story of the youthful David, son of Jesse
and successor to King Saul, sharing in the shepherding duties of that home
(1 Sam 16:11).

It is to the Old Testament Wisdom literature that we must turn to find a
theologizing of the importance of the individual household, especially as it
reflects on the economy and security of the Israelite people. R. E. Clements
remarks that

> individual households were seen to constitute the primary economic units
> within the community so that the prosperity of individuals was dependent
> upon the prosperity of the household in which they were resident.[12]

In the exercise of knowledge the most important person in the household is the husband and father. The author of Proverbs admonishes him to
grasp both the nature of his work and the needs of his family:

> Know well the condition of
>   your flocks,
>   and give attention to your
>   herds; . . .
>
> the lambs will provide your
>   clothing,
>   and the goats the price of a

field;
there will be enough goats' milk
    for your food,
    for the food of your household
    and nourishment for your
    servant girls. (Prov 27:23, 26-27)

As to the nature of work, *Qoheleth*, the author of Ecclesiastes, addresses the subject of the knowledge of the use of tools. He remarks:

If the iron is blunt, and one does
    not whet the edge,
then more strength must be
    exerted;
but wisdom helps one to
    succeed. (Eccl 10:10)

The very opposite of the industrious person is the slothful one. Proverbs expresses it thusly:

How long will you lie there,
    O lazybones?
    When will you rise from your
    sleep?
A little sleep, a little slumber,
    a little folding of the hands
    to rest,
and poverty will come upon you
    like a robber,
And want, like an armed
    warrior. (Prov 6:9-11)

We shall close out this section on the proper use of human knowledge with provisions for places and objects of worship. Surely this is an important way for humans to honor God through their God-given intelligence. The book of Exodus presents a lengthy account of the erection of the wilderness tabernacle, along with its furnishings and the clothing of the priests.[13]

Among other things, the Exodus account emphasizes that the pattern for the sanctuary and furnishings is from God; the materials (to be the very finest) for both sanctuary and furnishings shall be free-will offerings of the people, and the fashioning of everything shall exemplify the best skills of the workers (Exod 25–27, 30–31, 35–39). Among the materials the people bring are metals (such as gold, silver, and bronze), jewels (such as onyx), leather made of ram skins and goatskins, fine wood (especially Acacia), and cloths of various hews (such as blue, purple, and scarlet) (Exod 35:4-9).

The laborers are divided into three categories: two very talented overseers, other talented persons (including women), and willing persons who can perform perfunctory tasks.

> Then Moses said to the Israelites: See, the LORD has called by name Bezalel son of Uri son of Hur, of the tribe of Judah; he has filled him with divine spirit, with skill, intelligence, and knowledge of every kind of craft, to devise artistic designs, to work in gold, silver, and bronze, in cutting stones for setting, and in carving wood, in every kind of craft. And he has inspired him to teach, both him and Oholiab son of Ahisamach, of the tribe of Dan. He has filled him with skill to do every kind of work done by an artisan or a designer or by an embroiderer in blue, purple, and crimson yarns, and in fine linen, or by a weaver — by any sort of artisan or skilled designer. Bezalel and Oholiab and every skillful one to whom the LORD has given skill and understanding to know how to do any work in the construction of the sanctuary shall work in accordance with all that the LORD has commanded. (Exod 35:30–36:1)

> And let every able man among you come and make all that the LORD has commanded . . . (Exod 35:10 RSV)

> All the skillful women spun with their hands, and brought what they had spun in blue and purple and crimson yarn and fine linen . . . (Exod 35:25)

Daniel Boorstin's Contributions to our Understanding of Humanity's Quest to Know

In recent years Daniel Boorstin, considered by many to be one of America's twentieth-century literary giants, has published a trilogy on the history of knowledge: *The Discoverers* (1983), *The Creators* (1992), and *The Seekers* (1998). The trilogy contains a number of striking features. First, even though Boorstin does not mention it, the four main divisions of *The Discoverers* could have come right out of the opening chapters of Genesis: "Time," "The Earth and the Seas," "Nature," and "Society." Again, while Boorstin is obviously aware of the many diabolical uses humanity has made of its knowledge, he opts to put a positive spin on that use. For instance, he declares: "My hero is Man the Discoverer" (xv.). In this connection, he quotes with appreciation the following words of Francis Bacon, the seventeenth-century philosopher and statesman:

> Nay, the same Solomon the king, although he excelled in the glory of treasure and magnificent buildings, shipping and navigation, of service and attendance, of fame and renown, and the like, yet he maketh no claim to any of those glories, but only to the glory of inquisition of truth; for he saith expressly, "The glory of God is to conceal a thing, but the glory of the king is to find out" as if, according to the innocent play of children, the Divine Majesty took delight to hide his works, to the end to have them found out; and as if kings could obtain a greater honor than to be God's play-fellows in that game. (ix.)

Again, while not demeaning humanity's technological inventions, this aspect of its knowledge is not given a lot of attention. On occasion, Boorstin does refer to such inventions as the telescope, the microscope, magnetic compass, and the clock. He speaks of the latter as the "mother of machines." He explains it this way:

> Since clocks were the first modern measuring machines, clockmakers became the pioneer scientific-instrument makers. The enduring legacy of the pioneer clockmakers, though nothing could have been further from their minds, was the basic technology of machine tools. The two prime examples are the gear (or toothed wheel) and the screw. The introduction of the pendulum, by Galileo and then by Huygens, made it possible for clocks to be ten times more accurate than they had been, but this could be accomplished only by precisely divided and precisely cut toothed wheels. Clockmakers developed new, simpler, more precise techniques both for dividing the circumference of a circular metal plate into equal units and for cutting the gear teeth with an efficient profile. Clocks also required precision screws, which in turn required the improvement of the metal lathe. (64)

From the vantage point of Western civilization, Boorstin records the history of the discovery of other "worlds": the whole earth, the heavens and the microscopic world. He gives detailed discussions of such persons as Marco Polo, Columbus, Galileo, Newton, and Darwin. Realizing that the story of humankind's search for knowledge is never-ending, Boorstin remarks: "This is a story without end . . . . The most promising words ever written on the maps of human knowledge are *terra incognita* — unknown territory" (xvi).

Like *The Discoverers*, Boorstin's *The Creators*, while not ignoring humanity's technology, puts a heavier emphasis on humanity's artistic (in the larger sense) abilities and accomplishments. For instance, early artistic man saw that stones could be used to create a statue of himself and to erect — no one today knows for what purpose — such marvelous objects as Stonehenge in England.

Boorstin relates in detail the accomplishments of many artists. One such artist is Leonardo da Vinci, best known for his painting, "The Last Supper." Boorstin characterizes him as "scientist-artist-engineer" (400). Boorstin remarks that when Leonardo thought it necessary or expedient, he

> made the time to pursue his interests in anatomy, biology, mathematics, physics, and mechanics . . . . He . . . filled his notebooks with . . . [plans] for fantastic weapons, grand schemes of military architecture and hydraulic engineering. (400)

Perhaps it is because he, himself, is such an extraordinary "wordsmith" that Boorstin writes extensively about the historical use of words. Further, he rings the changes on the importance of the western printing press that has made it possible eventually to democratize literature.

From the earliest of times, words have been blended with the melodies of the human voice and those of man-made instruments. Contributing to such artistic blending have been such humans as Bach, Mozart, and Beethoven.

Just because an individual does not have the abilities of a Leonardo or a Bach does not mean that he is an insignificant person, insists Boorstin. There is sense in which every individual can be a creator-artist. Boorstin expresses it thusly:

> Man finally comes to himself as a rich raw material of creation. Not just the public notables whom Plutarch celebrated among the Greeks and Romans, but the idiosyncratic everyday person. Everyone is a subject, no act or feeling too intimate, too trivial, to be shaped into a biography — or autobiography. Not only the soul, which has engaged saints and priests and prophets, but the self in all its vagrancy. The wilderness within is not only a jungle of hopes and frustrations, but a place of mystery and beauty, of epic memories, bitter struggles and exhilaration, where the whole history of the human race is reenacted. From this vantage point are vistas never seen or revealed before. (553)

For some humans, there will be satisfaction in knowing a little of what is within them or around them or above them. For others, the probe must go deeper. They are *The Seekers*, as Boorstin puts it in the last book of his trilogy. They will carry out the search for their own satisfaction and some will pass the knowledge of their search on to others. In some cases, as with the Old Testament prophets, maybe it is not so much a search as it is their understanding of "Thus saith the Lord." In any case, Boorstin's last book covers such notable persons as Moses and Isaiah of the Old Testament; Socrates, Plato, and Aristotle of the ancient Greek philosophers; Jesus of the New Testament; Augustine (theologian) and Benedict (monastic founder) of the early Christian movement; Abelard and Aquinas of the medieval universities; Luther and Calvin of the Protestant Reformation; and Bacon, Locke, Jefferson, and Marx among those looking for a new way to understand society and the operation of government.

Perhaps it is significant, at least of interest, that the last book of Boorstin's trilogy ends without a formal conclusion. Rather, he tells the story of Einstein, whom he calls the "relentless Seeker" (258). With this in mind perhaps the following words of Einstein, quoted by Boorstin, can serve both as a suitable conclusion of Boorstin's trilogy and our summary presentation of that trilogy:

> The individual feels the futility of human desires and aims and the sublimity and marvelous order which reveal themselves both in nature and in the world of thought. Individual existence impresses him as a sort of prison and he wants to experience the universe as a single significant whole. (258)

Notes

Daniel Boorstin, *The Discoverers* (New York: Random House, 1983).
_____, *The Creators* (New York: Random House, 1992).
_____, *The Seekers* (New York: Random House, 1998).

Notes

[1] Gerald J. Janzen, *Job* in *Interpretation* (Atlanta: John Knox Press, 1985), 187.

[2] Claus Westermann, *Genesis 1–11*, vol. 1 (Minneapolis: Augsburg Press, 1984), 243-45.

[3] Augustine, *The City of* God, ed. Vernon J. Bourke (New York: Image Books, 1958), 526-27.

[4] See Gen 2:15, 3:17-18, 4:20.

[5] The Christian is reminded that the early church had to be scattered by persecution before it carried out Jesus' command to evangelize the earth. See Matt 28:18-20; Acts 1:8, 8:1, 11:9.

[6] Gerhard von Rad, *Genesis* (Philadelphia: The Westminster Press, 1972), 151.

[7] Westermann, 555.

[8] John T. Bunn, "Ezekiel," *The Broadman Bible Commentary*, vol. 6 (Nashville: Broadman Press, 1971), 314.

[9] Ibid.

[10] Ibid., 315.

[11] John Bright, *A History of Israel* (Philadelphia: Westminster Press, 1981), 217.

[12] R. E. Clements, *Wisdom in Theology* (Grand Rapids: Eerdmans, 1992), 126.

[13] It is possible that the Exodus description of the tabernacle blends features of Solomon's temple with those of the more simplistic wilderness tabernacle. In any case, the discussion will be based on the Exodus account as it now stands.

7

Tending God's World

The earth is the LORD's and all
    that is in it,
    the world, and those who live
    in it; . . . (Ps 24:1)

Then God said, "Let us make humankind in our image, according to our likeness, and let them have dominion over the fish of the sea, and over the birds of the air, and over the cattle, and over the wild animals of the earth, and over every creeping thing that creeps upon the earth." (Gen 1:26)

The LORD God took the man and put him in the Garden of Eden to till and keep it. (Gen 2:15)

Introduction

The above paradigm passages present in a summary fashion the unique relationship of God to creation, and particularly the special relationship of humanity to the rest of creation. While the Old Testament's presentation of the proper relationship of human beings to each other is quite extensive, the presentation of the proper relationship of humanity to non-human creation is not neglected. For instance, Habakkuk condemns the violence of one cruel nation toward weaker nations but also condemns that same cruel nation's violence toward forests, fields, and animals:

For the violence done to Lebanon [forests]
    will overwhelm you;
the destruction of the animals
    will terrify you —
because of human bloodshed and
    violence to the earth,
to cities and all who live in
    them. (Hab 2:17)

Dealing with a paucity of information on any given subject can cause a person to see information on that subject when it really isn't there. Among others, Lewis G. Regenstein, in his *Replenish the Earth*, is inclined to do this. For instance, the Mosaic law made provision for the tribe of Levi to be given a number of Palestinian towns in which to live in lieu of a special territory such as given to the other tribes:

In the plains of Moab by the Jordan at Jericho, the LORD spoke to Moses, saying: Command the Israelites to give, from their inheritance that they possess, towns for the Levites to live in; you shall also give to the Levites pasture lands surrounding the towns. The towns shall be for them to live in, and their pasture lands shall be for their cattle, for their livestock, and for all their animals. (Num 35:1-3)

Regenstein, in his discussion of this passage, fails to inform the reader that the land outside the given cities is for the Levites and their cattle. Rather he speaks of the specified land, as in some modern sense, being "a natural area, or greenbelt . . . to be used for the cities' public enjoyment."[1]

God's Care of and Care for Creation

The Old Testament does not always make it clear how humanity should relate to the so-called lower creatures and the inanimate created order. In light of humanity's stewardship, it seems obvious that understanding God's relationship to this creation would be a helpful place to begin, especially at those times and places where no human is present and not likely to be present. It is the Bible's testimony that God looks upon his creation as good (Gen 1:4, 9, 12, etc.) and tends his creation with loving care (Ps 104). What is disquieting, at least to some readers, is that the same God who condemns violence as depicted in the above Habakkuk passage sometimes uses violence, even predation.[2] Certainly a kind of super-romantic ideal concerning how

the various elements of creation should exist or live in harmony needs to be
tempered by such words as the following:

> The voice of the LORD breaks the
>   cedars;
>   the LORD breaks the cedars of
>   Lebanon.
> He makes Lebanon skip like a calf,
>   and Sirion like a young ox. . . .
> the voice of the LORD causes the
>   oaks to whirl,
>   and strips the forest bare;
>   and in his temple all say,
>   "Glory!" (Ps 29:5-6, 9)

> You cause the grass to grow for
>   the cattle,
>   and plants for people to use,
> to bring forth food from the earth,...
> You make darkness, and it is
>   Night,
>   when all the animals of the
>   forest come creeping out.
> The young lions roar for their
>   prey,
>   seeking their food from God.
> When the sun rises, they withdraw
>   and lie down in their dens. (Ps 104:14, 20-22)

Surely, we could have begun our approach in some more pleasant way
than discussing the ripping up of trees by their roots and the killing of
smaller animals by a lion. Yet, if a human can fathom what it means to be a
God of predation as well as a more benign God at other times, then maybe
that person will come to know what it means to properly hew down a tree in
a forest without severely over-cutting that same forest. Maybe that person
will come to know what it means to kill an animal for one's own use without
abusing the animals around him.

James A. Nash, in his *Loving Nature: Ecological Integrity and Christian
Responsibility*, insists that all humans are predators by nature, at least as he
defines predation:

I am using the word *predator* broadly to cover not only biological predation per se, but all forms of human destruction and consumption of other life forms and their habitats — both herbivore and carnivore, both as deliberate and unavoidable acts. Whether in a broad or narrow sense, however, predation is a primary condition of human existence.[3]

Further, Nash insists that it is up to humans to decide whether they become what he calls "profligate predators," on the one hand, or "creative predators" or "altruistic predators," on the other.[4] Nash further states,

We are the only creatures capable of intentionally creating and regulating our own environments — and, in fact, destroying every other creature's environment while recognizing the demonic effects of our actions. We are the only species that can create cultures, whether primary or complex, and a multitude of cultural artifacts, from artistic expressions to computer systems, from religious rituals to architectural structures, from moral designs to political order. *Only humans, according to traditional Christian doctrine, have the potential to serve as the image of God and to exercise dominion in creation.* Despite historical misinterpretations and abuse, these concepts recognize a basic biological fact: humans alone have evolved peculiar rational, moral, and, therefore, creative capacities that enable us alone to serve as responsible representatives of God's interests and values, to function as protectors of the ecosphere and deliberately constrained consumers of the world's goods.[5]

Nash admits that the "dominion" command of Genesis 1:26-28 has sometimes been misinterpreted and abused. However, the command is not to be faulted and discarded because of such misinterpretation and abuse. Rather, we should re-examine the passage, along with other passages such as the "tending" passage of Genesis 2:15, in the light of their history of interpretation, application, and our current scientific knowledge of misuse and abuse. For instance, Nash uses the first part of his book to discuss what he calls our present ecological crises under such headings as "pollution," "global warming," "ozone depletion," "resource exhaustion," and "extinctions of species."[6] One of the best books — perhaps the best — for examining the church's historical response to creation/nature is H. Paul Santmire's *The Travail of Nature: The Ambiguous Ecological Promise of Christian Theology.*[7]

Human Posture Toward Nonhuman Creation

Two important commands concerning humanity's posture toward nonhuman creation are recorded early in the book of Genesis (see the paradigm passages): the command for humans to subdue and have dominion over non-human creation (Gen 1:26-28) and the command to tend/till and keep the earth portion of creation (Gen 2:15). From a simple reading of these passages in an English translation, it is easy to read the first as giving humanity the right or mandate to dominate the rest of creation for the benefit of humanity, while the second passage instructs humankind to work with non-human creation for their mutual benefit.

Since, at least on the surface, the commands seem to present contrasting approaches, which shall be preferred and obeyed? When the "dominion" command is given priority, two opposite opinions often follow. First, there are those who insist that humans have the right arbitrarily to use nature however they please. Therefore, h*umans should not feel guilty or be made to feel guilty about so-called abuses.* On the other hand, there are those who insist that this command is a major cause — maybe *the* major cause — for all our present ecological problems. Of all the recent persons who have made this accusation, one stands out in particular. Lynn White delivered a speech in 1966 titled, "The Historical Roots of our Ecological Crisis." The following is a brief portion of that speech.

> The victory of Christianity over paganism was the greatest psychic revolution in the history of our culture . . . . What did Christianity tell people about their relations with their environment . . . . By gradual stages a loving and all-powerful God had created [everything including human and nonhuman] . . . . Man named all the animals, thus establishing his dominance over them. God planned all of this explicitly for man's benefit and rule: no item in the physical creation had any purpose save to serve man's purposes . . . . Christianity . . . insisted that it is God's will that man exploit nature for his proper ends . . . . But as we now recognize, somewhat over a century ago science and technology — hitherto quite separate activities — joined to give mankind powers which, to judge by many of the ecological effects, are out of control. *If so, Christianity bears a huge burden of guilt. . . .* The greatest spiritual revolutionary in Western history, Saint Francis, proposed what he thought was an alternative Christian view of nature and man's relation to it: he tried to substitute the idea of equality of all creatures, including man, for the idea of man's limitless rule of creation. He failed. Both our present science and our present technology are so tinctured

with orthodox Christian arrogance toward nature that no solution for our ecological crisis can be expected from them.[8]

But are there other avenues of approach concerning the "dominion" command besides using it as the basis for unrestricted power over nature or of attributing all ecological abuse to it? Reliable authors such as Loren Wilkinson insist there are.[9] One suggestion is to give priority to the "tending" command of Genesis 2. Wilkinson points out that the word "till" *avad* can be translated as "serve" and the word "keep" *shamar* as "watch over" or "preserve."[10] Wilkinson summarizes as follows:

> The significant thing about both words is that they describe actions undertaken not primarily for the sake of the doer but for the sake of the object of the action. The kind of tilling which is to be done is a *service* of the earth. The keeping of the garden is not just for human comfort but is a kind of *preservation*. Both verbs severely restrict the way the other two verbs — "subdue" and "rule" — are to be applied. Human ruling, then should be exercised in such a way as to *serve* and *preserve* the beasts, the trees, and the earth itself — all of which is being ruled. It is in such a relationship that we demonstrate the image of God — again, not as something which we are, but by carrying out a pattern of self-giving service demonstrated by the Creator.[11]

However, it is not necessary to give absolute priority to either command. For instance, it is possible to determine which command is going to have priority in a given situation.

This is the position taken by a Christian biologist and a Christian theologian, colleagues at Campbell University at the time, in an address titled "Subduing the Earth While Tending the Garden." One of the issues discussed in the address was that of disease. According to the authors, this is one situation that, for the sake of humans, some organisms must be destroyed. As the authors put it:

> Advances leading to greatly increased infant survival rates and the general increases in longevity for many human populations in the more developed parts of the world are clearly major triumphs. However, an important component of medicine is treatment of diseases, most of which are caused by microbes or invertebrate parasites. This involves killing creatures, including in some cases vectors and reservoir hosts as well as the infectious organism itself.[12]

In 1985 the senior author spent six weeks in a hospital with bacterial encorditis or a bacterial growth on a heart valve. By the valiant efforts of the physician in his use of modern medicine, the senior author survived while the bacterium causing the disease died. In such a situation, what was required was a kind of medical warfare rather than benign tending.

Caring About and Caring for Nature

Land and Plants

We begin with Old Testament materials dealing with caring about and for the land and plants. According to Mosaic law (Lev 25), even as humans and animals must be allowed to experience rest, so shall the land. Such a regulation as the one that follows helped to prevent overuse and the wearing out of the land:

> The LORD spoke to Moses on Mount Sinai, saying: Speak to the people of Israel and say to them: When you enter the land that I am giving you, the land shall observe a sabbath for the LORD. Six years you shall sow your field, and six years you shall prune your vineyard, and gather in the yield; but in the seventh year there shall be a sabbath for the LORD; you shall not sew your field or prune your vineyard. You shall not harvest the after-growth of your harvest or gather the grapes of your pruned vine: it shall be a year of complete rest for the land. (Lev 25:1-5)

Leviticus 25–26 included promises and warnings concerning the keeping of the land sabbath, as well as other regulations. One warning concerned the land being taken over by an enemy and the Israelites being scattered among the nations. In such desolation, the land would enjoy its sabbath by way of Israel's forfeiture of God's blessing:

> Then the land shall enjoy its sabbath years as long as it lies desolate, while you are in the land of your enemies; then the land shall rest, and enjoy its sabbath years. As long as it lies desolate, it shall have the rest it did not have on your sabbaths when you were living on it. (Lev 26:34-35)

Israel was admonished to feel about the land the same way that God did. As the Israelites were about to leave the desolate Sinai Peninsula, Moses painted for them a word picture of the land of Canaan they were about to enter. It was a land God loved and looked after just as he expected them to do:

But the land that you are crossing over to occupy is a land of hills and valleys, watered by rain from the sky, a land that the LORD your God looks
after. The eyes of the LORD your God are always on it, from the beginning
of the year to the end of the year. (Deut 11:11-12)

The Israelites were also admonished to care for the plants and trees that
grew on the land. For instance, the same Levitical Code that commanded a
sabbath for the land urged that fruit trees be given time to mature:

When you come into the land and plant all kinds of trees for food, then
you shall regard their fruit as forbidden; three years it shall be forbidden to
you, it must not be eaten. In the fourth year all their fruit shall be set apart
for the rejoicing in the LORD. But in the fifth year you may eat of their
fruit, that their yield may be increased for you; I am the LORD your God.
(Lev 19:23-25)

Further, during a time of war, fruit trees were to be spared while other trees
could be hewn down:

If you besiege a town for a long time, making war against it in order to take
it, you must not destroy its trees by wielding an ax against them. Although
you may take food from them, you must not cut them down. Are trees in
the field human beings that they should come under siege from you? You
may destroy only the trees that you know do not produce food; you may
cut them down for use in building siegeworks against the town that makes
war with you, until it falls. (Deut 20:19-20)

The book of Genesis contains a good deal of material about the actual
practice of agriculture, especially shepherding. After Genesis, the information continues but in more scattered form. While land and plants/trees are
mentioned, passages often contain little evaluation of humanity's stewardship. When evaluation is given, it is more-than-likely of a negative kind. For
instance, Isaiah contains a mocking statement against the king of Babylonia
who, like other kings, had abused the forest:

The cypresses exult over you,
        the cedars of Lebanon, saying,
"Since you were laid low,
        no one has come to cut us down." (Isa 14:8)

Surely there were those who loved the land and the plants/trees that grew on it and who practiced good stewardship. It is simply difficult to document this. There is the account of Jonah who became angry with God for destroying a bush that had provided Jonah with shade. However, Jonah was probably more sorry about the loss of the shade than the death of the bush (Jonah 4:6ff).

Animals

Besides land and plants, the Old Testament deals with caring for animals and birds. The ancient Israelites were expected to provide sustenance and rest for their animals as is expressed in the following passages:

> The righteous know the needs of
> their animals,
> but the mercy of the wicked is
> cruel. (Prov 12:10)

> You shall not muzzle an ox while it is treading out the grain. (Deut 25:4)

> Remember the sabbath day, and keep it holy. Six days you shall labor and do all your work. But the seventh day is a sabbath to the LORD your God; you shall not do any work — you, your son or your daughter, your male or female slave, your livestock, or the alien residents in your towns. (Exod 20:8-10)

Further, they were admonished not wantonly to destroy wild species:

> If you come on a bird's nest, in any tree or on the ground, with fledglings or eggs, with the mother sitting on the fledglings or on the eggs, you shall not take the mother with the young. Let the mother go, taking only the young for yourself. (Deut 22:6-7)

There have always been those who were either cruel or kind to animals. Examples are found in the stories of the patriarchs of Genesis. For instance, two of Jacob's sons, Simeon and Levi, were noted for their cruelty to animals as well as to humans. As Jacob lay on his deathbed, he spoke harshly about these two sons as follows:

> Simeon and Levi are brothers;
> > weapons of violence are their
> > swords.
> May I never come into their
> > council;
> > may I not be joined to their
> > company —
> for in their anger they killed men.
> > and at their whim they
> > hamstrung oxen. (Gen 49:5-6)

The opposite of the cruelty of Simeon and Levi is expressed in the kindness of the servant of Abraham delegated to find a proper bride for Isaac. The servant determined in advance that an important and necessary quality of the young lady would be kindness to animals. Rebekah demonstrated this kindness, to the satisfaction of Abraham's servant, by watering the camels of the servant. (Gen 24:10-21)

The Mosaic law that provided for animal sacrifices within Israelite worship also provided for some measure of humaneness within the rules of sacrifice. For instance, according to the book of Leviticus, newborn animals were to remain with their mothers for seven days after birth and were not to be slaughtered on the same day as the mother (Lev 22:26-28). The great medieval Jewish scholar, Maimonides, commented on this Levitical passage as follows:

> It is prohibited to kill an animal with its young on the same day, in order that people should be restrained and prevented from killing the two together in such a manner that the young is slain in the sight of the mother; for the pain of animals under such circumstances is very great. There is no difference in this case between the pain of man and the pain of other living beings.[13]

Sacrificing Animals

The above discussion on sacrifices needs to be addressed more fully. Just what is the Old Testament's testimony concerning its legitimacy? Without question, the book of Leviticus not only sanctions such sacrifice but goes into great details about its procedures (Lev 1:1ff).

On the other hand, the prophets not only seem to condemn such sacrifices for their day but some of them also seem to maintain that such sacrifices were wrong from the beginning. Representative of the prophetic position is the following declaration of Isaiah:

> What to me is the multitude of
>   your sacrifices?
>   says the LORD;
> I have had enough of burnt
>   offerings of rams; . . .
> I do not delight in the blood
>   of bulls,
>   or of lambs, or of goats . . .
> bringing offerings is futile;
>   incense is an abomination to
>   me.
> New moon and sabbath and
>   calling of convocation —
> I cannot endure solemn assemblies with iniquity . . .
> When you stretch out your hands,
>   I will hide my eyes from you;
> even though you make many
>   prayers,
>   I will not listen; . . .
> cease to do evil,
>   learn to do good;
> seek justice,
>   rescue the oppressed,
> defend the orphan,
>   plead for the widow. (Isa 1:11-17)

Did Isaiah and other prophets condemn animal sacrifices as wrong in all circumstances or only under certain ones? Many scholars hold to the latter opinion. They believe that the disapproval was based on the sacrifice being carried out for the wrong reason, such as a substitute for justice, or with the wrong inward attitude. For example, Roland de Vaux notes that if the Isaiah passage (along with such others as Jer 7:21-22; Amos 5:21-24; Mic 6:6-8, Hos 6:6) condemns all animal sacrifices, then it must condemn all pilgrimages and feasts, even all prayer. Concerning the latter, de Vaux remarks:

> Now since no one holds that the Prophets condemned prayer, the whole argument leads to an absurd conclusion and simply falls to pieces. These

biblical texts, therefore, cannot mean that the Prophets uttered condemna-
tions of sacrifice itself.[14]

Disagreeing with de Vaux are such interpreters as Lewis Regenstein who
insist animal sacrifices, such as those in Leviticus, were allowed by God as a
substitute for human sacrifice until God could reveal his higher will in the
prophets.[15] In fact, according to Regenstein, God finally revealed to his people that God "equates the killing of an animal with the murder of a
human."[16] He bases his position on Isaiah 66:3.

> Whoever slaughters an ox is like
>   one who kills a human being;
>   whoever sacrifices a lamb, like
>   one who breaks a dog's
>   neck;
> whoever presents a grain offering,
>   like one who offers swine's
>   blood;
> Whoever makes a memorial
>   offering of frankincense,
>   like one who blesses an
>   idol. (Isa 66:3)

The reader needs to take seriously the claim of Regenstein that God equates
the killing of an animal with the murder of a human. Further, the reader
needs to take seriously the prophet's declaration that Regenstein uses as proof
of his claim. Does the prophet really mean that "whoever slaughters an ox is
like one who kills a human being" as rendered in the New Revised Standard
Version? Many fine interpreters believe that a simple "yes" cannot be given to
that question. In fact, they would insist that a close study of the original
Hebrew text would show that such is not the prophet's meaning at all.
Typical of this latter position is the one of James Muilenburg. Since the
Hebrew text contains no word that can be translated "like," Muilenburg
translates the passage as follows:

> Who slaugthers an ox, who kills a man,
> Who sacrifices a lamb, who breaks a dog's neck.
> Who presents a cereal offering, who offers swine's blood,
> Who makes a memorial offering, who blesses an idol.[17]

A possible interpretation emerges from Muilenburg's translation: The same person who lawfully slaughters an ox for sacrificial purposes also unlawfully kills a human being for the same purpose. Muilenburg expresses his position as follows:

> They who offer the regular [approved] sacrifices of the first series also offer the unlawful sacrifice of the second. What is condemned is not sacrifice root and branch, but a sacrificial practice which has been debased by syncretism with corrupt pagan practices.[18]

Whatever the reader may think of Muilenburg's interpretation, his translation seems to be preferable to the translation provided in the New Revised Standard Version. To base such a radical position as that of Regenstein on a questionable text does not seem to be justified.

Living a Responsible Environmental Lifestyle

The authors hope that each reader is living (or can be encouraged to live) a responsible environmental lifestyle. At least three ingredients are required: a sound ideological base, informative scientifically-acceptable technological information, and the willingness to act responsibly.

While the authors believe that the Christian scriptures, properly interpreted, provide a solid base for exercising a responsible ecological life, they do not contend that a helpful ideology cannot be found elsewhere. Strange as it may seem, even some atheists function responsibly in this world without a belief in a creator god. Again, it is the contention of a group of ecologically-concerned individuals that the best ideological base is to be found in the blend of various worldwide systems of religion or philosophy. Two persons who espouse this view are Mary Evelyn Tucker and John Grim, who have published a collection of such views in *Worldviews and Ecology: Religion, Philosophy, and the Environment*. It is the position of Tucker and Grim that every group needs the wisdom of many other groups since there are fundamental flaws in the religious/philosophical systems of each group. Note the following quote from their preface:

> The premise of this book is . . . that no one religious tradition or philosophical perspective has the ideal solution to the environmental crisis. Our approach emphasizes plurality because...cosmological thinking is necessary. Furthermore, it is clear that theories and practices vary greatly when they are studied in historical context. In other words, Taoist wisdom regarding nature was not able to prevent deforestation of many parts of China, nor was Buddhist sensitivity to the interconnection of all reality able to prevent destruction of natural resources in Southeast Asia. The disjuncture between ideals and reality will temper our expectations; at the same time it will prod us toward more functional solutions. (11-12)

Since most of the readers of this text will have a Christian orientation, the authors recommend the readers consult Loren Wilkinson, editor, *Earthkeeping in the Nineties: Stewardship of Creation*, which weaves together sound scripture interpretation and the latest ecological data. One of the strengths of this work is the collaboration by a group of specialists in religion, philosophy, and the various sciences that were brought together by the Calvin Center for Christian Scholarship of Calvin College. The book first deals with the present state of our planet. The authors remark: "Threats to natural habitats occur on every continent, especially those areas of heavy rain forests where an incredible diversity of nature is manifest" (45). The second section is concerned with earthkeepers. The text provides a historical presentation of humankind's relationship to non-human creation from early times to the present. Concerning the present, the authors set forth the various attitudes that human beings have toward the rest of creation. The third section deals with God's ownership of creation and humanity's stewardship. The final section presents practical matters, including a presentation of twenty guidelines for the practice of Christian environmental stewardship. The following seven statements are a summary of those guidelines for Christian environmental stewardship:

1. Bases its attitudes and practices on awe of God's creation and a sense of humility as an integral part of that creation.
2. Makes the best use of land and natural resources.
3. Looks to the needs and feelings of animals, both wild and tame.
4. Carefully examines the varied processes (agricultural, mining, transportation, et cetera) necessary for the basic needs of humans and other creation.
5. Encourages changes of lifestyles of individuals.
6. Works for useful changes in social and economic structures.
7. Looks to the future as well as the present. (351ff.)

Notes

Mary Evelyn Tucker and John A. Grim, eds., *Worldviews and Ecology: Religion, Philosophy, and the Environment* (New York: Orbis Press, 1994).

Loren Wilkinson, ed., *Earthkeeping in the Nineties: Stewardship of Creation* (Grand Rapids: Eerdmans, 1991).

Notes

[1] Lewis G. Regenstein, *Replenish the Earth: A History of Organized Religion's Treatment of Animals and Nature* (New York: Eerdmans Publishing Company, 1991), 20.

[2] Predation can be defined as "The act or practice of plundering or marauding." William Morris, ed., *The American Heritage Dictionary* (Boston: Houghton Mifflin Company, 1976), 1031.

[3] James A. Nash, *Loving Nature: Ecological Integrity and Christian Responsibility* (Nashville: Abingdon Press, 1991), 146.

[4] Ibid., 149.

[5] Ibid., 149. Italics added.

[6] Ibid., 23ff.

[7] H. Paul Santmire, *The Travail of Nature: The Ambiguous Ecological Promise of Christian Theology* (Minneapolis: Fortress Press, 1985).

[8] Lynn White, "The Historical Roots of our Ecological Crisis," *Science* (vol. 155, March 1967), 1205-06. Italics added.

[9] Loren Wilkinson, ed., *Earthkeeping in the Nineties: Stewardship of Creation* (Grand Rapids: Eerdmans, 1991).

[10] Ibid., 287.

[11] Ibid.

[12] Raymond E. Grizzle and Michael Cogdill, "Subduing the Earth While Tending the Garden: A Proposal for a More Balanced Environmental Ethic," *Faculty Dialogue* (Winter, 1993–1994), 78.

[13] Quote as cited in Regenstein, 195-96.

[14] Roland de Vaux, *Ancient Israel*, vol. 2 (New York: McGraw Hill, 1968), 454.

[15] Regenstein, 45ff.

[16] Ibid., 45.

[17] James Muilenburg, "The Book of Isaiah: Chapters 40–66," in *The Interpreter's Bible*, vol. 5 (Nashville: Abingdon Press, 1956), 761.

[18] Ibid., 762.

8

Living in Community
Before God — Part I

Now Jericho was shut up inside and out because of the Israelites; no one came out and no one went in. The LORD said to Joshua, "See, I have handed Jericho over to you, along with its king and soldiers . . . . " On the seventh day they rose early, at dawn, and marched around the city in the same manner seven times . . . . When the priests had blown the trumpets, Joshua said to the people, "Shout! For the LORD has given you the city. The city and all that is in it shall be devoted to the LORD for destruction . . . . As for you, keep away from the things devoted to destruction, so as not to covet and take away any of the devoted things and make the camp of Israel an object for destruction . . . . " But the Israelites broke faith in regard to the devoted things: Achan son of Carmi son of Zabdi son of Zerah, of the tribe of Judah, took some of the devoted things; and the anger of the LORD burned against the Israelites . . . . So Joshua rose early in the morning, and brought Israel near tribe by tribe, and the tribe of Judah was taken. He brought near the clans of Judah, and the clan of the Zerahites was taken; and he brought near the clan of the Zerahites, family by family, and Zabdi was taken. And he brought near his household one by one, and Achan the son of Carmi son of Zabdi son of Zerah of the tribe of Judah, was taken. Then Joshua said to Achan, "My son, give glory to the LORD God of Israel and make confession to him. Tell me now what you have done; do not hide it from me." And Achan answered Joshua, "It is true; I am the one who sinned against the LORD, God of Israel. This is what I did: when I saw among the spoil a beautiful mantle from Shinar, and two hundred shekels of silver, and a bar of gold weighing fifty shekels, then I coveted them and took them. They are now hidden in the ground inside my tent, with the silver underneath." So Joshua sent messengers, and they ran to the tent; and there it was hidden in his tent with the silver underneath. They took them out of the tent and brought them to Joshua and all the Israelites; and they spread them out before the LORD. Then Joshua and all Israel with him took Achan son of Zerah, with the silver, the mantle, and the bar of gold, with his sons and daughters, with his oxen, donkeys, and sheep, and his tent and all that he had; and they brought them to the valley of Achor . . . . And all Israel stoned him to death; they burned them with fire, cast stones on them, and raised over him a great heap of stones that remains to this day. (Josh 6:1-2, 15-18; 7:1, 16-26)

Introduction

If as we have seen in the previous chapter, humans have a relationship with non-human creation, we have yet to consider more important relationships, namely human to God and human to human. One exception may be noted. Concerning human to human, in chapter 5 under the subject "humanity" we did consider the relationship between male and female. In this chapter we shall begin with a brief emphasis on the importance of human community. That will be followed with a discussion on community within an orderly universe and on sources of knowledge for God-approved community. In the remainder of this chapter, along with the chapter nine, we will consider various aspects of community, including necessary provisions for such community: community institutions, community leaders, community laws and regulations, and community worship. The intrusion of sin into community shall be reserved for its own special chapter.

Importance of Community

While it is not to be denied that there can be a one-on-one relationship between a human and God and between one human and another, the emphasis in this chapter and the following one is on community.

Paul D. Hanson, in his voluminous study titled *The People Called: The Growth of Community in the Bible*, quotes with appreciation the following lines from a T. S. Eliot poem:

What life have you if you have not life together?
There is no life that is not in community,
And no community not lived in praise to God.[1]

Hanson goes on to say that Eliot has "pointed to a truth verified both by social scientists and by our own practical experience: we receive life, we foster life, and we pass life on within the context of fellow humans."[2]

Community Within an Orderly Universe

Humanity, individually and corporately, needs a place to stand (sit, lie down, sleep, work, play, worship, etc.). The place needs to be well-organized, dependable, and reasonably friendly. To put it another way, it needs to be the kind of place that God called "good" in Genesis 1. As set forth in Genesis 1, along with other passages such as Psalm 104 and Job 38ff, it also needs to be a place we share with nonhuman creation. Note a portion of Psalm 104:

> Bless the LORD, O my soul . . .
> You set the earth on its
>   foundations,
> so that it shall never be shaken . . .
> You make springs gush forth in
>   the valleys;
> they flow between the hills,
> giving drink to every wild animal;
> the wild asses quench their
>   thirst.
> By the streams the birds of the
>   air have their habitation;
> they sing among the branches. . .
> You cause the grass to grow for
>   the cattle,
> and plants for people to use . . .
> and wine to gladden the human
>   heart,
> oil to make the face shine. (Ps 104:1, 5, 10-12, 14-15)

Sources of Knowledge for Formation
and Maintenance of Community

As a part of creation, humans not only need a place to stand, they also need their own methods of living with each other in wholesome, helpful, nondestructive ways. The Israelites gained this knowledge by their observation of the universe, by their God-given ability to think God's thoughts (see ch. 5), and by special knowledge God granted them at Sinai and other places.

Concerning the importance of the relationship of observance of the universe to a well-ordered life, individually and in community, the following words of Proverbs are instructive:

> The LORD by wisdom founded the
>   earth;
> by understanding he established
>   the heavens;
> by his knowledge the deeps broke
>   open,
> and the clouds drop down the
>   dew.
> My child, do not let these escape
>   from your sight:
> keep sound wisdom and
>   prudence,
> and they will be life for your soul
> and adornment for your neck. (Prov 3:19-22)

Over a period of time, Israel's sages or teachers gathered together and passed on the accumulated observations of Israel concerning the orderly universe and its relationship to an orderly community. Joseph Blenkinsopp remarks that one of the basic goals of Israelite sages, along with the sages of her neighbors, was:

> to bring human conduct into line with a cosmic law of regularity and order observable in the sequence of seasons, the movements of the heavenly bodies and the like. To be wise is, in a word, to live in conformity with the law of nature.[3]

Again, not only did humans learn by their God-given ability to observe the universe around them, they learned by experiencing their God-given ability to think God's thoughts, even if in some limited sense.[4] In her Wisdom literature (primarily Proverbs, Job, and Ecclesiastes), Israel has left a deposit of that understanding from her observation and intellect, an understanding she often shared with her neighbors who learned the basic art of living in the same way she did.

Beyond knowledge of humanity through observation of the universe and the development of inherent intellect, Israel testified she had been given an extra dimension of understanding the true nature of humanity by being chosen by Yahweh in some special sense.[5] She believed this extra measure of understanding came through God's special living presence with her and God's special rules for living in community given at Sinai and other places. This special relationship between God and Israel is set forth in the Pentateuch and other non-Wisdom literature.

It does not follow that ancient Israelites always had a direct word from God concerning every aspect of community. But they did have a special sense of God's presence in their community life. As Brevard Childs puts it:

> The biblical writers struggled to see the hand of God at work in their lives, and bore witness to its presence in all the concrete aspects of social life.[6]

The important thing in our day is not that we copy exactly every detail of Israelite social structure but that we see God at work in our own.

Community Institutions

One of the things Israel learned by way of observation, by way of God-given intellect, and by her special relationship to God was the value of institutions. These institutions might be social institutions such as family/household, clan, tribe, or tribal leagues (later becoming kingdoms) or they might be special institutions such as the military, cultic, etc.

A good example of the ever-widening social institutions from the family/household is contained in a story told in the book of Joshua, as seen in the paradigm passage for this chapter. Joshua, in a judicial process, moved in reverse order from tribe, through clan, to family, to individual to determine the guilty person responsible for taking forbidden spoils of war (things devoted to God) at the battle of Jericho, thus causing a loss in the following battle at Ai. The story in Joshua reads as follows:

> So Joshua arose early in the morning, and brought Israel near tribe [*shebat*] by tribe, and the tribe of Judah was taken. He brought near the clans [*mishpahah*] of Judah, and the clan of Zerahites was taken; and he brought near the clan of the Zerahites, family [*beth av*] by family, and Zabdi was taken. And he brought near his household one by one, and Achan son of

Carmi son of Zabdi son of Zerah, of the tribe of Judah, was taken. (Josh 7:16-18)

Household

The most basic institution was the family/household. What is meant by the word "household" (*beth av, bayat*) in the Old Testament differs from place to place and in the various time periods. As a general statement, the following words of Douglas A. Knight can suffice:

> Three types of family structure existed throughout Israel's history . . . . The smallest was the *nuclear family*, comprised of the parents, their children . . . . Larger was the *extended family* [including relatives such as grandparents] . . . . Beyond this was the *multiple-family household* . . . [such as] two or more married couples. [7]

One of the functions of the Israelite household was to provide for such economic needs as food, clothing, and housing. A careful reading of the story of the patriarchs in Genesis shows how all members of a household shared in its duties. For instance, Jacob's sons, including the youthful Joseph, shared in the shepherding duties. Also of interest are the culinary abilities of Esau and Jacob as well as their mother. Note words of Carol Myers concerning such households:

> [I]t is almost beside the point to quibble over whether males or females made the pots, pruned the trees, or baked the bread. The essential point is that in a household responsible for producing and processing nearly everything it needed for survival, the range of tasks was maximal and could not have been accomplished without the active involvement of all household members.[8]

Whereas the patriarchs, as roving shepherds, shared the grazing land of Palestine with other inhabitants of the land, provision was made in the Mosaic law for the distribution of Palestinian land for individual Israelite households/families during and following the days of Joshua. Each was to have its own inheritance (*nahala*) enabling each household to be economically sufficient. At least in principle, there was supposed to be a kind of financial equality among the various households. Further, provision was made to keep the household land together from one generation to the next.

If certain factors interfered, such as the death of the male heirs (through which land usually passed from one generation to another), the Mosaic law made provisions to pass the land on through a daughter (Num 27). The strong desire to keep the land within the specific household, even after the institution of kingship succeeded the twelve-tribe league, is seen in such cases as Naboth's refusal to sell his family property to King Ahab (1 Kgs 21).

Besides providing for the economic needs of individuals, family units also provided for the bonding of husband to wife and parent to child. Incentives and encouragement were given in such Mosaic provisions as the forbidding of adultery and the honoring of parents.

While ancient Israelite parents could no more be held responsible for all the evils of their children than can modern parents, they were expected to provide the proper setting for learning. We will have more to say about that below when discussing parental leadership.

Social Units Larger than the Household

In the period prior to the kingdom there were clans (composed of households) and tribes (composed of clans). According to Wright, the role of the clan might be described as protective and restorative. Among the leaders of a clan in its protective-restorative role was an individual who might be designated as a *goel*, "kinsman-redeemer." The "kinsman-redeemer" might be a member of a particular household as well as a clan person outside that household. Wright discusses four possible responsibilities of such a "kinsman-redeemer." First, he could serve as the avenger-executioner in the case of murder (Num 35:19). Second, he might marry a widow (of his brother or some other person) to raise-up a son for the deceased man who had no male heir. For instance, Boaz married Ruth for this purpose as told in the book of Ruth. Third, he might purchase land lost, or in danger of being lost, to a poor man of his clan (Lev 25:25). Finally he was supposed to aid the poor kinsman in any way possible, as well as purchasing the poor man's land. Such aid might even take the form of paying the ransom price for a person who found himself in slavery (Lev 25:35ff.).[9]

Above the households and the clans stood the tribes, often described as twelve in number.[10] Obviously, each tribe had some sort of organization, though the Old Testament is not always clear as to what that organization was. The most notable tribal leader was often called a judge (*shophet*). In the book of Judges, the judges are often broken down into what some would call major judges and minor judges. The so-called major judges, such as Ehud,

Deborah, Gideon, and Jephthah, served as military heroes who aided Israel
(or some part of Israel) in a time of distress (Judg 3, 4–5, 6–8, 11–12). The
so-called minor judges, such as Tola, Jair, and Elon, provided judicial
leadership in important cases, but are not described as military leaders in the
text (Judg 10, 12). Leaders such as Deborah seem to have exercised both
functions (Judg 4–5).

To what extent and how the various tribes cooperated in pre-kingdom
days is uncertain. There is at least some truth in scholarly argument that the
tribes were fashioned into some type of tribal league, bound together by a
covenant with their god, Yahweh. In such a case, they thought of Yahweh as
their king.

The time came when some Israelites looked with favor on the idea of an
earthly king like their neighbors. They approached Samuel, the last of the
judges, and expressed themselves as follows: "You are old and your sons do
not follow in your ways; appoint for us, then, a king to govern us, like other
nations" (1 Sam 8:5). Concerning what a kingdom of other nations might be
like, Keith Whitelam remarks:

> Monarchy is the most common form of government in agrarian societies
> throughout history. The development of the state with the king as the cen-
> tral symbolic figure represents a major stage in the evolution of political
> systems. The king was responsible for the maintenance of law and order
> within a defined territory through the use of a professional and permanent
> military force and a dedicated central bureaucracy. There is considerable
> evidence for Israel to suggest that the bureaucracy was modeled upon
> Egyptian patterns . . . . Such states were politically centralized societies
> based on social stratification and specialization and dependent upon the
> extraction of an agricultural surplus from the peasantry in order to provide
> for the subsistence needs of the royal elite and its religious and political
> specialists. The king had the power to command the payment of various
> forms of taxation, the rendering of services, and the obeying of law. The
> central bureaucracy provided a means whereby the king was able to control
> the various levels of government responsible for the military, economic,
> legal, and ritual activities of a network of urban centers and villages within
> the territorial boundaries of the state.[11]

Whitelam's words concerning the king's controlling power are echoed in
the following words of Samuel concerning what the Israelites might expect
from this new form of government ruled by a king:

These will be the ways of the king who will reign over you: he will take your sons and appoint them to his chariots and to be horsemen, and to run before his chariots; and he will appoint for himself commanders of thousands and commanders of fifties, and some to plow his ground and reap his harvest, and to make his implements of war and the equipment of his chariots. He will take your daughters to be perfumers and cooks and bakers. He will take the best of your fields and vineyards and olive orchards and give them to his courtiers. He will take one tenth of your grain and of your vineyards and give it to his officers and courtiers. He will take your male and female slaves, and the best of your cattle and donkeys, and put them to his work. He will take one tenth of your flocks, and you shall be his slave. (1 Sam 8:11-17)

While Samuel's prediction of harshness — at least for certain segments of society — came true, especially beginning with Solomon and continuing with many of the kings who followed him, the reality of kingship was not a total failure. Note the following assessment of Bright:

Solomon's projects, though state monopolies, must have given employment to thousands and stimulated others to private enterprise, thus raising the purchasing power of the entire nation and inducing a general prosperity. That many individuals grew rich either in Solomon's service or through personal efforts can hardly be doubted.[12]

Further, the following words of a psalmist express satisfaction in the institution of kingship:

I was glad when they said to me,
"Let us go to the house of the
      LORD!"
Our feet are standing
within your gates, O Jerusalem . . .
To it the tribes go up . . .
For there the thrones for judgment
      were set up,
the thrones of the house of
David. (Ps 122:1-2, 4-5)

Community Leaders

Within each family or larger social unit there were individuals who led or governed by principles and by rules/regulations they developed themselves, received from former generations, or received from God. It should be noted that in many ways Israelite leaders served the same functions as similar Gentile leaders. A major difference, of course, was Israel's commitment to Yahweh. Instructive are the words of Joshua to those Israelites who followed him into Palestine after the death of Moses:

> Now therefore revere the LORD [Yahweh], and serve him in sincerity and in faithfulness; put away the gods that your ancestors served beyond the River [Euphrates] and in Egypt, and serve the LORD. Now if you are unwilling to serve the LORD, choose this day whom you will serve, whether the gods your ancestors served in the region beyond the River or the gods of the Amorites in whose land you are living; but as for me and my household, we will serve the LORD. (Josh 24:14-15)

A question arises at this point concerning an adequate way of organizing this material. We shall begin by looking at Abraham as a model leader. We shall examine his relationship to members of his household/family, to the larger community, and to God. After that, since the institution of household existed in all times and places, we shall look at parental leadership. Following that, we shall examine the idea of Israelite leadership within a community especially chosen by God. Under this last heading we begin with the original founder of this group, namely Abraham. We follow that with an examination of Moses, Israel's unique architect, organizer, and overseer. Finally, we look at the roles of other Israelite leaders such as the military hero, king, prophet, priest, and sage.

Abraham: A Model Leader

Genesis makes clear that Abraham, as did other Near Eastern males, submitted to the leadership of his father during his father's lifetime. We are told that Terah, Abraham's father, along with Abraham and others, set out from the "Ur of the Chaldeans to go to the land of Canaan" (Gen 11:31). For whatever reason, rather than continuing on into Palestine, Terah settled down at Haran in upper Mesopotamia and remained there until his death. At that point, Abraham, along with his wife, Sarah, his nephew, Lot, and many servants made their way into Palestine, with Abraham assuming the role of family leader.

When Abraham began his journey to Palestine, he took under his wing his nephew, Lot (along with Lot's family, servants, and flocks), as Terah before him had done, because Haran, Lot's father, had died early in life. Abraham bestowed on Lot respect, honor, and protection. For instance, on one occasion, when Abraham's herds and herdsman and Lot's herds and herdsman were contending for the same grazing land, Abraham gave Lot first choice as to where their respective herds would graze. On another occasion, when Lot was captured by his enemies, Abraham sent his servants to rescue him (Gen 11–13).

Abraham's relation to his wives and other women ranged all the way from respect to misuse/abuse and manipulation. Early in his stay in Palestine he was forced to go into Egypt in search of grazing land. As they approached the borders of Egypt, he praised his wife for her beauty while at the same time putting her life into jeopardy by having her pretend that she was his sister rather than his wife. Later, back in Palestine, Sarah manipulated Abraham to sire a child by Hagar, Sarah's Egyptian slave girl. Several years later, out of jealousy over Hagar and Hagar's son, Ishmael, Sarah forced Abraham to cast out Hagar and Ishmael. The author of Genesis states: "The matter was very distressing to Abraham on account of his son [Ishmael], but he did Sarah's bidding anyway" (Gen 12, 16, 21).

Besides Ishmael (born to Hagar) and Isaac (born to Sarah), Abraham had other sons born to Keturah, his wife following Sarah's death. He probably loved all his sons, but he showed preference for Isaac. For instance, Abraham's chief overseer was given strict instructions concerning a bride for Isaac. In no case was Isaac to be allowed to marry a Canaanite girl (Gen 16, 21, 24, 25).

As Abraham, along with his family and servants, settled in Palestine, they became involved with other outsiders who had migrated at the same time and also with those native to the area. Three areas of cooperation are highlighted in Genesis.

When an alliance of four eastern kings captured portions of the territory adjacent to the Dead Sea, Abraham used his many servants to help bring relief to those living in the area (Gen 14). Following the victory, Abraham cooperated with the priest-king of Salem in the receiving of a blessing from the priest and the gift of a tithe to him (Gen 14). Finally there came a time when Abraham, who owned no property, had to secure a burial plot for his deceased wife, Sarah. Genesis 23 is an interesting account of the dickering that went on between Abraham and the owner of the property. The chapter closes as follows:

> So the field of Ephron in Machpelah, which was to the east of Mamre, the field with the cave that was in it and all the trees that were in the field, throughout its whole area, passed to Abraham as a possession in the presence of the Hittites, in the presence of all who went in at the gate of his city. After this, Abraham buried Sarah his wife in the cave of the field of Machpelah facing Mamre (that is Hebron) in the land of Canaan. The field and the cave that is in it passed from the Hittites into Abraham's possession as a burying place. (Gen 23:17-20)

All that Abraham did in the company of his family and the larger community, he did under the guidance and watchful gaze of God. He obeyed God's call to migrate to a new land where he would receive a blessing, a blessing to be shared with his Gentile neighbors. With the passing of time, when no offspring had been given to guarantee the blessing to his neighbors, he protested that God had not kept his promise. Further, he protested that God was too hard on his Sodomite neighbors. During the passing of the years, the bond between God and Abraham grew stronger and stronger until that day when God commanded Abraham to sacrifice his son, Isaac. Surely God was asking Abraham too much to ask him to destroy the very link of Israel's blessing to the Gentiles. With a leap of faith, Abraham obeyed. After all, it was God's plan (Gen 12).

Parental Leaders

The importance of parental leadership was emphasized in both Mosaic legislation and in the accumulated wisdom of the sages. Parents who give heed to careful teaching and children who heed such teaching not only bring forth mutual benefits to their families but give stability to the entire community. As the Mosaic Decalogue declares, there shall be long days in the land when sons and daughters (at whatever age) obey their parents (Exod 20:12).

In the book of Proverbs, the model of exemplary parental leadership passed on from one generation to the next is highlighted:

> When I was a son with my father,
> tender, and my mother's
>   favorite,

he taught me, and said to me,
"Let your heart hold fast my
      words;
keep my commandments,
      and live.
Get wisdom; get insight: do not
      forget, nor turn away
from the words of my mouth. (Prov 4:3-5)

The sages also insisted that the way parents lived their lives before their children was as important as how they taught them verbally. For instance, children were certainly influenced by the attitudes of the mother who was contentious toward her husband (Prov 21:19) or the mother who, according to one proverb, "does him [her husband] good, and not harm all the days of her life" (Prov 31:12).

Again, children were certainly influenced by the conjugal faithfulness of the husband to his wife. It was understood that a healthy infatuation with one's wife would bring a lifetime of marital bliss and provide for that kind of stable family in which children are born, grow, and mature. The following advice is given in Proverbs 5:

Drink water from your own
      cistern,
flowing water from your own
      well . . . .
Let your fountain be blessed,
and rejoice in the wife of your
      youth,
a lovely deer, a graceful doe . . .
may you be intoxicated always
by her love. (Prov 5:15, 18-19)

Finally, one more observation needs to be made. Parental teaching was expected to consist not only of family morals and history, but also the morals and history of the larger social unit called Israel. For example, note the following admonition of Moses:

When your children ask you in time to come, "What is the meaning of the decrees and the statutes and the ordinances that the LORD our God has commanded you?" then you shall say to your children, "We were Pharaoh's slaves in Egypt, but the LORD brought us out of Egypt with a mighty hand. The LORD displayed before our eyes great and awesome signs and wonders against Egypt, against Pharaoh and all his household. He brought us out from there in order to bring us in, to give us the land that he promised on oath to our ancestors." (Deut 6:20-23)

Israelite Leaders

In the course of time, God called out a people whom God hoped to develop into the kind of people God had intended when he first created humanity. God would bless this people with land, many offspring, and an understanding of the proper relationship with God's good earth, God's creatures, fellow humans, and with God. The people would be known as Israel and would settle in Palestine.

Abraham — Founder. It is the testimony of Genesis that the founder of this people was a man known as Abram/Abraham, whom we have examined in some detail above. There are hints that some of the people may have thought of Jacob/Israel as their founder since the people eventually bore his name and since they organized themselves into twelve tribes that bore the names of the sons of Jacob/Israel. However, the dominant testimony is that Abraham is the founder and original leader. Note the following passage from Genesis:

> Now the LORD said to Abram, "Go from your country and your kindred and your father's house to the land that I will show you. I will make of you a great nation, and I will bless you, and make your name great, so that you will be a blessing. I will bless those who bless you, and the one who curses you I will curse; and in you all the families of the earth shall be blessed."
> (Gen 12:1-3)

Moses — Unique Architect, Organizer, Overseer. No one descriptive word — not even the three used above — can fully describe Moses' role in Israel. Brevard Childs has expressed the situation this way:

> The most important point to make is that Moses was assigned a unique role within Israel, but one which at the same time encompassed such a rich diversity as to include practically every other office within Israel: deliverer, lawgiver, prophet, priest, psalmist, and sage. However, the central focus of Moses' unique place rested on his role as mediator of the covenant.[13]

If we may speak of Abraham as the founder of Israel, God's specially chosen, we may look upon Moses as the provider of the basic structures (political, societal, religious) that enabled Israel to carry out her divine calling in the land promised to her. Among other things, as provider, Moses served as architect, organizer, and overseer of Israel's general infrastructure. For instance, in the wilderness of Sinai he saw to the organization of Israel into tribal groups and later oversaw the erection of the tabernacle according to the plans given him by God. Further, he provided the Israelites with rules and regulations governing their daily affairs. We will have more to say about the tabernacle and various rules in the following chapter.

Joshua — Military Hero. Following the death of Moses, as the Israelites moved out of the wilderness into Palestine (the land of promise since the days of Abraham), they did not need another Mosaic architect and organizer. Rather, what they needed was a leader who could help them to possess the land and later leaders who could help them to preserve what had been possessed.

Joshua was the great military hero who enabled Israel to conquer and possess the land. Contrary to the views of some interpreters who hold that Joshua had little or no part in such a conquest, the position taken in this work is that some kind of conquest took place under Joshua even if modest gains were sometimes magnified into larger victories and even if, on occasion, Joshua was given credit for the accomplishments of lesser military figures, a practice probably typical even today. With this in mind, note the following words of God to Joshua:

> My servant Moses is dead. Now proceed to cross the Jordan, you and all this people, into the land that I am giving to them, to the Israelites . . . .
> Be strong and courageous; for you shall put this people in possession of the land that I swore to their ancestors to give them. (Josh 1:2, 6)

According to the book of Joshua, Joshua did enable the Israelites to possess enough of the land, even if mainly in the central hill country, to allow Joshua to distribute the Palestinian territory along tribal lines. Following the death of Joshua, the people often found their lives in jeopardy. Part of this can be attributed to God's displeasure of Israel's apostasy and part to the absence of a central leader from Joshua's death until the election of Saul as Israel's first king. Maybe at a later time God would abandon the idea of Israel on a God-given land, but not yet. So God raised up a series of "judges" (temporary military leaders) to rescue his people and thus preserve for them the promised land.

Kings. Yet there awaited for them a permanent military leader, namely a king. Aside from whatever military leadership they might exhibit, kings were expected to be administrators of God's justice — a justice that the king must live by and one tempered with compassion, a justice demonstrated within the sight of the nations/Gentiles (see Deut 17:14-20).

In our consideration of the king as the mediator of justice, we shall center our attention on King Solomon, who expresses the ideal of justice, a justice that he often forsook in actual practice, and King Josiah who actually practiced justice, while his sons, who succeeded him, did not. When early in his reign, God extended to Solomon the right to ask for any gift of his choosing, Solomon replied: "Give your servant therefore an understanding mind to govern your people, able to discern between good and evil; for who can govern this your great people?" (1 Kgs 3:9)

A short time later, Solomon showed great discernment in choosing between the rival claims of two harlots who both claimed to be the mother of the same child (1 Kgs 3:16-28). However, as his grandiose building projects took shape, Solomon exacted a harsh contribution from his citizenry in the form of conscripted labor. First Kings 5 records:

> King Solomon conscripted forced labor out of all Israel; the levy numbered
> thirty thousand men. He sent them to the Lebanon, ten thousand a month
> in shifts; they would be a month in the Lebanon and two months at home.
> (1 Kgs 5:13-14)

Solomon not only acted harshly toward his citizenry but also toward those who contested his right to rule. Among those he executed were the following: Adonijah, his brother; Joab, David's military commander-in-chief and supporter of Adonijah; Shemi, not a supporter of Adonijah, but one whom Solomon distrusted. He deposed priests and reorganized the office of priesthood to his own liking. Also of interest is the absence of any strong prophetic voice that confronted Solomon face-to-face as Nathan had done with David. Under such circumstances, it is not surprising that the author of 1 Kings can report: "So the kingdom was established in the hand of Solomon" (1 Kgs 2:46).

Paul Hanson critiques Solomon's reign as follows:

> Thus we discern a pattern that permeated all levels of Israelite society under Solomon, involving centralization of political power, which rescinded important rights earlier enjoyed by the people . . . . Finally, it is not surprising to discover that his pattern permeated temple worship as well, where the king was exalted to a level that threatened to divert attention of the worshippers away from the central quality of early Yahwism, sole worship of Yahweh . . . . His [Solomon's] heart, amid all this royal praise and splendor, became preoccupied with Solomon, not God. Israel's king clearly was a faithful example neither of true worship nor of godly righteousness nor of divine compassion.[14]

Unlike Solomon, some of the kings tended to keep one foot in the Mosaic covenant and the other in the newer Davidic covenant. Among such kings was Hezekiah. With appreciation, the author of 2 Kings says of him:

> He did what was right in the sight of the LORD just as his ancestor David had done . . . . He trusted in the LORD the God Israel . . . . he did not depart from following him but kept the commandments that the LORD commanded Moses. (2 Kgs 18:3-6)

What was said of Hezekiah can equally be said of King Josiah. Josiah's efforts to turn the Israelites back to the days of Moses was said to be based on some written document (perhaps our Deuteronomy or some form of it) that was discovered in his day. The author of 2 Kings describes Josiah's reaction to the newly-discovered document as follows:

> Then the king directed that all the elders of Judah and Jerusalem should be gathered to him. The king went up to the house of the LORD, and with him went all the people of Judah, all the inhabitants of Jerusalem, the priests, the prophets, all the people, both small and great; he read in their hearing all the words of the book of the covenant that had been found in the house of the LORD. The king stood by the pillar and made a covenant before the LORD, to follow the LORD, keeping his commandments, his decrees, and his statutes, with all his heart and all his soul, to perform the words of this covenant that were written in this book. All the people joined in the covenant. (2 Kgs 23:1-3)

Whatever reform Josiah was able to bear seems to have died with him a short time later on a battlefield at Meggido. His sons showed no interest in their father's reforms. This caused Jeremiah to warn them that without repentance, not only would their family come to an end, but also the same fate awaited the institution of kingship and the Davidic dynasty:

> Hear the word of the LORD, O king of Judah sitting on the throne of David . . . . Act with justice and righteousness, and deliver from the hand of the oppressor anyone who has been robbed. And do no wrong or violence to the alien, the orphan, and the widow, or shed innocent blood in this place. For if you will indeed obey this word, then through the gates of this house shall enter kings who sit on the throne of David, riding on chariots and on horses, they, and their servants, and their people. But if you will not heed these words . . . this house shall become a desolation. (Jer 22:2-5)

Prophets. Much could be said about the prophets as Israelite leaders. In keeping with the emphasis in this section on God's mission for his specially chosen people, we shall center our attention on the prophets as God's representatives in the calling of Israel to repentance so that she would not have to forfeit the right to her mission. It is noteworthy, for instance, that God does not send Elijah to some foreign place to bear witness to Israelite faith. Rather, he uses Elijah to challenge the Israelites to a true faith in Yahweh. From the top of Mount Carmel, his words ring out: "How long will you go limping with two different opinions? If the LORD is God, follow him; but if Baal, then follow him" (1 Kgs 18:21).

We saw above how Jeremiah pleaded with the sons of King Josiah to follow the administration of justice of their father for the sake of Judah, Israel's southern kingdom. Jeremiah's message went unheeded, except in some eschatological or messianic sense, and Jeremiah witnessed the fall of Judah to the Babylonians and the end of the Davidic dynasty.

Prior to the demise of Judah, Judah's sister nation to the north (known as Israel) had fallen to the Assyrians as predicted by Amos and Hosea. Just as the pleas of Jeremiah concerning repentance had gone unheeded, so had those of Amos and Hosea. Amos declares: "and Israel shall surely go into exile away from its land" (Amos 7:17). Amos's words are echoed by Hosea: "and in Assyria they shall eat unclean food" (Hos 9:3).

Priests. The priests carried out the dual role of intercession (prayer and sacrifice) and instruction of the Torah/Law of members of God's specially chosen people, the Israelites. Their cultic duties will be considered in the next chapter. In the wilderness, Yahweh addressed the following words to Aaron, Moses' brother and Israel's first high priest, concerning the teaching duties of the priests:

> And the LORD spoke to Aaron: Drink no wine or strong drink, neither you nor your sons, when you enter the tent of meeting, that you may not die; it is a statute forever throughout your generations. You are to distinguish between the holy and the common, and between the unclean and the clean; and you are to teach the people of Israel all the statutes that the LORD had spoken to them through Moses. (Lev 10:8-11)

By the time of Jeremiah, c. 600 BC, the priests were so sure of their role in Mosaic Torah instruction that they, along with prophets and wisdom teachers, challenged the mission and message of Jeremiah without fear of their role being stripped away from them. The book of Jeremiah states:

> Then they said, "Come let us make a plot against Jeremiah — for instruction ['Torah] shall not perish from the priests, nor counsel from the wise, nor the word from the prophet. Come, let us bring charges against him, and let us not heed any of his words." (Jer 18:18)

What the priests failed to understand was that whatever long-range plans God had for the priests relative to Torah, God could revoke any generation's right of priestly Torah instruction. To those Israelite priests in Babylonian bondage, God expressed it thusly through Ezekiel, a contemporary of Jeremiah:

> Disaster comes upon disaster,
> rumor follows rumor;
> they shall keep seeking a vision
>   from the prophet;
> instruction shall perish from
>   the priest,
> and counsel from the elders. (Ezek 7:26)

That this disruption was only temporary is made clear in the book of Malachi following Israel's return to Jerusalem from Babylonian Exile:

> For the lips of a priest should guard knowledge, and the people should seek instruction from his mouth, for he is the messenger of the LORD of host. (Mal 2:7)

Sages. As we come to the last of the Israelite leaders, namely the sages, the question arises concerning their actual existence. Was there a professional class of sages? James Crenshaw, a recognized authority in the field of biblical wisdom studies, concludes that there was.[15] The professional sage spent his time seeking out and proclaiming wisdom. Crenshaw states:

> For what, then did [biblical] ancient sages search from dawn to dusk? Perhaps nothing suffices to answer this important question but the word "life." Canonical sages went in pursuit of the good life in all its manifestations: health, wealth, honor, progeny, longevity, remembrance. These teachers never seemed to grow tired of promising such bounty to faithful listeners and of threatening fools with loss of life itself. In their eyes sufficient proof existed that life's goods accompanied wisdom . . . [16]

Thus, Israelite sages provided a body of knowledge and instruction that enabled God's specially chosen community to live full, good, and happy lives. When they did this in the presence of the Gentiles, they carried out a measure of God's mission for them. Eventually, the teaching of the sages was set down in written form. The final editor of the book of Proverbs declares that the teaching of Proverbs is:

> For learning about wisdom and
>   instruction,
> for understanding words of
>   insight,
> for gaining instruction in wise
>   dealing,
> righteousness, justice, and
>   equity
> to teach shrewdness to the simple,
> knowledge and prudence to the
> young. (Prov 1:2-4)

Notes

[1] Paul Hanson, *The People Called: The Growth of Community in the Bible* (New York: Harper and Row, 1986), 1.

[2] Ibid.

[3] Joseph Blenkinsopp, *Wisdom and Law in the Old Testament: The Ordering of Life in Israel and Early Judaism* (New York: Oxford Press, 1983), 19.

[4] See chapter five.

[5] As previously discussed in chapter two.

[6] Brevard S. Childs, *Old Testament Theology in a Canonical Context* (Philadelphia: Fortress Press, 1985), 187.

[7] Douglas A. Knight, "Family," *Mercer Dictionary of the Bible*, ed. Watson E. Mills et al. (Macon: Mercer University Press, 1990), 294.

[8] Carol Myers, *Discovering Eve: Ancient Israelite Women in Context* (New York: Oxford University Press, 1988), 145.

[9] C. J. H. Wright, "Family," *The Anchor Bible Dictionary*, ed. David Noel Freedman, vol. 2 (New York: Doubleday, 1992), 763.

[10] C. U. Wolf, "Tribe," *Interpreter's Dictionary of the Bible*, 4, 699ff. Wolf provides a discussion of the various lists of the number of tribes from less than twelve to more than twelve.

[11] Keith Whitelam, "King and Kingship," *The Anchor Dictionary of the Bible*, ed. David Noel Freedman, vol. 4 (New York: Doubleday, 1992), 40.

[12] John Bright, *A History of Israel* (Louisville: Westminster John Knox Press, 2000), 217.

[13] Childs, 109.

[14] Paul Hanson, *The People Called: The Growth of Community in the Bible*, 122-23.

[15] James L. Crenshaw, *Old Testament Wisdom: An Introduction* (Louisville: Westminster John Knox Press, 1998), 21.

[16] Ibid., 50.

9

Living in Community
Before God — Part II

Now this is the commandment — the statutes and the ordinances — that the LORD your God charged me to teach you to observe in the land that you are about to cross into and occupy, so that you and your children and your children's children may fear the LORD your God all the days of your life, and keep all his decrees and his commandments that I am commanding you, so that your days may be long. Hear therefore, O Israel, and observe them diligently, so that it may go well with you, and so that you may multiply greatly in a land flowing with milk and honey, as the LORD, the God of your ancestors, has promised you. (Deut 6:1-3)

Praise the LORD!
Praise God in his sanctuary;
praise him in his mighty
    firmament!
Praise him for his mighty deeds;
praise him according to his
    surpassing greatness!
Praise him with trumpet sound;
praise him with lute and harp!
Praise him tambourine and
    dance;
praise him with strings and
    pipe!
Praise him with clanging cymbals;
praise him with loud clashing
    cymbals!

Let everything that breathes praise
   The LORD!
Praise the LORD! (Ps 150)

Introduction

In this chapter we shall close out our study of Community with
"Community Laws and Regulations" and "Community Worship." While at
first there may seem to be little connection between the two subjects, they
are closely woven together in the various legal codes of the Pentateuch. For
instance, the Mosaic Decalogue (treating it for our purposes as a law code)
includes a command about worship along with such societal prohibitions as
killing and stealing (Exod 20). Again, the so-called Covenant Code of
Exodus includes a body of legal matter that is introduced by and concludes
with cultic instructions (Exod 20:21–23:19). Furthermore, the passage
sometimes spoken of as the Deuteronomic Code combines both societal and
worship instructions (Deut 12–26).

Community Laws and Regulations

If a community, such as Israel, is to survive and prosper, it needs to observe
such proper conduct that blesses all of its members. Further, if it also is to be
a source of God's blessing to the Gentiles, it must observe those special
requirements that set it morally and spiritually above its Gentile neighbors.

While various specialized codes for living may be included or at least
alluded to here and there outside the Pentateuch, the Pentateuch contains
the most systematic collections (including, namely the Decalogue [Exod
20:1-17; Deut 5:6-21], the Covenant Code [Exod 21:1–23:33], and the
Deuteronomic Code [Deut 12–26]). Therefore we will primarily depend on
these three codes for our current presentation. However, it is important to
recognize that in order to grasp the theological significance of the law codes
of the Pentateuch, including the Decalogue, they must be studied in the context of the entire Old Testament. Applying this principle of interpretation to
the Decalogue, Brevard Childs remarks:

> In my judgment, it is an important task of an Old Testament theology to
> sketch the range of interpretation within the whole Old Testament in order
> to understand how the Decalogue functioned within Israel, and to discern
> both the dynamics of its movement and the nature of its actualization. For
> example, . . . the story of the temptation of Joseph by Potiphar's wife offers

one interpretation of the prohibition of adultery within a concrete situation . . . . Conversely, biblical law serves an important function in any reading of the narrative material by preventing the reader from simply moralizing the stories and thus failing to see the true nature of human existence with its potential for both good and evil in the light of the divine will.[1]

For the sake of presentation, selected laws and regulations of the Pentateuch shall be organized under the following categories: dealing with homicide, bodily harm, and harm to property; dealing with the marginalized; and dealing with fairness/justice in the workplace, marketplace, and the courts.

Dealing with Homicide, Bodily Harm, and Harm to Property

The breaching of the various codes brings harm to the individual and one's society. For instance, killing is the ultimate harm to the individual. At the same time, the trouble brought on by the killing of one individual may escalate into serious problems for many. If the victim is a husband and father, the family may not only lose its primary economic provider, but the widow and her children may become a burden on the other members of society. If the victim is a male leader of a larger group such as a clan or tribe, the whole group may find itself shattered. Furthermore, if the members of the deceased family decide to avenge the death, many persons may eventually die before the matter is settled. Consider the case of Dinah's (daughter of Jacob and Leah) rape by Shechem, a Gentile, and the subsequent slaughter of Shechem, his family, and other acquaintances for the deed by Simeon and Levi, Dinah's brothers (Gen 34). In the eyes of some Israelites, if not all, rape was tantamount to death since the female victim might be considered unfit for marriage.

While the Decalogue might simply declare "You shall not murder" (Exod 20:13), other codes dealt with human killing more specifically. For instance, the Covenant Code declares:

Whoever strikes a person mortally shall be put to death. If it was not premeditated, but came by an act of God, then I will appoint for you a place to which the killer may flee. But if someone willfully attacks and kills another by treachery, you shall take the killer from my altar for execution. (Exod 21:12-24)

Even though this code provides more details concerning the actual settling of the matter than does the Decalogue, there is still much that is not spelled out. The code does make a distinction between intentional and unintentional killing as well as provide protection for a possible innocent person (notice the cities of refuges in Deut 4:41ff) until the matter could be fairly decided by the proper authorities. How the latter is to be done is not stated in the passage. Further, if the person is found guilty of murder, we are not told how he shall be executed, or by whom.

Some of the details that are absent in the Covenant Code are supplied by the Deuteronomic Code. For instance, we are given more details about the cities of refuge, an illustration of an unintentional killing, and the proper person to administer the death penalty:

> [Y]ou shall set apart three cities in the land that the LORD your God is giving you to possess . . . so that any homicide can flee to one of them.
>
> Now this is the case of a homicide who might flee there and live, that is, someone who has killed another person unintentionally when the two had not been at enmity before: Suppose someone goes into the forest with another to cut wood, and when one of them swings the ax to cut down a tree, the head slips from the handle and strikes the other person who then dies; the killer may flee to one of these cities and live . . . .
>
> But if someone at enmity with another lies in wait and attacks and takes the life of that person, and flees into one of these cities, then the elders of the killer's city shall send to have the culprit taken from there and handed over to the avenger of blood[2] to be put to death. Show no pity; you shall purge the guilt of innocent blood from Israel, so that it may go well with you. (Deut 19:2-5, 11-13)

Concerning the above passage, along with others, Mark Biddle remarks:

> The Old Testament, then, advocates a very high respect for human life. The murderer who means to kill must be punished for an action that strikes at the very heart of human society and that destroys one made in the very image of God. All other killers, however, must be protected. The loss of precious human life in an accident cannot be compensated by further shedding of blood. The desire for revenge must be controlled.[3]

Various laws of the Pentateuch recognized that violence must be properly dealt with even when death was not involved. Further, intention and attitude were important considerations when dealing with these matters. Of course, the most that the various codes can do is include selective cases. For instance, if during an altercation between men, one is hurt, the offending party shall pay the victim for time lost and the cost of recovery (Exod 21:18-19). Walter Brueggemann points out that the aim of the law goes beyond individual restitution to a settling of the quarrel for the sake of the community: "the community metes out punishment that is equitable without vengeance. The community sets a limit on vengeance and thereby seeks to control violence."[4] The legal codes of the Pentateuch dealt with property loss as well as loss of life and health. Of particular importance was the question of responsibility. Suppose, for instance, an individual is responsible for the death of a neighbor's animal in an open pit that the owner had failed to secure. According to the Covenant Code, the guilty party shall "make restitution, giving money to its owner, but keeping the dead animal" (Exod 21:34). In the case of the loss of an owner's crop because of a careless neighbor, the law stipulates:

> When someone causes a field or vineyard to be grazed over, or lets livestock loose to graze in someone else's field, restitution shall be made from the best of the owner's field or vineyard. (Exod 22:5)

Property laws not only dealt with the harm that one neighbor could do to another; they also dealt with the responsibility to be of help to a neighbor, even one's enemy:

> When you come upon your enemy's ox or donkey going astray, you shall bring it back. When you see the donkey of one who hates you lying under its burden and you would hold back from setting it free, you must help to set it free. (Exod 23:4-5)

We turn again to Brueggemann for helpful remarks: "These two commands indicate that for the sake of the neighbor i.e., for the health of the community, one has obligations that override one's emotional propensity."[5]

Dealing with the Marginalized

While some individuals experienced situations that brought on death, bodily harm, and harm to property, others experienced situations that affected their station in life. The latter persons are also dealt with in various legal codes in the Pentateuch. For instance, some persons found themselves economically bound over for a period of time as debt slaves.[6] The law concerning such debt slaves reads as follows: "When you buy a male Hebrew slave, he shall serve six years, but in the seventh he shall go out a free person, without debt" (Exod 21:2). Others such as widows and orphans often found themselves vulnerable for long periods of time. The law codes also make provisions for them. For one thing, the community was admonished not to take advantage of them:

> You shall not abuse any widow or orphan. If you do abuse them, when they cry out to me, I will surely heed their cry; my wrath will burn, and I will kill you with the sword, and your wives shall become widows and your children orphans. (Exod 22:22-24)

Further, they, along with the poor in general, were to benefit from the annual fruits of the harvest through gleaning and from the fruits that grew on their own (without cultivation) every seventh year:

> When you reap the harvest of your land, you shall not reap to the very edges of your field, or gather the gleanings of your harvest. You shall not strip your vineyard bare, or gather the fallen grapes of your vineyard; you shall leave them for the poor and the alien: I am the LORD your God. (Lev 19:9-10)

> For six years you shall sow your land and gather in its yield; but the seventh year you shall let it rest and lie fallow, so that the poor of your people may eat; and what they leave the wild animals may eat. You shall do the same with your vineyard and with your olive orchard. (Exod 23:10-11)

In order that the widow not be forced to a lifetime of poverty, provision was made for her to marry a brother or some other near kin of her deceased husband. The provisions of the law are given in Deuteronomy 25 and an example of such an arrangement is told in the book of Ruth concerning the marriage of Boaz and Ruth.

Dealing with Fairness/Justice in the Workplace, Marketplace, and the Courts

Of particular interest are the provisions made in the various codes concerning fairness in the workplace, marketplace, and the courts. For instance, it was important that those whose welfare depended on their daily labors be paid daily. The Deuteronomic code stipulated:

> You shall not withhold the wages of poor and needy laborers, whether other Israelites or aliens who reside in your land in one of your towns. You shall pay them their wages daily before sunset, because they are poor and their livelihood depends on them; otherwise they might cry to the LORD against you, and you would incur guilt. (Deut 24:14-15)

As for the marketplace, it was important, especially for the poor and other vulnerable people, that sellers use honest means of measuring out their products. The Deuteronomic Code also addresses this matter:

> You shall not have in your bag two kinds of weights, large and small. You shall not have in your house two kinds of measures, large and small. You shall have only a full and honest weight, . . . so that your days may be long in the land that the LORD your God is giving you. For all who do such things, all who act dishonestly, are abhorrent to the LORD your God. (Deut 25:13-16)

When necessity required that matters of dispute be settled in the courts, it was important that all persons be treated fairly. For instance, the courts were to show partiality neither to the rich nor the poor. The Covenant Code speaks of this matter as follows:

> You shall not spread a false report. You shall not join hands with the wicked to act as a malicious witness. You shall not follow a majority in wrongdoing; when you bear witness in a lawsuit, you shall not side with the majority so as to pervert justice; nor shall you be partial to the poor in a lawsuit . . . . You shall not pervert the justice due to your poor in their lawsuits. Keep far from a false charge, and do not kill the innocent and those in the right, for I will not acquit the guilty. You shall take no bribe, for a bribe blinds the officials, and subverts the cause of those who are in the right. (Exod 23:1-3, 6-8)

Walter Brueggemann summarizes the above passage as follows:

> The entire section of vv. 1-9 portrays a passionate commitment to the maintenance of a community in which all members are safe and respected, in which due process is guaranteed, and in which selfish interest is curbed

for the sake of the weaker, more vulnerable members of society. This section powerfully reflects, in legal form, the ongoing passion of the community of liberation.[7]

Basic Principles Undergirding the Law

According to Paul Hanson, the Israelites developed under the leadership of Moses three principles/beliefs that served to undergird the multifaceted laws/rules binding their community together. Hanson speaks of a triadic wedding of *righteousness/justice, compassion*, and *worship*. Israel is to be righteous because God is righteous. Israel is to be compassionate because God is compassionate. Israel is to recognize that the true bonding of righteousness and compassion is to be found in her worship of Yahweh (the LORD) her God. The following is one of Hanson's summaries of the triadic concept:

> [A] triad of qualities underlies the early Yahwistic notion of community. In their interrelationship, they clarify the dynamism discernible in Israelite community in the premonarchial period. The righteousness of God represented a universal standard of justice that ordered life, defined the realm in which Yahweh's . . . [peace] could be received, and gave rise to ordinances and institutions that formed a protective wall around the people that sheltered it from life-threatening dangers. Compassion allowed righteousness in Israel to maintain its stringency as a clear and dependable standard by giving it a heart, and by wedding its just requirements with openness and concern for the salvation of all members of God's family. Finally the two were able to work together as a life-enhancing polarity in maintaining an ordered but open society by finding their unity in worship of the one holy God, the Judge of the wicked and the Redeemer of the repentant and the innocent oppressed.[8]

Community Worship

We begin our opening remarks on Israelite worship with the following trenchant words of James Muilenberg:

> Worship is holy meeting. In worship, man enters into the sphere of holiness, into the presence of the Holy one. Israel was born in the hour of the covenant to be a holy nation or people. In her worship she remembers God's self-witness, "I, the Lord, am holy," and to it she responds confessionally, "The Lord our God is holy." (Ps 99)[9]

In the discussion that follows we shall examine holy days, holy seasons, holy places, sacrifices, offerings, specialized worship personnel, and Israel's exalted hymnal (the Psalter). Before we move further, two matters of importance need to be considered, namely to what extent was free, spontaneous worship approved alongside of prescribed ritualistic worship, and whether animal sacrificial worship was approved or condemned.

Free Worship and Ritualistic Worship

During the period of the Exodus, Moses both prescribes rituals to be followed in seasonal worship as the Passover and leads his people in a free celebration of the exodus experience.

Among the fixed rituals of worship were such yearly celebrations as Passover. All of the books of the Pentateuch, except Genesis, have stipulations about the Passover ceremony. Together, instructions are given concerning such matters as the length of the ceremony, the season of the year, the place where offered, and proceedings (see Exod 23, 24; Lev 23; Num 28-29; Deut 16).

There is evidence that the Passover, along with Pentecost and Tabernacles, developed in stages, at first being agricultural rites. The three stages of the Passover may be classified as: harvest, exodus, and messianic. Concerning the last stage, even today an empty chair is placed at the Passover table in anticipation of the coming of Elijah, the forerunner of the Messiah.[10]

The Israelites often broke out in free, spontaneous acts of worship expressing emotions such as joys of victory. Following Israel's deliverance from Egypt, both Moses and Miriam led the people in expressions of praise. Note Miriam's role:

> Then the prophet Miriam, Aaron's sister, took a tambourine in her hand;
> and all the women went out after her with tambourines and with dancing.
> And Miriam sang to them:
> "Sing to the LORD for he has
>   triumphed gloriously;
> horse and rider he has thrown into
>   the sea." (Exod 15:20-21)

Animal Sacrifices — Authorized and Commended or Condemned?

Certain elements of Israelite worship, such as animal sacrifices, are both authorized/commended and seemingly condemned in the Old Testament. Illustrative of the former position is the following stipulation from the book of Leviticus:

> The LORD summoned Moses and spoke to him from the tent of meeting, saying: Speak to the people of Israel and say to them: When any of you bring an offering of livestock to the LORD, you shall bring your offering from the herd or from the flock . . . . If your gift for a burnt offering is from the flock, from the sheep or goats, your offering shall be a male without blemish . . . the priest shall offer the whole and turn it into smoke on the altar; it is a burnt offering, an offering by fire of pleasing odor to the LORD. (Lev 1:1-2,10, 13)

On the surface, the prophets seem to condemn such sacrifices. However, they more than likely did not completely condemn them except when they became a substitution for such things as justice (Jer 7:1ff) or when practiced by rote without any proper inward attitude (Isa 29:13).[11]

Sacred Time (Days and Seasons)

Sabbath. We shall not try to determine, as some have done, whether sacred time or sacred space/place is more important. Concerning sacred time, we begin with the sabbath. For ancient Israelites, as with many today, there was a need for a time set aside weekly to contemplate on God's good creation and amazing grace. The Decalogue as preserved in Exodus emphasizes the former and as preserved in Deuteronomy emphasizes the latter:

> Remember the sabbath day, and keep it holy . . . . For in six days the LORD made heaven and earth, the sea, and all that is in them, but rested the seventh day; therefore the LORD blessed the sabbath day and consecrated it. (Exod 20:8, 11)

> Observe the sabbath day and keep it holy, as the LORD your God commanded you . . . . Remember that you were a slave in the land of Egypt, and that the LORD your God brought you out from there with a mighty hand and an outstretched arm; therefore the LORD your God commanded you to keep the sabbath day. (Deut 5:12, 15)

Passover. Coming in spring, Passover is the earliest seasonal cultic celebration among the other Israelite seasonal religious experiences such as Pentecost, the Day of Atonement, and the Feast of Tabernacles. Concerning the Passover, Hayyim Schauss remarks:

> *Pesach*, usually called Passover, is first in the calendar of Jewish festivals. It is the greatest of Jewish festivals. For over two thousand years it has been more than a holiday; it has been *the* holiday, the festival of redemption. In addition, *Pesach* is the oldest of Jewish festivals. Jews observed it in the most ancient of times, in the days when they were still nomadic shepherds in the wilderness.[12] (Italics added)

Schauss' last remark reminds us that as the Passover celebrated the deliverance from Egypt, it also was associated with the celebration of the coming of spring with the birth of kids and lambs and ripening of grain. Thus, to this day, Passover is celebrated in early spring.[13]

Pentecost. For fifty days after the Passover, the Israelites celebrated Pentecost (Greek for "fifty"). Like the Passover, it began as an agricultural celebration (see Deut 16:9-10) and remained as such throughout the Old Testament period. By the first century AD it had taken on the symbolism of God's pact with Noah and God's gift of the Torah to the Israelites at Sinai. In recent years, Pentecost has taken on an added dimension, especially among the Reformed Jews, at which time spiritual confirmation (about the ages of 12 to 13) takes place for the young men and ladies.[14]

Day of Atonement. Whereas the Passover and Pentecost were important spring celebrations, the Day of Atonement and Feast of Tabernacles were important ones in the fall. The Day of Atonement (*Yom Kippur* in Hebrew), provided for a time of spiritual renewal for all Israelites. According to Leviticus 16, the high priest was to make atonement in the following order: for himself, his spiritual staff, the holy tabernacle (later temple), and finally for all the Israelites. Note the appropriate sections of Leviticus 16 below:

> Thus shall Aaron come into the holy place with a young bull for a sin offering . . . for himself . . . and for his house [spiritual staff] . . . he shall make atonement for the sanctuary.... Then Aaron shall lay both his hands on the head of the live goat, and confess over it all the iniquities of the people of Israel, . . . putting them on the head of the goat, and sending it away into the wilderness. (Lev 16:3ff)

Tabernacles. While pre-first century AD Jews celebrated other sacred days such as Purim and Hannukah,[15] we shall close our studies with the Feast of Tabernacles/Booths (*Sukkoth* in Hebrew) which was celebrated a few days after the Day of Atonement. It was the most joyous of the three harvest festivals (Passover, Pentecost, Feast of Tabernacles), including a celebration of the harvest of grapes (to be made into wine) as well as the harvest of fall grain. While all of the celebrations were subject to abuse, the Feast of Tabernacles was probably the most susceptible to excesses. Schauss states the celebration "often became a tumultuous, wild bacchanalia."[16]

As the Passover celebrated the freedom from Egypt and Pentecost the giving of the Law at Sinai, in time Tabernacles celebrated Israel's wilderness wanderings following her sojourn at Sinai (Lev 23).

Sacred Places: Geographical Places

There is a sense in which all things (time, place, etc.) may be considered sacred because God created them. On the other hand, certain of these — trees, streams, rocks — may have a special significance because they instill in humanity a sense of awe. Perhaps God will be found in those places or be met there. Furthermore, some places take on significance because of a God-human encounter at those places. For instance God met Jacob at a certain mountain place called Luz (Gen 28). Jacob renamed the place Bethel (house of God) and later returned there under the behest of God:

> God said to Jacob, "Arise, go up to Bethel, and settle there. Make an altar there to the God who appeared to you when you fled from your brother Esau." (Gen 35:1)

Like Jacob, Israelites would continue to go to that same spot to celebrate their ancestor's experience and to develop their own. For instance, so important did Bethel become as a place of worship that King Jeroboam chose it as one of his spiritual capitals as a substitute for Jerusalem (1 Kgs 12).

From among the special places of worship we shall examine four — Shechem, Bethel, Sinai, and Jerusalem — two, and perhaps three, that are related to the lives of the Patriarchs.

Shechem. We begin with Shechem, located in the central hill country of Palestine. It was at Shechem that Abraham was informed by God that he was standing on the God-promised land. To celebrate the occasion and the place,

Abraham erected an altar there. The book of Genesis records the experience as follows:

> Abram passed through the land to the place at Shechem, to the oak at Moreh . . . . . Then the LORD appeared to Abram, and said, "To your off-spring I will give this land." So he built there an altar to the LORD, who had appeared to him. (Gen 12:6-7)

It is certainly possible that the oak tree was already sacred to the Canaanites before Abraham arrived there. Abraham may have even been awestruck by it. In any case, it was his experience with God that caused him to erect the altar. When many years later Joshua, in his old age, gathered tribes together for a covenant renewal at Shechem, did they gather around Abraham's altar? We don't know. We would like to think that they did, but the book of Joshua offers no assurance concerning the matter. In any case, the fact that Joshua chose Shechem for such a momentous occasion is significant (Josh 24). The city continued to be important, even if not always of spiritual significance, up to approximately 100 BC when it was obliterated by the Romans.[17]

Bethel. Located to the south of Shechem in Palestine's hill country, Bethel was made spiritually important by Jacob's first major encounter with God. Having tricked his brother, Esau, out of Esau's blessing, Jacob fled northward toward Haran to escape Esau's wrath. While he experienced a troubled sleep at Luz (later Bethel), in a dream he saw heavenly beings and he heard God addressing him. The promise of blessing and the vocation of a mission to the Gentiles, which had originally been spoken to his grandfather, Abraham, were now spoken to Jacob. Upon awakening, he renamed the site *Beth-el* (house of God) and tremblingly accepted God's challenge to bless the Gentiles through him:

> So Jacob rose early in the morning, and took the stone that he had put under his head and set it up for a pillar and poured oil on the top of it. He called that place Bethel; but the name of the city was Luz at first. Then Jacob made a vow, saying, "If God will be with me, and will keep me in this way that I go, and will give me bread to eat and clothing to wear, so that I come again to my father's house in peace, then the LORD shall be my God, and this stone, which I have set up for a pillar, shall be God's house;

and of all that you give me I will surely give one-tenth to you." (Gen 28:18-22)

Like Shechem before it, Bethel remained an important worship center long after the time of the Patriarchs. Following Jacob's example, faithful Israelites visited or went on pilgrimages there according to 1 Samuel 10. According to Judges 20, sacrifices were offered there and for a time the Ark of the Covenant was kept there.

Jerusalem. We have discussed the two worship centers — Shechem and Bethel — which, according to the book of Genesis, had their Israelite beginnings in the lives of the Patriarchs. A third, Jerusalem, is more problematic in its relationship to the Patriarchs. The problem hinges on the relationship of the land of Moriah, the site of Abraham's near sacrifice of Isaac (Gen 22), to Jerusalem. Second Chronicles 3 states that Solomon erected the Jerusalem temple on Mount Moriah. It is not clear that Mount Moriah and the land of Moriah are identical. Morever, the book of 2 Chronicles does not mention Abraham in its account. However, it should be noted that Josephus, a first century AD Jewish historian, along with a number of Jewish rabbis, and Jerome, the Christian translator of the Latin Vulgate Bible, did accept the view that the site, later known as Jerusalem, was the place of Abraham's near sacrifice of Isaac.[18]

Another connection of Abraham with the site of later Jerusalem is his experience with Melchizedek, priest-king of Salem, after Abraham's war involvement with non-Palestinian intruders. There is fairly strong evidence that Salem should be identified with Jerusalem. An Israelite psalmist puts it this way:

> In Judah God is known,
> his name is great in Israel.
> His abode has been established in
>   Salem,
> his dwelling place in Zion [Jerusalem].
> There he broke the flashing
>   arrows,
> the shield, the sword, and the
>   weapons of war. (Ps 76:1-3)

A modern author declares:

The position of Salem on Abram's return route from Damascene to the Hebron area, and the proximity to it of the Valley of Shaveh also speak in favor of its identity with Jerusalem.[19]

However, the best hope of connecting Jerusalem as a place of worship with the Patriarchs is still to be found in the Moriah passage, since there is more reason to believe that the Israelites would have established Jerusalem as a place of worship based on the near sacrifice of Isaac than on an experience with a Gentile priest.

Whatever the final decision on the connection of Jerusalem as a place of worship with the Patriarchs, we are on more solid ground with David's involvement. After David had been inaugurated as king over all the tribes, he conquered the ancient Jebusite city of Jebus and made it his political capital, renaming it Jerusalem. Further, he moved the Ark of the Covenant there and temporarily housed it in a tent as he made plans for a more permanent dwelling. Frustrated in his plans for the latter, the erection of the temple awaited the inauguration of Solomon, David's successor (2 Sam 5-7; 1 Kgs 6).

There is no way that David or Solomon could have envisioned the future historical importance of Jerusalem, with its magnificent temple, as a great worship center. How could they possibly have imagined the thousands of persons flooding its streets during the days of Isaiah, Jeremiah, or Jesus of Nazareth? What marvel would greet their eyes today as they witnessed Jews, Christians, and Muslims vying for the privilege of giving it their reverence.

Sinai. We close our discussion of sacred places with Sinai, the place where God made his covenant with Israel (Exod 19ff). One cannot but wonder what significance Sinai would have had across the centuries if it had not been so geographically inaccessible. Would it have vied with Jerusalem as the great center of worship?

While Sinai's inaccessibility might have prevented many ordinary believers from visiting there, it did not hinder those intrepid pilgrims who considered all of its hardships worthwhile. For instance, the Old Testament tells the story of the prophet, Elijah, who fled there from Queen Jezebel (1 Kgs 19). In the fourth century AD, Egeria made a pilgrimage there and later wrote of the experience. Reflecting on Egeria's experience, an author recently wrote:

> In the centuries since Egeria toured the Holy Land, many pilgrims have retraced her difficult walk: They travel to St. Catherine's Monastery, which

was built by the emperor Justinian as a fortress in the sixth century CE at the foot of Jebel Musa, a 7,500 -foot peak in the southern Sinai peninsula, and trek before dawn up the jagged granite mountainside. Near the top, they must traverse thousands of steps before they reach the summit. But most find the exertion well worth the effort, for they believe they have reached one of the places on earth where the Lord revealed himself to humankind: where the Bible says Moses spent 40 days encountering God and receiving the Ten Commandments, where the Israelites, encamped below, demanded of Aaron the high priest that he fashion for them a golden calf, and where an enraged Moses shattered the first tablets of the Law in response to the Israelite's sins.[20]

The problem is, as the author of the above quotation points out, that they might not be standing where Moses stood. The author goes into some detail to present the view, a view held by a number of Jews and Christians across the centuries, that the actual site was on the east side, rather than the west side, of the Gulf of Aqaba.[21] Still others have thought that Mount Sinai was actually in what is now modern Sinai but in a more northern region.[22] Perhaps it is enough to believe, as the modern pilgrim does, that he stands where ancient Israel stood as she made her covenant with her God. There, in some mysterious fashion, modern pilgrims join hands with ancient Israelites as they worship their God.

Sacred Places — Buildings

We now turn our attention from such places as Bethel and Jerusalem to special edifices or buildings within those places. Among the number of sacred Israelite edifices/buildings were Moses' wilderness tabernacle, Solomon's Jerusalem temple, and Ezekiel's ideal Jerusalem temple.

The first thing to be understood is that we are not dealing with auditorium-like structures that house people who have come to worship. Among other things, the edifices housed an object such as the Ark of the Covenant that served as God's earthly throne. They also contained rooms where the priests could carry out their various functions. The people gathered outside in the open courtyard where they might worship through such activities as prayer, song, dance, etc.

Moses's Tabernacle. One of the interesting things concerning the three edifices under consideration is that they were neither made of cheap materials nor hastily thrown together with slipshod labor. According to the book of

Exodus, the architect of the tabernacle's blueprints was God, stipulating only the finest materials should be used in the construction of the tabernacle. The book of Exodus devotes ten chapters for the planning and erection of the sacred tent. For a fuller discussion see chapter 6.

Solomon's Temple. As grand as the wilderness tabernacle might have been, it could not match the splendor of Solomon's Jerusalem temple. Among other things, the latter consisted of the finest stone, wood, and precious metals. As the author of 1 Kings remarks, Solomon "overlaid the whole house [temple] with gold in order that the whole house might be perfect" (1 Kgs 6:22).

One of the outstanding differences between the tabernacle and the temple was the method of providing for the building materials and the labor. Concerning the gathering of the materials for the tabernacle, it was said: "Take from among you an offering to the LORD; let whoever is of a generous heart bring the LORD's offering: gold, silver, bronze, . . . (Exod 35:5).

As for much of the building materials for Solomon's temple, they came from Tyre (ancient Phoenecia; modern Lebanon), paid for by taxes from the Israelite people. Further, construction was overseen by Phoenician artisans. For instance, a certain Hiram was said to have overseen the making of the many bronze temple objects (1 Kgs 7). As for ordinary Israelites (those that did not become leaders in Solomon's government), many were conscripted (along with Gentile slaves) into forced-labor units to do the laborious work. Some were even sent away from Palestine for a month at a time (1 Kgs 5:13ff; 9:15ff; 11:26ff).

Ezekiel's Idealized Temple. Ezekiel's idealized Jerusalem temple, which he sees in a vision, is glorious in that the glory of God is everlastingly present (at least when humanity is cultically and morally faithful). Further, there flows from the idealized glorious temple a healing stream that heals all of broken humanity that it touches. Unlike the beauty of Solomon's temple that was expressed in terms of gold, the beauty of Ezekiel's temple was expressed in its wonderful geometrical design (Ezek 40ff).

Sacrifices and Offerings

A significant aspect of Israelite worship was sacrifices/offerings. There were basically two kinds: (1) animal offerings with an emphasis on shedding of blood, burning of flesh, and eating of flesh and (2) grain/cereal offerings that included the burning of the offering. Much more detail is given to the how of the offerings than to the meaning or symbolism of the offerings. Zimmerli puts it this way: "Unfortunately, the instructions for sacrificial worship . . . say very little about the intentions of the worshippers."[23] However, three purposes of the sacrifices/offerings are fairly apparent. First, they are acts that honor God. According to the book of Leviticus, they are a pleasing "odor to the LORD" (Lev 1:9; 2:2). Second, the offerings serve as acts of communion between God and man and between man and man. The book of Deuteronomy records:

> But you shall seek the place the LORD your God will choose out of all your tribes as his habitation to put his name there. You shall go there, bringing there your burnt offerings and your sacrifices, your tithes and your donations, your votive gifts, your freewill offerings, and the firstlings of your herds and flocks. And you shall eat there in the presence of the LORD your God, you and your households together, rejoicing in all the undertaking in which the LORD your God had blessed you. (Deut 12:5-7)

Third, the offerings serve as acts of repentance for sins. The following instructions are given in the book of Leviticus:

> When you realize your guilt in any of these, you shall confess the sin that you have committed. And you shall bring to the LORD, as your penalty for the sin that you have committed, a female from the flock, a sheep or a goat, as a sin offering; and the priest shall make atonement on your behalf for your sin. (Lev 5:5-6)

Specialized Worship Personnel

Like modern worshippers, ancient Israelites had to determine if specialized officiants were important, *even necessary*, to carry out certain functions. For instance, in the same way that modern Roman Catholicism may insist on a specialized leader in the celebration of the Mass, there were those among the Israelites who insisted on special leaders in such activities as animal sacrifice.

During the days of the Patriarchs, Abraham could offer up his own sacrifice, as was the case when he offered up a ram in the place of Isaac, his son (Gen 22). Such was still the case several hundred years later when a judge by the name of Jephthah sacrificed his daughter as the fulfillment of a rash vow to God (perhaps he expected to see an animal upon his arrival from a successful battle) (Judg 11). Nothing is said in the story about his using the services of a priest, though priests/Levites are mentioned in the book of Judges.

At what time special priestly leadership was generally accepted as a rule of conduct is difficult to determine from the various Old Testament texts. According to the Pentateuch, at least in some rudimentary form, priests from the days of Moses were considered special and Levites labored beside them (Lev 8ff).

An important matter that would eventually have to be dealt with was the right of the king to exercise priestly duties. For instance, in fear of being overwhelmed in battle against the Philistines, King Saul offered up a burnt offering. This act was thoroughly condemned (the Old Testament does not make clear why) by Samuel, the priest (1 Sam 13). On the other hand, David moved the Ark of the Covenant — without seemingly any priestly protest — to Jerusalem, leading the grand procession, wearing a priestly linen ephod, and even sacrificing animals (2 Sam 6). The book of 1 Chronicles makes it clear that whatever leadership role David chose to exercise, he did not ignore the priestly prerogatives of two important priests, Zadok and Abiathar, and their levitical aides (1 Chron 15).

An important feature of Israelite worship, especially after the establishment of the kingdom, was instruction given to and by specialized worship leaders. Included among such leaders were the levitical instructors of sacred music. Alfred Sendry, a modern authority in ancient Israelite music, speaks of "a regular school for liturgical education with religious music as the main subject of its curriculum in which hundreds of students were continuously trained for a professional career."[24]

One of the best examples of true Israelite worship (including its music) during the kingdom period is described in the book of 2 Chronicles concerning the renewal of acceptable temple worship by the recently installed king, Hezekiah. He removed all of the unacceptable objects of worship that King Ahaz, his father, had placed in the temple and cleansed the temple by sacrificing prescribed Levitical offerings. This was followed by a grand celebration.

> He stationed the Levites in the house of the LORD with cymbals, harps, and Lyres, according to the commandment of David and of Gad the king's seer and of the prophet Nathan, for the commandment was from the LORD through the prophets. The Levites stood with the instruments of David, and the priests with the trumpets. Then Hezekiah commanded that the burnt offering be offered on the altar. When the burnt offering began,

the song of the LORD began also, and the trumpets, accompanied by the instruments of King David of Israel. The whole assembly worshiped, the singers sang, and the trumpeters sounded; all this continued until the burnt offering was finished. When the offering was finished, the king and all who were present with him bowed down and worshiped. King Hezekiah and the officials commanded the Levites to sing the praises to the LORD with the words of David and of the seer Asaph. They sang praises with gladness, and they bowed down and worshiped. (2 Chron 29:25-30)

The Psalter — Israel's Hymnal

It is probably impossible to place too much emphasis on the book of Psalms as Israel's hymnal. James Muilenberg expresses it this way:

> The Psalter is preeminently the Book of Prayer and Praise. Many of the songs, hymns, prayers, and laments have their setting in the cult [worship], and they were employed in its exercise. It is seldom that we can be sure precisely what function they played in Israel's worship, and this is a grievous loss to us. For the psalms are not the product of human artifice and genius, but the modes of expression employed by Israel in all the various and manifold exigencies of daily life and historical existence, when she stood in the presence of her covenant-keeping Lord, . . . In the Psalter, we listen to the way of Israel's speaking in the presence of the Holy One.[25]

It would be hard to imagine any experience of the Israelites, as individuals or community, that is not mentioned in the various Psalms. These experiences include reflection on the nature of God, the nature of humanity, and humanity's proper relationship to God and all God's creation. If they felt sad, there was a lament psalm (such as Ps 13 or 137) to express their feelings. Likewise, there was a psalm to express their feeling of praise (such as Ps 30 or 149), chagrin at sin (Ps 51), et cetera. There were psalms to express Israel's heritage as God's people (Ps 105) and psalms to be used in the coronation of a king (Ps 2).

There were not only psalms that could be used as a part of a worship service; there also were psalms that addressed various matters about worship. For instance, Psalm 15 addresses proper preparation for worship.

O LORD, who may abide in your
    tent?
Who may dwell on your holy

hill?
Those who walk blamelessly, and
do what is right,
and speak the truth from their
heart;
who do not slander with their
tongue,
and do no evil to their friends,
nor take up a reproach against
their neighbors;
in whose eyes the wicked are
despised,
but who honor those who fear
the LORD;
who stand by their oath even to
their hurt;
Who do not lend money at
interest,
and do not take a bribe against
the innocent.
Those who do these things shall
never be moved. (Ps 15:1-5)

There are psalms that speak of the joy that comes from being in the presence of God, especially in or near the temple. Illustrative of this type of psalm is Psalm 84.

How lovely is your dwelling
place,
O LORD of hosts! . . .
For a day in your courts is better
than a thousand elsewhere.
I would rather be a doorkeeper in
the house of my God
than to live in the tents of
wickedness. (Ps 84:1, 10)

Typical of the psalms that speak of the sorrow felt by one who is no longer able to be a pilgrim leader to the temple is Psalm 42:

My soul is cast down within me;

therefore I remember you
from the land of Jordan and of
        Hermon,
from Mount Mizar.
Deep calls to deep
at the thunder of your cataracts;
all your waves and your billows
have gone over me . . . .
I say to God, my rock,
"Why have you forgotten me?
Why must I walk about
        mournfully
because the enemy oppresses
        me?"
As with a deadly wound in my
        body,
my adversaries taunt me,
while they say to me continually,
"Where is your God?" (Ps 42:6-7, 9-10)

Whatever note of sadness may be expressed in Psalm 42, the Psalter ends
with a loud, crashing, crescendo of praise as witnessed in the concluding
verses of Psalm 150:

Praise him with clanging cymbals;
praise him with loud clashing
        cymbals!
Let everything that breathes praise
        the LORD!
Praise the LORD! (Ps 150:5-6)

Notes

[1] Brevard S. Childs, *Old Testament Theology in a Canonical Context*
(Philadelphia: Fortress Press, 1988), 64.

[2] See discussion dealing with the "avenger of blood" in chapter eight under
"clan."

[3] Mark E. Biddle, "Murder," *Mercer Dictionary of the Bible*, ed. Watson E. Mills
et al. (Macon: Mercer University Press, 1990), 589.

[4] Walter Brueggemann, "Exodus," *The New Interpreter's Bible*, vol. 1 (Nashville:
Abingdon Press, 1994), 873.

[5] Ibid., 870.

[6] The book of Genesis tells that Jacob bound himself to Laban as a debt slave for 14 years for the favor of marriage to Rachel and Leah. See Gen 29.

[7] Brueggemann, 870.

[8] Hanson, *The People Called: The Growth of Community in the Bible* (New York: Harper and Row, 1986), 75.

[9] James Muilenburg, *The Way of Israel: Biblical Faith and Ethics* (New York: Harper Torchbooks, 1961),108.

[10] Hayyim Schauss, *Guide to Jewish Holy Days: History and Observance* (New York: Schocken Books, 1938), 38ff.

[11] For further discussion, refer to earlier chapter titled, "Tending God's World," where the question of animal sacrifice is discussed.

[12] Schauss, 38.

[13] For Christians it is important to remember that Jesus instituted the Lord's Supper as he ate the Passover meal with his disciples. The New Testament also demonstrates the close relationship between the Passover and the Feast of Unleavened Bread in the Gospel accounts of the Lord's Supper. (See Mt 26:17-19 or Mk 14:12-15)

[14] Ibid., 86-95.

[15] Ibid., 208ff., 237ff.

[16] Ibid., 173.

[17] William G. Dever, "Shechem," *Mercer Dictionary of the Bible*, ed. Watson E. Mills et al. (Macon: Mercer University Press, 1990), 816-19.

[18] Walter E. Brown, "Moriah, Mount," *Mercer Dictionary of the Bible*, ed. Watson E. Mills et al. (Macon: Mercer University Press, 1990), 583.

[19] Michael C. Astour, "Salem," *The Anchor Dictionary of the Bible*, edited by David Noel Freedman, vol. 5 (New York: Doubleday, 1992), 905.

[20] Allen Kerkeslager, "Mt. Sinai — in Arabia?" in *Bible Review*, vol. 16, no. 2 (April 2000), 32-33.

[21] Ibid., 33ff.

[22] Duane L. Christensen, "Sinai," *Mercer Dictionary of the* Bible, ed. Watson E. Mills et al. (Macon: Mercer University Press, 1990), 828-29.

[23] Walter Zimmerli, *Old Testament Theology in Outline* (Atlanta: John Knox Press, 1978), 149.

[24] Alfred Sendry, *Music in Ancient Israel* (New York: Philosophical Library, 1969), 489.

[25] Muilenburg, 110.

10

Sin

Happy are those whose
     transgression is forgiven,
whose sin is covered.
Happy are those to whom the
     LORD imputes no iniquity,
and in whose spirit there is no
     deceit.
While I kept silence, my body
     wasted away
through my groaning all day
     long.
For day and night your hand was
     heavy upon me;
my strength was dried up as
     by the heat of summer.
Then I acknowledge my sin to
     you,
and I did not hide my iniquity;
I said, "I will confess my
     transgressions to the LORD,"
and you forgave the guilt of
     my sin.
Therefore let all who are faithful
offer prayer to you;
at a time of distress, the rush of
     mighty waters
shall not reach them. (Ps 32:1-6)

Have mercy on me, O God,
according to your steadfast love;
according to your abundant mercy
blot out my transgressions.
Wash me thoroughly from my
     iniquity,
and cleanse me from my sin . . .
Create in me a clean heart,
     O God,
and put a new and right spirit
     within me. (Ps 51:1-2, 10)

Introduction

In the previous chapter we noted that there are psalms in the Israelite Psalter
that speak to almost every human experience and feeling. For instance, there
are psalms that address human sinfulness, sin's disruptive consequences, and
human expressions of regret. There are other psalms that address disrupted
losses brought on by so-called "acts of God" (earthquakes or disease for
example). Again, there are those that speak of hope for a better life. All of the
above ideas need to be explored more fully than has been done thus far in
this theology. This chapter deals primarily with sin in the lives of individuals
and community.

Our paradigm passages are an excellent place to begin our study of sin in
the Old Testament. First, they use several of the many words in Israel's
vocabulary for sin. Second, if they reflect David's affair with Bathsheba, as
they may, we are reminded that historical context is important for the study
of any theological idea — in this case, sin. Third, they address the idea of the
psalmist's original reluctance to confess his sin, which leads to a searing conscience. Fourth, they speak of God's forgiveness of the psalmist, leading to
the feeling of peace and security that swept over him.

The outline for the remainder of this chapter shall follow in a general
way the above reflections on the paradigm passages. We shall first examine
sin as expressed in Old Testament vocabulary. That shall be followed by
reflections based on Wisdom, Mosaic, Prophetic, and narrative literature.
After that we shall examine humanity's and the Deity's attitudes toward sin.

We close out this introductory section with a word about the titles or
superscriptions of the individual psalms. It is generally understood that the
titles were assigned at a time when various smaller collections were being

formed rather than assigned by their authors. According to these titles, over half of them are related to David in some fashion. The Hebrew term *le+david* may be translated as "by, to, or for David." This is true of our two paradigm passages, Psalms 32 and 51. The superscription of Psalm 51 adds "when the prophet Nathan came to him after he had gone into Bathsheba." Further, it is suggested by some interpreters that Psalm 32 follows Psalm 51 as an expression of David's blessed condition upon experiencing God's forgiveness. It seems safe to say that these Psalms can profitably be read in this way, whatever the final decision concerning David's authorship and historical context. During the course of this chapter when the two psalms are being discussed, the reader is invited to read them in this way.[1]

Sin Terminology

Concerning terminology, Robin Cover points out that the Old Testament contains over fifty words for sin.

> Israelite literature draws upon a rich thesaurus for terminology relating to sin. One may count over fifty words for "sin" in biblical Hebrew, if specific as well as generic terms are isolated . . . . The plethora of Hebrew terms and their ubiquitous presence in the Hebrew Bible testify to the fact that sin was a dominant concern of the Israelite theologians. Indeed, their highlighting of human failure, deficiency, or offense in the cultic, ethical, and moral spheres constitutes a central theme of Old Testament theology.[2]

Four of the most important Old Testament words for sin are joined together in close fashion in the opening verse of Psalm 32. We shall limit our discussion on sin terminology to them. First, listen to the psalmist:

Happy are those whose
    transgression [*Pesha*] is forgiven,
whose sin [*(C)Hata*] is covered.
Happy are those to whom the
    LORD imputes no iniquity [*Avon*],
and in whose spirit there is no
    deceit [*Remiyah*]. (Ps 32:1-2)

Transgression

The first word for sin used in the passage is "transgression" (*Pesha*). Perhaps a stronger and more meaningful word for *pesha* would be "rebellion." While the word *pesha* is not used by the Genesis storyteller concerning Adam and Eve's misdeeds in the garden, the word is appropriate. Robin Cover points out that *pesha* "signifies willful, knowledgeable violation of a norm or standard."[3] Certainly this would apply to such a Decalogue command as "You shall not steal" (Exod 20:15). Perhaps it cannot be said that the couple in the garden violated such a norm. It was more the violation of a specific command pertaining to their situation.

Iniquity

The translators of the New Revised Standard Version render the Hebrew word *avon* as "iniquity," a rather fuzzy English word. As Cover points out, the word *avon* may carry with it the idea of some deliberate moral error or the guilt and/or punishment that follows. For instance, the New Revised Standard Version renders *avon* as "punishment" in the Genesis account of Cain's slaying of Abel. Is Cain saying in the following passage that he cannot bear his sin, or his guilt, or his punishment: "My punishment is greater than I can bear"? (Gen 4:13). Robin Cover remarks:

> In Genesis 4:13, . . . it [*avon*] clearly signifies "guilt" (forensic and psychological) or "punishment," (penal), and probably connotes both.[4]

Sin

The all encompassing Old Testament word for "sin" is neither *pasha* (transgression, rebellion) nor *avon* (iniquity, guilt). Rather it is *[C]Hata*, often simply translated as "sin." It means something like missing a road or a mark (like the bull's-eye on a target). Concerning the latter, see Judges 20:16 on the exploits of proficient archers who do not miss the mark or bull's-eye. Concerning missing the way, note the following words in Proverbs:

> Desire without knowledge is
>   not good,
> and one who moves too
>   hurriedly misses the way. (Prov 19:2)

The word *hatah* is so broad in its meaning or scope that it can include deeds, as Cover states, that are "unconscious, inadvertent, or unavoidable."[5] Another way of stating this is to say that God demands perfection.[6] It should be noted that the author of Psalm 32 was convinced that the same God who demanded perfection also provided the full measure of grace needed to deal with sin. See more about grace later in the chapter.

Deceit

We close out our study of the words in Psalm 32 with *Remiyah,* rendered "deceit" in the New Revised Standard Version. Does the psalmist mean that a person who is honest with himself or one who is honest with others is blessed? Perhaps the two cannot be separated.

In closing out our section on terminology, we will do well to heed the words of Robin Cover who insists that the four words examined, along with others, are often used interchangeably. As he puts it, it may be that the words "have lost some of their crisp distinctiveness, and are employed as virtual synonyms."[7] In any case, together they help us to understand the Israelite concept of sin.

Sin in Wisdom, Mosaic, Prophetic, and Narrative Literature

As we approach sin from the standpoint of Israelite literature, the reader should expect no hard and fixed distinctions in the various kinds of literature. For instance, while Wisdom literature (Proverbs, Job, and Ecclesiastes) speaks more of the sense of sin based on observation than it does the infraction of laws, it does not follow that various contributors to the Wisdom literature were unaware of such statutes. Likewise, if the Mosaic legal system addresses itself more often to specific demands of God than it does observation, it does not follow that Moses, and other contributors of the law, were unaware of the latter.

Sin in Wisdom Literature

The teachers of wisdom are more likely to speak of the keeping of proper codes of conduct than the keeping of specific laws. For instance, there are codes of conduct within the family where respect of all family members is expected (Prov 4:1ff; 12:4; 11:29). There are also codes of conduct for members of the community (Prov 11:1ff; 22:22ff; 24:23ff).

Rather than carry on an exhaustive organized discussion of sin based on selected passages from the Wisdom literature, we now turn our attention to a lengthy speech in Job 31 in which Job seeks to justify his integrity. Prior to this speech he has been informed by three special friends that his sinfulness is the cause of his suffering. During the same time, Job has been complaining that his suffering is the result of God's faulty judgment.

When Job maintains in his speech (Job 31) that *if* he has done so and so, he means that he *has not done* those things. In other words, he has not breached the community's code of conduct. By observing the elements of the community's code of conduct that he claims not to have breeched, we arrive at a sort of select summary of that code. In many ways it parallels the laws contained in the law codes in the Pentateuch examined in the previous chapter. As the reader reads Job 31, along with the summary of that chapter that follows below, the reader needs to keep in mind that Job is depicted in the opening part of the book of Job as quite likely a non-Israelite or a Gentile (Job 1:1). However, as Carol Newsom points out, this fact may play no significant role in the book as it now stands:

> Whatever the origins of the figure of Job, his story has been naturalized into Israelite religious culture, so that Job is presented unself-consciously as a worshipper of Yahweh (1:21).[8]

We begin the summary of Job's community code of conduct, based on Job's speech, by noting that nothing is to be given priority over God (Job 31:24-28). Further, the code demands integrity in the community's basic institution, namely, the family. Spouses must be utterly faithful to each other (31:1, 9-12). Concerning the larger family, servants (including slaves) must be treated with fairness and respect (31:13). The destitute (widows, orphans, strangers) must not be mistreated but rather must be aided in every possible way in terms of lodging, food, clothing, et cetera (31:16-21, 32). The community elite (court leaders) must be absolutely fair in all dealings (31:4-7). Landowners must be good stewards of their land (31:38-40).

Sin in the Mosaic Legal Code

Whereas Job can claim he has not been guilty of apostasy or moral error without going into detail about specific laws or rules that he has not broken, such laws are set forth in some detail in that portion of the Pentateuch beginning with the book of Exodus. Since in the previous chapter we have dealt with Mosaic laws and regulations concerning apostasy and moral error, it will not be necessary to repeat that information here. However, some comments need to be made concerning sin dealing with uncleanness in Mosaic legislation. Even though the laws of the Pentateuch that address uncleanness are not considered as important for modern Christians as they are for modern Jews, Christians at least need to be aware of them.

The Mosaic legislation (especially in its Levitical statements) makes no hard and fast distinction between apostasy, moral errors, and uncleanness. Take for examples some stipulations from the book of Leviticus:

> When any of you sin in that you have heard a public adjuration to testify and . . . does not speak up, you are subject to punishment. Or when any of you touch any unclean thing — whether the carcass of an unclean beast . . . . Or when you touch human uncleanness . . . . Or when any of you utter aloud a rash oath . . . . When you realize your guilt in any of these, you shall confess the sin that you have committed. And you shall bring to the LORD, as your penalty for the sin that you have committed, a female from the flock, a sheep or a goat, as a sin offering; and the priest shall make atonement on your behalf for your sin. (Lev 5:1-6)

The Mosaic law concerning uncleanness may be classified under four headings: persons, animals/food, places, objects. For example, three types of personal uncleanness are highlighted: that caused by male discharge (semen) and female discharge (blood), that caused by contact with dead bodies, and that caused by skin eruptions such as leprosy. All of these were considered serious enough to cause the individual to be excluded for a period of time from the tabernacle/temple in particular or from society in general. The book of Numbers expresses it thusly:

> The LORD spoke to Moses, saying: Command the Israelites to put out of the camp everyone who is leprous, or has a discharge, and everyone who is unclean through contact with a corpse; you shall put out both male and female, putting them outside the camp; they must not defile their camp, where I shall dwell among them. (Num 5:1-3)

As to human uncleanness related to food animals, the problem could involve such matters as to how the animal died and whether there remained blood in the animal. The Levitical Code states:

You shall not eat the blood of any creature, for the life of every creature is its blood; whoever eats of it shall be cut off. All persons, citizens or aliens, who eat what dies of itself or what has been torn by wild animals, shall wash their clothes, and bathe themselves in water, and be unclean until evening; then they shall be clean. But if they do not wash themselves or bathe their body, they shall bear the guilt. (Lev 17:14-16)

Besides the aforementioned matters, some creatures, by their very nature, were considered unclean. Animals, fish, birds, and insects were divided into clean and unclean categories as seen in the following words of Deuteronomy 14:

Yet of those [animals] . . . you shall not eat these: the camel, the hare, and the rock badger . . . they are unclean for you. And the pig . . . is unclean for you . . . . Of all that live in water . . . whatever does not have fins and scales you shall not eat; it is unclean for you. . . . These are the ones [birds] that you shall not eat: the eagle, the vulture, the osprey, the buzzard, the kite . . . And all winged insects are unclean for you. (Deut 14:7ff)

In most cases, places and objects could be considered clean until made unclean by touching something unclean. For instance, Leviticus 14 gives some idea of how and to what extent a house becomes unclean by contact with a leprous body, and what should be done with it. If, upon examination, the priest found greenish or reddish spots on the wall caused by leprosy, he might have the spots scraped off the wall and the house vacated for a period of time. If that did not correct the situation, he might have the house torn down and otherwise destroyed (Lev 14:33ff).

We close out this section on Mosaic legalism as it involved uncleanness. Consider the remarks of L. E. Toombs:

The God who had delivered the nation, and who as its king gave the nation his law, had included the purity laws as part of his will. There was, therefore, no possibility of evading them as trivial or of regarding them as of lesser importance than the moral laws. They were part of the constitution of Israel's national life, and their observance was an inescapable necessity if the obligations of the covenant were to be met.[9]

Sin in the Prophets

When we move from "Sin in the Mosaic Legal Code" to "Sin in the Prophets," we move from something like a system of laws to an indictment of those who break the laws. The book of Hosea relates,

> Hear the word of the LORD,
>   O people of Israel;
>   for the LORD has an indictment
>   against the inhabitants
>   of the land. (Hos 4:1)

While we might expect a prophet such as Hosea to say, "You are being indicted for breaking such and such Mosaic law," that is not the case. On the other hand, it is hard to imagine that Hosea was unfamiliar with the various Mosaic laws. He does accuse the priests, who were required to teach the Torah, of forgetting "the law [*Torah*] of God" (Hos 4:6). While the term "law" in this passage may be a general reference to instruction, surely it includes Mosaic instruction. It would be hard to believe otherwise when Hosea in the same passage indicts the Israelites of swearing, lying, murder, stealing, and adultery (Hos 4:2).

Just as the Mosaic Decalogue divides its rules into two broad categories of human relationships to God on the one hand, and human relationships to humanity on the other, so we find the same divisions in the Prophets. There is no better evidence for this point than the words of Jeremiah.

> For if you truly amend your ways and your doings, if you truly act justly one with another, if you do not oppress the alien, the orphan, and the widow, or shed innocent blood in this place, and if you do not go after other gods to your hurt, then I will dwell with you in this place, in the land that I gave of old to your ancestors for ever and ever. (Jer 7:5-7)

While the prophets held that all persons are responsible to other humans (especially the unfortunate), persons in authority and those with special assets bore an extra heavy responsibility. Note the terrible indictment that Micah brought on these persons of special authority (kings, prophets, priests):

Thus says the LORD concerning
     the prophets
who lead my people astray,
who cry "Peace"
when they have something to
     eat,
but declare war against those
who put nothing into their
     mouths....
Hear this, you rulers of the house
     of Jacob
and chiefs of the house of Israel,
who abhor justice
and pervert all equity,
who build Zion with blood
and Jerusalem with wrong!
Its rulers give judgment for a
     bribe,
its priests teach for a price,
its prophets give oracles
     for money. (Mic 3:5, 9-11)

In various places in his prophetic message, Amos speaks out strongly against the economically powerful who abuse their power:

Thus says the LORD:
For three transgressions of Israel,
     and for four, I will not revoke
     the punishment;
because they sell the righteous
     for silver,
     and the needy for a pair of
     sandals —
they who trample the head of
     poor into the dust of
     the earth. (Amos 2:6-8)

Sin in Narrative Literature

One of the most interesting and instructive approaches to a study of sin in the Old Testament is through narrative. Since the presentation of many sin stories would be overwhelming, another approach will be necessary. First, we shall list ten separate sin stories that express a variety of types, followed by a longer discussion of David and Bathsheba, and Adam and Eve.

Ten Selected Stories
1) Adam and Eve's eating of the forbidden fruit (Gen 3)
2) Cain's killing of Abel (Gen 4)
3) The extreme corruption of the people of Noah's era (Gen 6)
4) Pharaoh's enslavement of the Israelites (Exod 1)
5) Israelite apostasy in the making of the golden calf (Exod 32)
6) Achan's stealing of the forbidden war booty (Josh 7)
7) Citizens of Bethel's violent rape of a concubine (Judg 19)
8) David's affair with Bathsheba (2 Sam 11)
9) Solomon's worship of foreign gods (1 Kgs 11)
10) Jezebel's ruthless destruction of Naboth (1 Kgs 21)

David and Bathsheba. At a time in his life when David had established a kingdom composed of all the tribes and was in the process of securing rule over several adjoining kingdoms, he had an adulterous affair with Bathsheba. Second Samuel introduces the story as follows:

> In the spring of the year, at the time when kings go out to battle, David sent Joab with his officers and all Israel with him; they ravaged the Ammonites, and besieged Rabbah. But David remained at Jerusalem. It happened, late one afternoon, when David rose from his couch and was walking about on the roof of the king's house, that he saw from the roof a woman bathing; the woman was very beautiful. David sent someone to inquire about the woman. It was reported, "This is Bathsheba daughter of Eliam, the wife of Uriah the Hittite." So David sent messengers to get her, and she came to him, and he lay with her. (2 Sam 11:1-4)

Upon learning that Bathsheba was pregnant, David set in motion a process that eventually would result in Uriah's death. At first, David ordered Uriah, Bathsheba's husband and one of David's mercenary soldiers, to be sent home from the battlefield and to report to David. David instructed Uriah to go home apparently in the hope that Uriah would be thought to be the father of Bathsheba's baby. When Uriah refused to go home, even after David had made him drunk, David sent Uriah back to the battlefront and ordered his military commander to place Uriah in an extremely dangerous place where he would die at the hands of the enemy.

When it was reported to David that Uriah was dead, David quickly made Bathsheba one of his wives. At this point, Nathan, David's court prophet, accused David of sin and foretold that terrible calamities would befall David's family. As an old saying goes, David had sown the wind and he will reap the whirlwind. (2 Sam 11)

Adam and Eve and the Primal Sin. The first of the Old Testament sin narratives tells the story of Adam's and Eve's eating of the fruit of the forbidden tree. Whereas God had warned them that disobedience would bring death, a crafty serpent assured them that nothing of the sort would happen. In fact, he said that the tree would bestow on them the rich benefits of being "like God, knowing good and evil" (Gen 3:5). Upon eating of the fruit, the couple did acquire new knowledge, among other things, knowledge of their nakedness. This was followed by devastating alienation: alienation from each other, their bodies, and from God.

The couple's sin is designated as primal not because it is thought of as the fountainhead from which thereafter all human sins flow, but simply because it is the first of many more like it. It should be made clear that there are interpreters who choose not to see the couple's act as sin; at least, they feel that the couple's disobedience should not dominate our thinking about the story as it is recorded. Typical of this position is that of Carol Myers as set forth in her work *Discovering Eve*.

> None of the words that are part of the Hebrew vocabulary for sin and transgression are present in the story. Even when God utters the fateful words leading to the banishment of the primeval couple from their idyllic life in the well-watered garden, only the specific act — the eating of the fruit of a tree that was forbidden — is cited. Interpreters may label this act as disobedient; exegetes may consider it sinful. But *God* does not provide such a judgement within either the narration or the discourse of Genesis 3.[10]

But if sin is rebellion against God (*pesha*) or the failure to walk the path intended by God (*[C]Hata*), then surely sin is involved in the story even if not so designated by the Hebrew vocabulary for sin.

Before leaving the subject, it should be noted that there are those who look upon the couple's action as necessary for the maturing of the human race. Among the variety of positions on this view is the one posited by Ellen

Wolde, who sees the expulsion from the garden (brought on by the eating of the forbidden fruit) as a God-planned (at least, God approved) step toward human maturity. After all, the home that God ultimately intended for the couple was not the garden-home but the earth-home. The following section sufficiently demonstrates Wolde's position:

> The moment that one begins to realize that [Genesis] 2:24 is an account of the man's growing up and that a similar kind of behavior can be seen in the human being towards God, the reader can ask whether Genesis 2–3 as a whole is not a reflection of this process of growing up or becoming adult. In that case this account of the garden of Eden is a picture of a harmonious youth in which the human being is a unity with the world around him/her. The limits which God sets, the prohibition and the sanction on the transgression of the prohibition, are comparable to the position occupied by parents. The limits which they set are there to protect them against pain, misery and death. The phase of the transgression of the prohibition then stands for puberty, in which the woman and the man come to years of discretion . . . . In puberty, in the years of going beyond the limits which have been set, girls and boys acquire capacities for discernment, sexual awareness and the capacity to procreate. It is a necessary phase, since precisely by going beyond the set limits which were intended to protect them as children, they attain insight and autonomy. In this way the necessary conditions for an adult life and for the maintenance of life are fulfilled. Finally, the period of adulthood begins with the man and woman being driven out of the garden. The unity with things is lost; differences and pain takes its place; continuity becomes discontinuity and simplicity complexity. And so the story of paradise can be read as a parable about the human maturation process.[11]

While the above interpretation with its positive spin is very appealing, the following words of Terence Fretheim must also be considered.

> There are, in fact, few signs that the human lot improves [with the human sin and divine expulsion], from either the divine or human perspective. All signs are that death (in the comprehensive sense) has become a pervasive reality with which humanity must deal, and that far from being marked by a new maturity or freedom, human life now entails broken relationships with God and every other creature.[12]

God's Attitude and Response to Sin

As we close out this study of sin, we examine God's attitude and response to sin before we look at that of humanity, because God will have both the first and last word about humanity's misdeeds. God is the provider of the order humanity is expected to observe and also of special laws and regulations that humanity is to obey. This order and these laws have been previously discussed — *to breech them is to sin.*

When humans breech God's universal or special laws they set in motion tragic consequences on themselves individually, corporately, and on the rest of creation. Over and over again the Old Testament expresses God's disappointment at humanity's actions. Of necessity, punishment will follow. Such punishment will not be capricious. Rather, it will be designed to restore harmony to God's entire creation. Further, it will be tempered by God's compassion. Note the following words of God to Moses upon Moses's receipt of the second set of stone tablets (the ten commandments) following Moses's angry destruction of the first set upon seeing the golden calf erected by the people:

> "The LORD, the LORD,
> a God merciful and gracious,
> slow to anger,
> and abounding in steadfast love
>   and faithfulness,
> keeping steadfast love for the
>   thousandth generation,
> forgiving iniquity and
>   transgression and sin,
> yet by no means clearing the
>   guilty, . . . " (Exod 34:6-7)

Similar words of God concerning his compassion are cited by Hosea.

> How can I give you up, Ephraim?
> How can I hand you over,
>   O Israel?
> How can I make you like Admah?
> How can I treat you like
>   Zeboiim?
> My heart recoils within me;

my compassion grows warm
    and tender.
I will not execute my fierce anger;
I will not again destroy
    Ephraim. (Hos 11:8-9)

In Psalm 51, David appeals to God on the basis of God's compassionate nature:

Have mercy ([c]*hanan*) on me, O God,
according to your steadfast love (*[C]Hesed*);
according to your abundant mercy [motherly compassion] (*rahamim*)
blot out my transgression. (Ps 51:1)

God's compassion, however, is not just an expression of God's own nature. It is also an expression of God's understanding of the nature of humanity. For instance, after almost wiping out humanity by the flood during the days of Noah, God declares never again to exercise such drastic measures because it will serve no ultimately good purpose since humanity by nature will continue to sin. "I will never again curse the ground because of humankind, for the inclination of the human heart is evil from youth" (Gen 8:21).

A similar idea is expressed by one of the psalmists who assesses Israel's see-saw (faithful/unfaithful) historical relationship to God:

When he killed them, they sought
    for him;
they repented and sought God
    earnestly.
They remembered that God was
    their rock,
the most High God their
    redeemer.
But they flattered with him their
    mouths;
they lied to him, with their
    tongues.
Their heart was not steadfast
    toward him;
they were not true to his
    covenant.

> Yet he, being compassionate,
> forgave their iniquity,
> and did not destroy them;
> often he restrained his anger,
> and did not stir up all his wrath.
> He remembered that they were
> but flesh. (Ps 78:34-39)

The word flesh (*basar*) used above does not of necessity in this case refer to a sinful inclination. It may simply refer to humanity's weakness in comparison with God's strength. In any case, humanity, in its weakness, is prone to temptation leading to sin.

In the numerous Old Testament sin stories we are told of God's involvement. Note the following examples from the Pentateuch: to Adam and Eve, God inquires, "Where are you?" (Gen 3:9); to Cain, God asks, "Where is your brother?" (Gen 4:9); to Noah, God says, "I have determined to make an end of all flesh." (Gen 6:13); and concerning the Israelites, God speaks to Moses, "Now let me alone, so that my wrath may burn hot against them" (Exod 32:10).

When God speaks of burning divine wrath in the above passage, God seems to be referring to some direct punishment awaiting Israel. However, it is true that God's punishment is sometimes brought about by God's standing aside to allow life to take its natural course. How shall we, for instance, read God's words to Adam and Eve after they ate of the forbidden fruit? How shall the following words to Eve be taken?

> "I will greatly increase your pangs
>   in childbearing;
> in pain you shall bring forth
>   children,
> yet your desire shall be for your
>   husband,
> and he shall rule over you." (Gen 3:16)

While the passage seems to be saying that God is destining Eve to pain in childbirth and dominance by her husband, there are interpreters who see this as God's letting sin naturally work itself out in their lives. For instance, Phyllis Trible, working closely with the Hebrew text, claims that the sin of Adam and Eve brought about a situation that was allowed by God rather than directly caused by God. She states, "God describes this consequence but does not prescribe it as punishment."[13]

Humanity's Attitude and Response to Sin

When humans sin, they either do so because they choose to do so, or they inadvertently slip into some misdeed. In our discussion above concerning the Hebrew word [C]Hastah, "sin," we noted that the term is so broad in its meaning that it can include "unconscious, inadvertent, or unavoidable deeds."[14] However, it can safely be said that sin is more often Pesha, "transgression." That is to say, the transgressor knows that he/she is living outside the will of God.

How does the sinner react once he/she has been made to confront sin directly by God or indirectly by the troubles brought on by his/her misdeeds? In the case of Adam and Eve, they began immediately to respond: they covered their nakedness, they hid from God, and they placed blame on the other rather than self. As for Cain, when God confronted him about Abel's absence, he acted like God had unfairly pointed an accusing finger in his face. The story of David, as recorded in 2 Samuel, indicates that he began a cover-up as soon as he learned of Bathsheba's pregnancy (2 Sam 11). According to Psalm 32, David speaks of this time as a time of silence followed by a time of admission and confession (Ps 32:3, 5).

Between the sin and the confession, David experiences a searing conscience (like a desert heat), which he attributes to God. He speaks of God's heavy hand on him. During the experience he claims that his body wasted away, whether literally or figuratively we do not know. His groaning, as he expresses it, was like the warnings of a roaring lion. Such an oppressive conscience eventuates into a confession to God (Ps 32:3-5).

Pricked by his conscience, David longs for forgiveness and re-creation. In his prayer as recorded in Psalm 51, he begs for both an inward and outward cleansing. Inwardly he asks God to create within him a clean heart and a right spirit. Outwardly he asks that he be sprinkled with a hyssop branch and be thoroughly washed. David's request for outward cleansing reminds us of the Mosaic instructions concerning cleansing in connection with some terrible disease such as leprosy (Lev 14, Num 19).

Having experienced the forgiveness and re-creation for which he had prayed (Psalm 51), David could then joyously say (Ps 32):

> Happy are those whose
>   transgression is forgiven [lifted up] (*nasa*)
> whose sin is covered. (*Kesu*)
> Happy are those to whom the
>   LORD imputes no (*[c]hashav*) iniquity,
> and in whose spirit there is no
>   deceit. (Ps 32:1-2)

In Psalm 32, David expresses what God has done for him in three ways. First, he says that God "imputes no (*[c]hashav*) iniquity." That is to say, God does not charge him with sin or no longer holds him accountable for sin. We may consider this an image from the financial world. The same God who makes provisions for humans no longer to be held accountable for human debt at the end of seven years, in order to give the debtor another chance, could hardly be expected to do less (Deut 15).

In the second place, David speaks of God covering (*Kesu*) his sins. God even provided the Israelites a special cultic day when such covering took place. We know it as the Day of Atonement or *Yom Kippur*, "Day of Covering." Thus, what God declares to be covered, man should do likewise.

Third, the forgiveness [lifted up] (*nasa*) of which David speaks is also closely related to the Day of Atonement. When he declares that his sin has been forgiven, he means that it has been taken up and carried away as it was done by the ritual ceremony of the scapegoat who, on the Day of Atonement, carries the sins of the people into the wilderness (Lev 16).

In Psalm 51 David has said that if God would forgive him and create in him a new heart, he would instruct other sinners so that many of them could return to their God. Having experienced that forgiveness, he can declare in Psalm 32 that he is now ready to teach them in the way they should go. Having opened the psalm with an expression of happiness for God's gracious activity in the past, David closes the psalm with an invitation for other forgiven sinners to rejoice with him:

> Be glad in the LORD and rejoice,
>   O righteous,
>   and shout for joy, all you
>   upright in heart. (Ps 32:11)

Biblical Sin and English Literature

The Bible probably has had a more formative influence on English literature than any other single book. One of the prominent themes dealt with in both is sin. Among the valuable sources that deal with the Bible and English literature is *A Dictionary of Biblical Tradition in English Literature*. The title of the aforementioned book is somewhat of a misnomer since the work is much broader than what the title suggests. Besides discussion of various examples of English literature, most entries (like the entry for "Cain") also contain some biblical exegesis and the historical usage of the subject by great leaders of the church such as Augustine, Aquinas, Luther, and Calvin.

The book is large, containing hundreds of entries in over 800 pages. An extra 100 pages deal with such bibliographic matters as concordances, Hebrew and Greek grammars, commentaries, history of Bible translations, influence of the Bible on English literature, and English authors and their works. Included among the authors are Bunyan, Byron, Coleridge, Dickens, Faulkner, Frost, Hawthorne, Hemingway, Joyce, Lawrence, Longfellow, Melville, Milton, Shakespeare, and Wordsworth. From the entries related to sin, we choose two that reflect humankind's inhumanity to each other and the resulting estrangement that follows: Cain and Absalom.

The entry on "Cain" is written by James M. Dean. Among the works that Dean discusses is Byron's drama "Cain: A Mystery." According to Dean, Byron "exploits the moral and psychological complexities of Cain's situation after his brother's death at Cain's hand, and Cain's subsequent wandering in search of fertile ground following God's curse of Cain's land." As Dean explains, Byron's play depicts Cain as not only cut off from his beloved soil but his family as well. Dean continues: "Cain bitterly criticizes his parents for depriving him of his inheritance, Eden, and for preferring Abel to him . . . . After the murder, Eve delivers a terrible curse on her firstborn, banishing him from the Adamic fellowship" (122). Like the story of Cain, the story of Absalom deals with fratricide. Absalom, a son of King David, ordered his half brother Amnon killed for Amnon's rape of Tamar, half sister of Amnon and full sister of Absalom. Absalom probably also contemplated the assassination of his father as part of a conspiracy to dethrone David. In the end, the uprising failed, Absalom was killed, and David deeply mourned Absalom's death. (2 Sam 13–18)

The entry on "Absalom" is written by Frans De Bruyn, who summarizes Faulkner's novel *Absalom, Absalom!* A part of the summary follows:

> Faulkner's profound reenactment of the narrative in his novel *Absalom, Absalom!* (1936) is centered around the triad of Thomas Sutpen, his son Henry, and Henry's half-brother Charles Bon, a triangle reflecting the David/Absalom relationship in 2 Samuel 13. Like Absalom, who murders his half-brother Amnon in revenge for the latter's drunken rape of Absalom's sister Tamar, Henry kills Charles to forestall his incestuous and miscegnational marriage to Henry's sister Judith . . . . Sutpen's house, like David's is doomed to play out the consequences of the father's sin . . . . In both families the failure of love ends in fratricide and civil war. (14)

Notes

James M. Dean, "Cain," in A Dictionary of Biblical Tradition in English Literature.
Frans De Bruyn, "Absalom," in A Dictionary of Biblical Tradition in English Literature.
David Lyle Jeffrey, ed., A Dictionary of Biblical Tradition in English Literature (Grand
Rapids: William B. Eerdmans Publishing Company, 1992).

Notes

[1] For a fuller treatment of the Psalm titles in general and those of our two paradigm passages in particular, see J. Clinton McCann, Jr., "Psalms," in *The New Interpreter's Bible*, vol. 4 (Nashville: Abingdon Press, 1996), 641ff.

[2] Robin C. Cover, "Sin, Sinner," *The Anchor Bible Dictionary*, vol. 6 (New York: Doubleday, 1992), 31.

[3] Ibid., 32.

[4] Ibid.

[5] Ibid.

[6] No wonder Paul can assert that "All have sinned and come short of the glory of God" (Rom 3:23).

[7] Cover, 32.

[8] Carol A. Newsom, "Job," *The New Interpreter's Bible*, vol. 4 (Nashville: Abingdon Press, 1996), 345.

[9] L. E. Toombs, "Clean and Unclean," *Interpreter's Dictionary of the Bible*, vol. 1, 648.

[10] Carol Myers, *Discovering Eve: Ancient Israelite Women in Context* (New York: Oxford University Press, 1988), 87.

[11] Ellen van Wolde, *Stories of the Beginning: Genesis 1–11 and Other Creation Stories*, trans. John Bowden (Ridgefield CT: Morehouse Publishing, 1996), 60-61.

[12] Terence E. Frethiem, "The Book of Genesis," *The New Interpreter's Bible*, vol. 1 (Nashville: Abingdon Press, 1994), 368.

[13] Phyllis Trible, *The Rhetoric of Sexuality* (Philadelphia: Fortress Press, 1978), 128.

[14] Cover, 32.

11

Living Life Under Threat and with Distress

There was once a man in the land of Uz whose name was Job. That man was blameless and upright, one who feared God and turned away from evil. There were born to him seven sons and three daughters. He had seven thousand sheep, three thousand camels, five hundred yoke of oxen, five hundred donkeys, and very many servants, so that this man was the greatest of all the people of the east . . . . One day when his sons and daughters were eating and drinking wine in the eldest brother's house, a messenger came to Job and said, "The oxen were plowing and the donkeys were feeding beside them, and the Sebeans fell on them and carried them off, and killed the servants with the edge of the sword; I alone have escaped to tell you." While he was still speaking, another came and said, "The fire of God fell from heaven and burned up the sheep and the servants, and consumed them; I alone have escaped to tell you." While he was still speaking, another came and said, "The Chaldeans formed three columns, made a raid on the camels and carried them off, and killed the servants with the edge of the sword; I alone have escaped to tell you." While he was still speaking, another came and said, "Your sons and daughters were eating and drinking wine in their eldest brother's house, and suddenly a great wind came across the desert, stuck the four corners of the house, and it fell on the young people, and they are dead: I alone have escaped to tell you . . . . So Satan went out from the presence of the Lord, and inflicted loathsome sores on Job from the sole of his foot to the crown of his head. Job took a potsherd with which to scrape himself and sat among the ashes.

Then his wife said to him, "Do you still persist in your integrity? Curse God, and die. "But he said to her, "You speak as any foolish woman would speak. Shall we receive the good at the hand of God, and not receive the bad?" In all this, Job did not sin with his lips.

Now when Job's three friends heard of all these troubles that had come upon him, each of them set out from his home — Eliphaz the Temanite, Bildad the Shuhite, and Zophar the Naamathite. They met together to go and console and comfort him. When they saw him from a distance, they did not recognize him, and they raised their voices and wept aloud; they tore their robes and threw dust in the air upon their heads. They sat with him on the ground seven days and seven nights, and no one spoke a word to him, for they saw that his suffering was very great. (Job 1:1-3, 13-19; 2:7-13)

Introduction

According to the Old Testament, humanity is now living in the "in-between" times, between an ideal past and an ideal future. Isaiah pictures the ideal new age as reflective of the original ideal Eden:

> The wolf shall live with the lamb,
> the leopard shall lie down with
>   the kid,
> the calf and the lion and the
>   fatling together
> and a little child shall lead them . . .
> The nursing child shall play over
>   the hold of the asp,
> and the weaned child shall put
>   its hand on the adder's den (Isa 11:6, 8)

The time in which humanity now lives may be characterized by, among other things, disease, distress, sorrow, and hardship. Some of these things humanity has brought on itself by sin as we noted in the last chapter. Others may come from the so-called acts of God. In any case, some of the things are those caused by God directly or they are ones that God permits.

We close out our studies of Old Testament theology with "Living Life under Threat and with Distress" (ch. 11) and with "Living Life With Hope" (ch. 12).

Among the ways that a threat may be considered are: warning (for example, "click it or ticket" relative to auto seat belts), and danger or risk (for example, hurricanes in the United States are more likely during the summer seasons than the winter ones). Distress refers to some stress or burden a person is already experiencing such as interpersonal fractures, extreme poverty, illness, etc. Hope, characterized by such attitudes as expectation, confidence, and trust, shall be examined in the next chapter.

Like all the previous chapters, this one shall follow an organizing principle different from that used in the Old Testament. In any case, the approach must be rational and reasonable. For instance, we might begin with the question concerning the nature of the threat or the distress. One such threat or distress that runs through the entire Old Testament is violence. Again, we might organize the materials around the persons who suffer such violence. Finally, we could include a recitation of a narrative such as that of Cain and Abel, with commentary.

Rather than use the latter approaches, we shall use the first dealing with the nature of the threat or distress and weave into it the stories of persons. Concerning the nature of the threat or distress, we shall use a very simple two-part, overlapping outline: (1) interpersonal ruptures, and (2) deprivation and loss. What needs to be said about interpersonal ruptures is covered in some minimal fashion in the paradigm passage from the book of Job along with other passages from that book. For instance, death brings rupture between Job and his children. Moreover, the four areas on deprivation and loss to be covered below are also found in the book of Job: (1) poverty and economic loss; (2) humiliation and loss of honor; (3) disease and loss of health; (4) death and loss of life.

Interpersonal Ruptures

Family: Marital

One type of interpersonal rupture is marital rupture. Rupture is narrated very early in the Old Testament. Rupture plays an integral part in the story of Adam and Eve who, through sin, alienated themselves from each other and from God. The ultimate rupture might come through unfaithfulness of one of the spouses or through death. Concerning the latter, consider the fact that when Naomi lost her husband (along with her two sons) by death, she wished no longer to be known as Naomi (Hebrew for "pleasant") but Mara (Hebrew for "bitter") (Ruth 1:20).

Family: Parents and Children

The Old Testament is filled with examples of interpersonal ruptures between parents and their offspring. On his death bed, for example, Jacob gathers around him his sons and gives them his evaluation of each of them. He expresses great disappointment in Reuben, his firstborn, for having sexual relations with Bilhah, one of his concubines:[1]

> Reuben, you are my firstborn,
> my might and the first fruits of
>   my vigor,
> excelling in rank, and excelling
>   in power.
> Unstable as water, you shall no
>   longer excel
> because you went up unto your
>   father's bed; . . . (Gen 49:3-4)

Jacob's bitter feelings against Reuben, however, did not compare with his abhorrence at the cruelty and violence of Simeon and Levi towards humans and beasts as expressed in the following words;

> Simeon and Levi are brothers;
> weapons of violence are their
>   swords . . .
> For in their anger they killed men,
> and in their whim they
>   hamstrung oxen. (Gen 49:5-6)

The ruptures that come between parents and children are not always brought on by wrongdoing, at least not intentionally. For instance, the rupture that came between Jephthah and his unnamed daughter was brought on by an ill-conceived rash vow that Jephthah made to God and foolhardily kept. He vowed that if God would give him victory over the Ammonites he would sacrifice the first thing/person coming out of his dwelling. To his dismay, it was his daughter who met him (Judg 11).

Family: Siblings

The Old Testament is laced with stories of sibling rivalry, often with tragic results. For instance, Cain murdered his brother Abel out of extreme jealousy

(Gen 4). Again, Jacob, through sharp practice and deception, obtained his brother Esau's birthright and blessing. This led to thoughts of murder on Esau's part and flight on Jacob's part (Gen 25–27). Jacob's rivalry with Esau was later reflected in the rivalry between Jacob's own children. The latter rivalry became so intense that the brothers made arrangements for Joseph, one of the brothers, to be sold into slavery in Egypt (Gen 37–39). The sibling rivalry was not always limited to brothers. Such was the case between Moses and his sister Miriam. In the wilderness of Sinai, Miriam (along with her brother Aaron) publicly challenged Moses' authority as follows: "Has the LORD spoken only through Moses? Has he not spoken through us also?" (Num 12:2) God chided Miriam and Aaron for their challenging of Moses' authority and afflicted her with a disease for seven days (Num 12).

Gerstenberger summarizes the tragedy of family ruptures as follows:

> Thus according to the Old Testament, self-destructive forces are at work even in the most intimate circles of human society . . . . When a man cannot escape suffering even where of all places he might be secure, how then can he survive in other, that is, in larger and more impersonal contexts.[2]

Institutional Ruptures within a Group

The last sentence in the above quotation reminds us that ruptures take place in "larger and more impersonal contexts" as well as the local or nuclear family. This may take place within an authoritative group, between two authoritative persons or groups (prophets, priests, kings), and between those in authority and those under their authority.

Prophets. Clashes with invectives sometimes broke out within a particular authoritative institution such as the prophets. A good example of this is the conflict that took place between the prophet Jeremiah and the prophet Hananiah during the early years of the Babylonian intrusion into Judea. Hananiah declared that such "vessels of the LORD's house" carried into Babylonia would soon be returned. Jeremiah retorted that not only would those vessels not be returned but that other vessels would be taken away as well. Hananiah fought back by breaking a wooden yoke that Jeremiah wore around his neck as a symbol of the control that the Babylonians would eventually have over Judah and her neighbors. This was followed, in turn, by Jeremiah's prediction of Hananiah's impending death, which shortly occurred (Jer 27–28).

Priests. The narrative sections of the Old Testament do not have as strong an attestation of the conflict that took place within the priestly institution as the prophetic one. However, it can be found. For instance, the book of Numbers recounts how a very early Israelite priestly faction under the leadership of a certain Korah not only rebelled against the general leadership of Moses but also against the cultic leadership of Aaron. Hear the words, which Moses addresses to Korah and his followers:

> Then Moses said to Korah, "Hear now you Levites! Is it too little for you that the God of Israel has separated you from the congregation of Israel, to allow you to approach him in order to perform the duties of the LORD's tabernacle, and to stand before the congregation and serve him? He has allowed you to approach him, and all your brother Levites with you; yet you seek the priesthood as well! Therefore you and all your company have gathered together against the LORD. What is Aaron that you rail against him? (Num 16:8-11)

Kings. Generally, the conflict that took place within the institution of Israelite kingship was not between two kings but between a king and a military general who aspired to leadership. The most notable example is Jehu's coup against the Omri dynasty (Omri, his son Ahab, and his grandsons). Jehu killed Joram (Jehoram), son of Ahab, while he was recuperating from battle wounds. He followed that act by having Jezebel (Ahab's wife and Joram's mother) thrown from a window where she was trampled by horses and eaten by dogs. Wishing to make sure that neither he nor his dynasty could be so easily deposed, he ordered the death of seventy sons of Ahab (their heads were carried to Jezreel where Naboth had died by the orders of Ahab), along with forty-two Judean (southern kingdom) princes who were visiting in Israel (northern kingdom). Besides these, he destroyed numerous Baal prophets and worshippers of Baa. (2 Kgs 9–10). Biblical evaluation of his actions is mixed. Concerning the slaughter at Jezreel, the author of 2 Kings reports:

> The LORD said to Jehu, "Because you have done well in carrying out what I consider right, and in accordance with all that was in my heart have dealt with the house of Ahab, your sons of the fourth generation shall sit on the throne of Israel." (2 Kgs 10:30)

On the other hand, the book of Hosea reports that Hosea was instructed by God to name his son Jezreel as a symbol of God's punishment of Jehu's blood purge at Jezreel:

> And the LORD said to him [Hosea], "Name him Jezreel; for in a little while I will punish the house of Jehu for the blood of Jezreel, and I will put an end to the kingdom of the house of Israel." (Hos 1:4)

Institutional Ruptures between Groups

Sometimes the disruptive conflicts arose between authoritative persons or groups such as prophet and priest or prophet and king.

Prophet and Priest. Concerning prophet and priest, no conflict is more vividly presented than that between the headstrong prophet, Amos, and the equally headstrong priest of Bethel, namely, Amaziah:

> And Amaziah said to Amos, "O seer, go, flee away to the land of Judah, earn your bread there, and prophesy there; but never again prophesy at Bethel, for it is the king's sanctuary, and it is a temple of the kingdom."
> Then Amos answered Amaziah, . . .
> "Now therefore hear the word of
>   the LORD.
> You say, 'Do not prophecy against
>   Israel,
> and do not preach against the
>   House of Isaac.'
> Therefore thus says the LORD:
> 'Your wife shall become a
>   prostitute in the city,
> and your sons and your
>   daughters shall fall by
>   the sword,
> and your land shall be parceled
>   out by line;
> you yourself shall die in an
>   unclean land,
> and Israel shall surely go into
>   exile away from its land." (Amos 7:12-17)

Prophet and King. No contest between a king and a prophet is presented more graphically and with greater detail than as the one between King Ahab and the prophet Elijah. The story of the encounter between them, as narrated in the book of 1 Kings, begins with a recitation of the words of Elijah to the king, concerning an approaching three-year drought. This is followed three years later by a confrontation over Ahab's support of Baal worship, a contest on Mount Carmel between Elijah and 450 prophets of Baal, and the ultimate slaying of those prophets. When Elijah hears that Jezebel, Ahab's wife, has threatened to kill him in retaliation for the death of the Baal prophets, he flees hundreds of miles to the south to Mount Sinai. The narrator recites one more decisive confrontation between the two men. The last one deals with Ahab's confiscation of Naboth's vineyard. The words of the two men on that occasion, as quoted by the narrator, summarize very well the feelings that each man had for the other:

> Ahab said to Elijah, "Have you found me, O my enemy?" He answered, "I have found you. Because you have sold yourself to do what is evil in the sight of the LORD, I will bring disaster on you; I will consume you, and will cut off from Ahab every male, bond or free, in Israel; and I will make your house like the house of Jeroboam son of Nebat, and like the house of Baasha son of Ahijah, because you have provoked me to anger and have caused Israel to sin." (1 Kgs 21:20-22)

Deprivation and Loss

Poverty and Economic Loss

We move from interpersonal ruptures to deprivation and loss as an expression of threat and distress. We begin with poverty and economic loss. While the book of Job does not cover the whole spectrum of the Old Testament's presentation of economic loss or the nature and cause of poverty, it does offer a good place to begin. For instance, the opening prose chapters suggest the following possibilities: (1) plunderers/brigands might steal a person's animals (1:14-15, 17); (2) natural calamities might kill a person's animals or destroy his buildings (1:16, 18-19); some type of heavenly being, with God's permission, might be in control of the above tragic events (1:6-12).

Once we get into the lengthy poetic section of Job, other suggestions are made: according to Job's friends, economic loss is due to Job's own sin (4:7-8); according to Job, economic loss and poverty are due to God's unfair treatment (10:1-7); again, according to Job, poverty is due to the abuse of the poor by the wealthy, an abuse seemingly condoned by God who stands aside while the wealthy do their wicked deeds. Concerning the latter, Job remarks:

> The wicked remove the landmarks;
>   they seize flocks and pasture
>   them.
> They drive away the donkey of
>   the orphan;
> they take the widow's ox for a
>   pledge...
> From the city the dying groan,
>   and the throat of the wounded
>   cries for help;
> yet God pays no attention to
>   their prayer...
> They harm the childless
>   woman,
> and do no good to the widow.
> Yet God prolongs the life of the
>   mighty by his power;
> they rise up when they despair
>   of life.
> He gives them security, and they
>   are supported;
> his eyes are upon their ways. (Job 24:2-3, 12, 21-23)

It is true that the Old Testament as a whole holds God responsible in some fashion for economic loss or poverty, even if not unfairly as Job supposes. (Jeremiah entertains a view similar to that of Job as demonstrated in Jer 12:1ff.) God may do this directly by some natural calamity such as drought or indirectly by allowing the rich to abuse the poor. Of course, it may be that God's standing by while the rich abuse the poor may be due to his patience as well as his lack of compassion. In any case, it is difficult to draw a sharp line between such direct and indirect causes on God's part.

Certainly, the Deuteronomic code makes it clear that God is the source of economic loss or poverty when Israel disobeys God's laws. That Israel could expect prosperity in times of obedience and curses in times of disobedience is dramatically set forth in a series of blessings and curses that Moses addresses to the people near the end of their wilderness wanderings. The blessings and curses are introduced as follows:

> If you will only obey the Lord your God, by diligently observing all his commandments that I am commanding you today, the LORD your God will set you high above all the nations of the earth; all these blessings shall come upon you and overtake you, if you obey the LORD your God: But if you will not obey the LORD your God by diligently observing all his commandments and decrees, which I am commanding you today, then all these curses shall come upon you and overtake you. (Deut 28:1-2, 15)

As indicated in the blessing–curse passage of Deuteronomy 28, sin on the part of humans can be the cause of economic loss or poverty. The sin may be committed by the poor person or against him by someone else. For instance, the poor person may bring trouble on himself/herself by the lack of self-discipline in slackness of effort or misuse of finances. Note an instructive passage in the book of Proverbs:

> A little sleep, a little slumber,
> a little folding of the hands
>   to rest,
> and poverty will come upon you
>   like a robber,
> and want, like an armed
>   warrior. (Prov 6:10-11)

Of course, the Israelite sages knew that poverty was sometimes brought on by the hands of others rather than by the poor themselves. The following remarks are typical:

> Do not rob the poor because they
>   are poor,
> or crush the afflicted at the gate [place of political/economic jurisdiction];
> for the LORD pleads their cause
> and despoils of life those who
>   despoil them. (Prov 22:22-23)

This theme, concerning the mistreatment of the poor and unfortunate, runs throughout the Old Testament. Representative of the prophets are the following words of Micah:

> They [the rich and powerful] covet fields, and seize them;
> houses, and take them away;
> they oppress householder
>   and house,
> people and their inheritance. (Mic 2:2)

Humiliation and Loss of Honor

Erhard Gerstenberger and Wolfgang Schrage, in their book titled *Suffering*, remark:

> One can say that in ancient Israel, property was a "highest good," with which perhaps only "honor" could compare in the scale of social values.[3]

Nowhere in the Old Testament is the idea of shame and humiliation more poignantly expressed than in Phinehas's wife naming of her newly born son Ichabod (no glory) as she lay dying. Israel had just lost many of her soldiers to the Philistines in the battle of Aphek. Furthermore, those same Philistines had captured Israel's Ark of the Covenant and killed the priest Phinehas who had escorted the Ark to the battlefield. Eli, the high priest and the father of Phinehas, died of shock upon hearing all the tragic news. The glory of every married woman was the gift of a son to her husband. But what good is the gift of son to a father who died in disgrace?

> Now his [Eli's] daughter-in-law, the wife of Phinehas, was pregnant, about to give birth. When she heard the news that the ark of God was captured, and that her father-in-law and her husband were dead, she bowed and gave birth, for her labor pains overwhelmed her. As she was about to die, the women attending her said to her, "do not be afraid, for you have borne a son." But she did not answer or give heed. She named the child Ichabod, meaning, "The glory has departed from Israel," because the ark of God had been captured and because of her father-in-law and her husband. She said "The glory has departed from Israel, for the ark of God has been captured." (1 Sam 4:19-22)

Job's numerous remarks on his loss of honor, along with his wealth, confirm Gertstenberger's and Schrage's position as cited above:

Terrors are turned upon me;
my honor is pursued as by the
     wind,
and my prosperity has passed
     away like a cloud. (Job 30:15)

Concerning people in general, Job remarked that he had become a "byword," and that disrespect for him was shown by spitting (Job 17:6). Concerning his friends (though not necessarily his three special visitors), he had become a "laughingstock" (Job 12:4). He declared that even members of his family had become "estranged" from him (Job 19:13). Furthermore, when addressing himself directly to God, he declared that he was "filled with disgrace" (Job 10:15).

In a long speech, recorded in chapters 29 and 30 of the book of Job, Job wishes for the good old days when persons showed him honor and respect. Selections of the speech follow:

"O, that I were as in the months
     of old, . . .
When I went out to the gate of
     the city,
when I took my seat in the
     square,
the young men saw me and
     withdrew,
and the aged rose up and stood;
     the nobles refrained from talking,…
But now they make sport of
     me,
those who are younger than I
whose fathers I would have
     disdained
to set with the dogs of my
     flock. (Job 29:2, 7-9; 30:1)

One of the interesting aspects of Job's attitude toward his former honor and present dishonor is Job's insistence on his deserving of the previous honor because of his proper relationship to God and his fellow human beings. However, the above passage depicts Job's haughtiness as unbecoming to one claiming the right to such honor.

During the course of their history, the descendants of Abraham experienced periods of humiliation such as their enslavement in Egypt. Later they were humiliated by the Philistines at the battle of Aphek, as related above, followed by further shame at the battle of Gilboa with the death and subsequent beheading of King Saul. The author of 1 Samuel depicts the latter humiliation as follows:

> The next day, when the Philistines came to strip the dead, they found Saul and his three sons fallen on Mount Gilboa. They cut off his head, stripped off his armor, and sent messengers throughout the land of the Philistines to carry the good news to the houses of their idols and to the people. They put his armor in the temple of Astarte; and they fastened his body to the wall of Beth-shan. (1 Sam 31:8-10)

The prophets claimed that most of the nationalistic humiliations were instigated by God for Israel's failure to abide by God's covenant. Prophets like Jeremiah hearkened back to former times of humiliation to urge the people of their day to repent of their transgressions. Jeremiah tied his prophecy of doom concerning Jerusalem and its temple to Shiloh and its temple during the Philistine humiliation of Israel in the period of the judges. As we sometimes remark today, "what goes around comes around."

> Go now to my place that was in Shiloh, where I made my name dwell at first, and see what I did to it for the wickedness of my people Israel. And now because you have done all these things, says the LORD, and when I spoke to you persistently, you did not listen, and when I called you, you did not answer, therefore I will do to the house that is called by name, in which you trust, and to the place that I gave to you and to your ancestors, just as I did to Shiloh. And I will cast you out of my sight, just as I cast out all your kinfolk, all the offspring of Ephraim. (Jer 7:12-15)

If the people experienced humiliation or dishonor because of their disobedience to God, the prophets often experienced dishonor at the hands of the Israelite people for their obedience to God. For instance, some like Hosea experienced verbal abuse as the people declared, "the prophet is a fool" (Hos 9:7). For prophets like Amos it was threat of expulsion (Am 7:10-13). For prophets like Jeremiah it was physical threat, whippings, and imprisonment (Jer 20:2; 37:13-16).

In spite of the prophets' courage and willingness to suffer on behalf of God, there was still the feeling of mortification or wounded pride. This was particularly true of Jeremiah who, more than most of the prophets, wore his feelings on his sleeves. On one occasion he begged God to protect him from shame and dismay brought on by his adversaries:

> Let my persecutors be shamed,
> but do not let me be shamed;
> let them be dismayed,
> but do not let me be dismayed;
> bring on them the day of disaster;
> destroy them with double
> destruction! (Jer 17:18)

Jeremiah was aware, however, that all of the blame of his misery could not simply be laid at the doorstep of his enemies. God was responsible in the sense that God was the one who commissioned him and who continually insisted that Jeremiah stay the course, whatever might happen to him. On one occasion, Jeremiah addressed God as follows:

> O LORD, you have enticed me,
> and I was enticed;
> you have overpowered me,
> and you have prevailed.
> I have become a laughingstock all
> day long; (Jer 20:7)

We began this section on the loss of honor with a remark by Gerstenberger and Schrage. We close with another by them:

> An Israelite whose honor was assailed felt that his life was in danger. Honor was something like the psychic skeleton of a man.... If it collapsed, death could seize one.[4]

Disease and Loss of Health

To whatever extent Israel's understanding of economic loss and loss of honor are similar to our modern views, the understanding of the loss of health would be quite dissimilar. This is bound to be so since modern medical concepts, including such views as germ theory, are so different from that of Israel. While the Old Testament presents sin as a prominent cause of economic loss and loss of honor, it makes sin an even more prominent cause of illness than we do. For instance, soon after Israel entered the Sinai wilderness following its escape from Egypt, God spoke these words:

> There the LORD made for them a statute and ordinance and there he put them to the test. He said, "If you will listen carefully to the voice of the LORD your God, and do what is right in his sight, and give heed to his commandments and keep all his statutes, I will not bring upon you any of the diseases that I brought upon the Egyptians; for I am the LORD who heals you." (Exod 15:25-26)

Some forty years later, at the end of the wilderness journey, Moses announced a series of curses designed to destroy the Israelites if they failed to obey God's commandments. Concerning illness, Moses declared: "The LORD will afflict you with consumption, fever, inflammation, with fiery heat, and drought, with blight and mildew" (Deut 28:22).

There are ample Old Testament testimonies of Israel's God afflicting both Gentiles and Israelites. An example of the former relates the affliction that came on the Philistines for capturing and publicly displaying Israel's sacred Ark(1 Sam 5:6-12). As to the nature of the afflictions, two suggestions have been made: dysentery or bubonic plague.[5]

From among the many examples of the testimonies of illness as a means of God's judgment on the Israelites, we choose that of the painful illness and death of King Jehoram of Judah. Jehoram, married to Athaliah, a descendent of Omri of Israel,[6] turned aside from Yahweh and led his people to do likewise. Moreover, in order to solidify his hold on the kingdom, he murdered his brothers and other rivals. So incensed was Elijah by Jehoram's actions that he wrote him a letter denouncing his actions and pronouncing a series of judgments on him, including a horrible disease leading to death (2 Chron 21:12-15).[7]

> A letter came to him from the prophet Elijah, saying: "Thus says the LORD . . . [you] have led Judah and the inhabitants of Jerusalem into unfaithfulness, as the house of Ahab led Israel into unfaithfulness, and because you have also killed your brothers, members of your father's house, who were better than yourself, see the LORD will bring a great plague on your people, your children, your wives, and all your possessions, and you yourself will have a severe sickness with a disease of your bowels, until your bowels come out, day after day, because of your disease." (2 Chron 21:12-15)

The curse of God came to pass in the form of Gentile raids on the kingdom, including the destruction of Jehoram's family, and his agonizing illness and death (2 Chron 21:16-19).

The deteriorating bodily functions, which accompanied the normal aging process, seem to have been taken in stride by most of the Israelites. For instance, the Old Testament narratives remark as a simple matter of fact that when Isaac was old his "eyes were dim" (Gen 27:1) and that when Eli was ninety-eight "his eyes were set" (1 Sam 4:15). When David returned to Jerusalem after the abortive coup by Absalom, he invited a certain aged man by the name of Barzillai to escort him back to Jerusalem. Barzillai graciously declined the king's offer because of his age. He singled out especially the loss of the senses of taste and hearing. Note the narrator's account in the book of 2 Samuel:

> But Barzillai said to the king, "How many years have I still to live, that I should go up with the king to Jerusalem? Today I am eighty years old; can I discern what is pleasant and what is not? Can your servant taste what he eats or what he drinks? Can I still listen to the voice of singing men and singing women?" (2 Sam 19:34-35)

If most of the Israelites accepted the physical conditions of old age without too much complaint, the author of Ecclesiastes, who always seemed to march to the beat of a different drummer, did not. The book of Ecclesiastes presents a melancholy figurative description of the failing body in old age. Note the following passage:

> Remember your creator in the days of your youth, before the days of trouble come, and the years draw near when you will say, "I have no pleasure in them"; before the sun and the light of the moon and the stars are darkened and the clouds return with the rain, in the day when the *guards* of the house tremble, and the *strong men* are bent, and the *women who grind* cease working because they are few, and those who look through the *windows* see dimly; when the *doors on the street* are shut, and the sound of the grinding is low, and one rises up at the sound of a bird, and all the daughters of song are brought low; when one is afraid of heights, and terrors are in the road; the *almond tree* blossoms, and the *grasshopper drags* itself along and desire fails; because all must go to their eternal home and the mourners will go about the streets; before the silver cord is snapped, and the golden bowl is broken, and the pitcher is broken at the fountain, and the wheel broken at the cistern, and the dust returns to the earth as it was, and the breath returns to God who gave it. (Eccl 12:1-7) (Italics added)

Each of the italicized symbolic words can be interpreted as follows: (1) "guards," failing arms; (2) "strong men," failing legs; (3) "women who grind," failing teeth; (4) "windows," failing eyes; (5) "door on the street," failing ears; (6) "almond tree," gray hair; (7) "grasshopper drags," failing vitality.[8]

If most Israelites took the bodily failings of age with some sort of acceptance, they did not look upon illness in children in the same fashion. An instructive example is David's attitude toward the illness of his son born to him and Bathsheba:

> The LORD struck the child that Uriah's wife bore to David, and it became very ill. David therefore pleaded with God for the child; David fasted, and went in and lay all night on the ground. The elders of his house stood beside him, urging him to rise from the ground; but he would not, nor did he eat food with them. On the seventh day the child died. (2 Sam 12:15-18)

The book of Kings narrates the stories of the extreme illness (leading to death) of two boys, their distraught mothers, and the ministries to them by the prophets Elijah and Elisha (1 Kgs 17; 2 Kgs 4). It is significant that a later prophet looked forward to the day when no child would have to suffer such extreme illness and no parent would have to suffer such anguish. The prophet remarks:

> No more shall there be in it
> an infant that lives but a
>   few days, . . . (Isa 65:20)

Death and the Loss of Life

Whatever may be the lot of humans concerning poverty, humiliation, and disease, death is sure for all. For some it may come very early in the form of being stillborn or dying in the process of being born, as Job, in his extreme pain, wished had been his case (Job 3). For others, like Moses, it may come very late in life (Deut 34:1ff). For still others it might come at any time as the result of illness, accident, or perhaps murder.

Attendant with the death of a loved one was mourning. The Old Testament narrators may feel that it is sufficient simply and briefly to record the fact of the mourning. Such is the case of Israel's mourning the death of Moses: "The Israelites wept for Moses in the plains of Moab thirty days; then the period of mourning for Moses was ended" (Deut 34:8). On the other hand, another author did not feel that such a short statement was sufficient in expressing David's grief concerning the loss of many Israelites at the hands of the Philistines, especially the death of his friend, Jonathan. The narrator thinks that it is important to tell the reader that David composed a funeral dirge and that he commanded it to be taught to the Israelites. Furthermore, the narrator preserves the hymn in written form so that the reader may enter into the bereavement experience. A portion of the hymn follows:

> Your glory, O Israel, lies slain
>   upon your high places!
> How the mighty have fallen . . .
> Saul and Jonathan, beloved and
>   lovely!
> In life and in death they were
>   not divided;
> they were swifter than eagles,
> they were stronger than lions.
> O daughters of Israel, weep over
>   Saul, . . .
> How the mighty have fallen
> in the midst of the battle! (2 Sam 1:19, 23-25)

The grief experienced by David can be felt both by those who believe in a glorious heavenly existence after death and equally by those who believe in no such existence or perhaps only a shadowy one. While we cannot be sure about David's beliefs, he probably believed in a shadowy existence in a place that the Israelites called Sheol. Isaiah 14 is representative of the above view. It is partially cited below:

> The cypresses exult over you [dead tyrant],
> the cedars of Lebanon, saying,
> "Since you were laid low,
> no one comes to cut us down."
> Sheol beneath is stirred up
> to meet you when you come;
> it rouses the shades to greet you, . . .
> All of them will speak
> and say to you:
> "you too have become as weak

as we!
You have become like us! (Isa 14:8-10)

The words "shades" (shadows) and "weak" in the above passage depict an
after-death existence that is lower than anything that the human has experienced while alive. The deceased is said to have fellowship with other shadows
while nothing is said about fellowship with God. There are some passages,
like the one quoted below, that seemingly express the idea of abandonment
by God in Sheol.

I am counted among those who
 go down to the Pit [Sheol];
I am like those that have no
 help,
like those forsaken among the
 dead,
like the slain that lie in the
 grave,
like those whom you remember
 no more,
for they are cut off from your
 hand. (Ps 88:4-5)

Before closing out this section on death, it needs to be pointed out that
there are passages that could be taken to mean that death brings on a cessation of any kind of existence. Such is the following passage from Psalm 39.[9]

"Hear my prayer, O LORD,
and give ear to my cry;
do not hold your peace at my
 tears.
For I am your passing guest,
an alien, like all my forebears.
Turn your gaze away from me,
 that I may smile again,
before I depart and am no
 more." (Ps 39:12-13)

Notes

[1] Bilhah is sometimes referred to as Rachel's maid as in Genesis 30:3; sometimes as Jacob's concubine as in Genesis 35:22; and sometimes as Jacob's wife as in Genesis 37:2.

[2] Erhard S. Gerstenberger and Wolfgang Schrage, *Suffering*, trans. John E. Steely (Nashville: Abingdon Press, 1977), 48.

[3] Ibid., 23.

[4] Ibid., 34.

[5] Max Sussman, "Sickness and Disease," *Anchor Bible Dictionary*, vol. 6 (New York: Doubleday, 1992), 6-15.

[6] There is debate concerning the ancestral heritage of Athaliah. 2 Kings 8:26 and 2 Chronicles 22:2 describe her as a "daughter of Omri." But in 2 Kings 8:18 and 2 Chronicles 21:6, she is called a "daughter of Ahab." Attempts at reconciling these differences have led some scholars to favor the view that Athaliah is the granddaughter of Omri, while others scholars favor describing Athaliah as the sister of Ahab. For further discussion see Winfred Thiel, "Athaliah," *Anchor Bible Dictionary*, vol. 1 (New York: Doubleday, 1992), 511-12.

[7] There is some question whether Elijah could have written the letter since he seems to have died earlier. See 2 Kings 1–3.

[8] See Wayne E. Peterson, "Ecclesiastes," *The Broadman Bible Commentary*, vol. 5 (Nashville: Broadman Press, 1971), 126-27; Sibley W. Towner, "Ecclesiastes," *New Interpreters Bible*, vol. 5 (Nashville: Abingdon Press, 1997), 354-55; Ludwig Koehler, *Old Testament Theology*, trans. A. S. Todd (London: Lutterworth Press, 1953), 42.

[9] See also Job 7:21; Ecclesiastes 3:18-19; 12:7.

12

Living Life with Hope

The Lord blessed the latter days of Job more than his beginning; and he had fourteen thousand sheep, six thousand camels, a thousand yoke of oxen, and a thousand donkeys. He also had seven sons and three daughters . . . . In all the land there were no women so beautiful as Job's daughters; and their father gave them an inheritance along with their brothers . . . . And Job died, old and full of days. (Job 42:12-17)

Surely he [the Servant] has borne our infirmities
and carried our diseases;
yet we accounted him stricken,
struck down by God, and
afflicted.
But he was wounded for our
transgressions,
crushed for our iniquities;
upon him was the punishment that
made us whole,
and by his bruises we are
healed. (Isa 53: 4-5)

Introduction

What was the basis for Israelite hope? We shall briefly consider the following: the universe's natural order, rules and regulations, the human ability to assess the past, and God's promises.

Hope and the Natural Order

In terms of threat or distress, as examined in the previous chapter, there are certain things a person can hope for or expect because they are built into the very order of life. For instance, basic to the order is its consistency. This consistency allows persons, for example, both to prevent disease or to bring cure to illness. The following proverbs are typical:

> A tranquil mind gives life to
>   the flesh,
> but passion makes the bones
>   rot. (Prov 14:30)

> A cheerful heart is a good
>   medicine,
> but a downcast spirit dries up
>   the bones. (Prov 17:22)

Again, take the matter of time, which just in itself can be a source of hope. Note the following encouraging words from the psalmist:

> For his anger is but for a moment;
> his favor is for a lifetime.
> Weeping may linger for the night,
> but joy comes with the
>   morning. (Ps 30:5)

Hope and Rules and Regulations

Simple "rules to live by," as we sometimes say, may be included under the above heading. The book of Proverbs contains hundreds of such sayings, often based on observation. One will suffice: "A soft answer turns away wrath, but a harsh word stirs up anger" (Prov 15:1). Surely numerous Israelites experienced the good life and the hope for its continuance by living according to the simple rules contained in the book of Proverbs and other Wisdom sources.

More formal rules than those in Proverbs are contained in the various Mosaic codes that we examined rather extensively in chapter nine. Not only are Mosaic rules more precise than those of Proverbs, so are the promised blessings and curses relative to those rules. If one hoped for the good life by way of God's blessings, he must obey the rules. Otherwise, he will suffer curse. This is set forth clearly in Deuteronomy 28:

> If you will only obey the LORD your God, by diligently observing all his commandments . . . all these blessings shall come upon you . . . .
> Blessed shall you be in the city, and blessed shall you be in the field.
> Blessed shall be the fruit of your womb, the fruit of your ground, and the fruit of your livestock. (Deut 28:1-4)

> But if you will not obey the LORD your God by diligently observing all his commandments . . .
> all these curses shall come upon you . . . .
> Cursed shall you be in the city, and cursed shall you be in the field.
> Cursed shall be your basket and your kneading bowl. (Deut 28:15-17)

Hope and the Ability to Assess the Past

An important ingredient in Israelite hope was the ability of both the individual Israelite and the community to assess the past properly. For instance, Job (though probably not an Israelite) had difficulty finding even a small ray of hope in his illness. However, he was aware of his former good life and he was convinced that he had been true to humanity and to God. Whatever hope he had, at least it had to begin with his understanding of his past.

The senior author of this work remembers a time many years ago when he went to a friend for advice and consolation during a difficult period in his life. The friend reminded the author that he seemingly had forgotten how God had walked with him earlier in a similar situation. *Hope is often bound-up in memory.*

Like individuals, the people of Israel, in times of distress, needed to remember the great days of their ancestors: for instance, the times of the Patriarchs, Moses, and David. Second Isaiah (prophet of the exile) encouraged his people in exile to look to Abraham and Sarah, whom God had blessed, and to David, who received from God an everlasting covenant (Isa 51:2, 55:3). The Israelites found great hope in singing praises to God for his salvation from Egypt. Psalm 136 is a paean of praise recited (or sung) antiphonally by a leader and congregation. The following lines are a sample:

> O give thanks to the LORD, for he
>   is good,
> for his steadfast love endures

> forever . . . .
> but [the LORD] overthrew Pharaoh and his
>   army in the Red Sea,
> for his steadfast love endures
>   forever; . . . (Ps 136:1, 15)

Hope and God's Promises

Scattered throughout the Old Testament are promises of God that serve as grounds for hope. Concerning general provisions for human needs is God's first recorded promise to humanity:

> God blessed them, and God said to them, "Be faithful and multiply, and fill the earth and subdue it; and have dominion over the fish of the sea and over the birds of the air and over every living thing that moves upon the earth." God said, "See, I have given you every plant yielding seed that is upon the face of all the earth, and every tree with seed in its fruit; you shall have them for food." (Gen 1:28-29)

A later promise gave humanity a similar reason to hope:

> [T]he LORD said . . .
> As long as the earth endures,
> seed time and harvest, cold and
>   heat,
> summer and winter, day and
>   night,
> shall not cease. (Gen 8:21-22)

There are also promises of God related to humanity's penchant to sin. For instance, God promises Adam and Eve and their descendants that they will not be helpless in the presence of evil's temptations (Gen 3:15). One of the most gripping and encouraging Old Testament promises is the following recorded in 2 Chronicles:

> If my people who are called by my name humble themselves, pray, seek my face, and turn from their wicked ways, then I will hear from heaven, and will forgive their sin and heal their land. (2 Chron 7:14)

Hope for the Israelite Individual

Hope for the Poor

We begin with hope for the poor. There was reason for Israel's poor to hope for something better, if the observations of the seers were heeded, the Mosaic code followed, and the prophetic pronouncements taken to heart. According to the seers, as we saw in the previous chapter, the lazy among the destitute could help themselves by changing their lifestyle. Furthermore, the wealthy could help to ameliorate the situation of the poor rather than making it worse as they so often did (Prov 6:6ff; 22:9,16ff). In chapter nine above we examined in some detail Mosaic regulations dealing with such persons as the poor in general, debt slaves, and widows. It was noted that daily laborers were to be paid daily and that debt slaves were to be given financial freedom after seven years, with a chance to begin anew. Likewise, widows were accorded socially-approved means to improve their station in life through prescribed remarriage. Again, the indigent were to be aided through such provisions as gleaning at harvest time. Finally, the poor were always to be treated fairly in the courts of law.

The prophets declared that the poor's hope for the better depended a great deal on their treatment by the wealthy, especially those in positions of leadership. But alas, as Jeremiah put it, little hope could be expected from them.

> They [wealthy leaders] know no limits in deeds of
>   wickedness;
> they do not judge with justice
> the cause of the orphan, to make
>   it prosper,
> and they do not defend the
> rights of the needy. (Jer 5:28)

Hope for the Diseased

As the Israelites entered the wilderness of Sinai following their escape from Egypt, God promised them that obedience on their part would guarantee that the kinds of diseases that the Egyptians experienced would not befall them. In fact, God insisted: "I am the LORD who heals you" (Exod 15:26). In other words, God desires health rather than disease. Surely if obedience prevents disease, repentance restores health. (Whatever truth there was in such a simple formula, Job had trouble applying it to his own condition. See Job 6.)

The most vocal cries for respite are found in the book of Psalms. In some of these Psalms, if not all, the psalmists are clear that suffering is deserved because of sin. They may feel, however, that suffering has gone on long enough. One of the most poignant and yet uplifting of these psalms is Psalm 102. The psalmist, who seems to be extremely ill, begs God not to take him away at the midpoint of his life. It seems that his days are hastening away like smoke. As for his body, his bones are ready to protrude through his skin. In fact, he remarks: "I am too wasted to eat my bread" (Ps 102:4).

Of great interest and importance is this psalmist's concern — amid his own sickness — for others, including his people, Israel. The psalmist is certain that whatever happens to him, God will care for the "destitute" and even for those "yet unborn." The psalmist puts it this way:

> He will regard the prayer of the
> > destitute,
> and will not despise their
> > prayer.
> Let this be recorded for a
> > generation to come,
> so that a people yet unborn may
> > praise the LORD. (Ps 102:17-18)

Hope for the Dead

From a Christian point of view, the Old Testament concept(s) of an after-death existence was bleak. Seemingly, some Israelites thought that existence ceased at death. On the other hand, most Israelites seemingly felt that existence continued in Sheol (an underground abode) with the vitality of that existence at a very low ebb. (See previous chapter.)

If we picture this latter view as the sky on a dark night, can we discern any flickering stars of hope that offer a better life after death? In an excursus at the end of this chapter we shall examine that dark sky fading away in the bright light of Christian resurrection. In the meantime, we may note that there are some Old Testament passages (Ps 16, 49, 73) that seem to present an after-death existence with the presence of God at least as fulfilling, if not more so, than presently enjoyed by individuals. For instance, the author of Psalm 49 declares that the wicked shall "waste away" in sheol. As for himself:

> But God will ransom my soul
>> from the power of Sheol,
> for he will receive me. (Ps 49:15)

Perhaps it would be too little to say that the above psalmist only refers to God's snatching him away from the edge of the grave to live awhile longer. On the other hand, perhaps it would be too much to declare that the psalmist presents a clear picture of a blessed life with God after death as might be found in later Jewish or Christian writings. Clinton McCann expresses it this way:

> While v. 15 probably does not represent a developed doctrine of resurrection or afterlife, it certainly does...push beyond the normal limits (see also Ps 16:10-11). The Psalmist trusts that nothing, not even death, will finally be able to separate the faithful from God.[1]

If some of the psalmists felt that God was somehow going to provide for them a blessed life beyond the present one, they did not bother to explain how God was going to do this. There are hints by others that God is going to do this by some type of resurrection. We examine one uncertain passage and one with more certainty.

The uncertain passage comes from the book of Job. We hear Job say:

> For I know that my Redeemer
>> lives,
> and that at the last he will
>> stand upon the earth;
> and after my skin has been
>> destroyed,
> then in my flesh I shall see
> God. (Job 19:25-26)

H.H. Rowley remarks that the above passage should not be simply brushed aside by insisting that the passage speaks only of a vindication in this life, nor should it be seen as teaching the resurrection doctrine of a later time. Rowley closes with these words:

> There is no hint here of more than a momentary consciousness of his vindication by the God in whom he trusted, in spite of all his complaint

against him. He seems to me to be reaching out after something more sat-
isfying than the common view, but not yet to have grasped it securely.[2]

According to Rowley, the one "clear and undisputed reference to the resurrection of the dead"[3] is the following from the book of Daniel:

> Many of those who sleep in the dust of the earth shall awake, some to ever-
> lasting life, and some to shame and everlasting contempt. (Dan 12:2)

Hope for the Israelite Community

Pre-exilic Hope

Not only did individual Israelites express hope for a better life, so did the
community of Israel. Such hope might be expressed by the whole community or through one of its leaders. Further, it took on different expressions
across Israel's history. We begin with one such situation, namely Israel's
anguished cry amid her Egyptian bondage. We would like to think that
Israel's cry was addressed to God. However, that does not seem to be the
case.[4] On the other hand, to insist that none of the Israelites hoped that God
would hear their moaning also seems to be going too far. In any case, we are
told that God heard and acted on behalf of his people. Consider and reflect
on the incident as recorded in Exodus:

> After a long time the king of Egypt died. The Israelites groaned under their
> slavery, and cried out. Out of the slavery their cry for help rose up to God.
> God heard their groaning, and God remembered his covenant with
> Abraham, Isaac, and Jacob. God looked upon the Israelites and took notice
> of them (Exod 2:23-25)

Israel later would have other occasions to cry out in times of bondage, *with
her cry often directed to God.* Such was the case during the period of the
Judges when Israel had to submit to a number of her neighbors such as the
Moabites. The author of Judges reports: "But when the Israelites cried to the
LORD, the LORD raised up for them a deliverer, Edud" (Judg 3:15).

On some occasions Israel, rather than crying out to God, decided for
herself how God could save her from bondage. She might, for instance, find
her hope in the Ark of the Covenant as she did during Israel's struggle with
the Philistines at the battle of Aphek. The Ark was escorted by two priest
from the temple at Shiloh to the battlefield. Whatever saving power the Ark

might have at a particular time, it proved to be useless that day. In fact, the Ark was actually captured by the enemy and displayed in its towns as a battle trophy (1 Sam 5).

With the coming of David as king, the Israelites no longer had to experience submission to some other power. At least that was the case until the kingdom of Israel (consisting of the ten northern Israelite tribes following Solomon's death) had to submit to encroachment by and finally complete submission to the Assyrians during the eighth century BC. We might suppose that under these conditions they might cry out to God in repentance for salvation. Based on the account in 2 Kings, seemingly they did not do so. Were they blind to their sinfulness or to their dire situation? More than likely, both (2 Kgs 17). The closest they came to a prayer of repentance and a plea for help was through the prophet, Hosea, who invited his people to join him in such a prayer:

> "Come, let us return to the LORD;
> for it is he who has torn, and he
>   will heal us;
> he has struck down, and he will
>   bind us up.
> After two days he will revive us;
> on the third day he will raise
>   us up,
> that we may live before him." (Hos 6:1-2)

Whatever impact Hosea's plea had on his people it was so ephemeral that God replied:

> Your love is like a morning cloud,
> like the dew that goes
>   away early. (Hos 6:4)

When the Assyrians completely subjected the kingdom of Israel during the eighth century BC, the kingdom of Judah (consisting of two southern Israelite tribes following Solomon's death) retained its identity but as a vassal state. When Judah finally succumbed to a fate similar to that of Israel, it was at the hands of the Babylonians during the sixth century BC.

If Hosea had tried to lead his people to a community act of repentance and a plea for help, Jeremiah was commanded not to do this for the people of Judah during their last days of independence. This command of God left Jeremiah with mixed feelings for at least two reasons. First, he was of the opinion that it was God's nature to change God's announced actions if a people repented. If that were not so, what meaning did his trip to the potter's house have? As Jeremiah watched the potter refashion a misshapen piece of clay, God said to Jeremiah:

> Can I not do with you, O house of Israel, just as this potter has done? says the LORD. Just like the clay in the potter's hand, so are you in my hand, O house of Israel. At one moment I may declare concerning a nation or a kingdom, that I will pluck up and break down and destroy it, but if that nation, concerning which I have spoken, turns from its evil, I will change my mind about the disaster that I intended to bring on it. (Jer 18:6-8)

If Jeremiah believed that it was God's nature to change, it was difficult for him to believe that his people were neither capable of repenting nor had any intention to do so. For instance, when King Zedekiah begged Jeremiah to beseech God on behalf of Judah, Jeremiah had every reason to believe that Zedekiah made his request in sincerity. However, God's reply that the Babylonians were going to destroy Jerusalem, just as God had previously announced, meant that either Zedekiah's request was not sincere or that the situation had deteriorated beyond hope (Jer 37).

In any case, Jeremiah was extremely moved by all that was going on around him: the sinfulness of his people, God's declared intention to punish them severely, and his own inability to change anything. He wished that he might multiply his tears and that he might find some hiding place where he could forget it all:

> O that my head were a spring of
>   water,
> and my eyes a fountain of tears,
> so that I might weep day and
>   night
> for the slain of my people!
> O that I had in the desert
> a traveler's lodging place,
> that I might leave my people
> and go away from them! (Jer 9:1-2)

Hope in and beyond Exile

God might give Jeremiah profuse tears as requested in the above passage, but God would not grant Jeremiah a place of asylum. However, God did do something for Jeremiah that would benefit his people in the long run even if not Jeremiah himself. He gave him a message of hope for his people in exile and their return to Palestine. Of course, the doomed people did not look upon Jeremiah's message as a gift of hope, because in that message he encouraged those already in Babylonia and those who would follow later to make peace with their exilic situation and with their overlords who were responsible for their deportation. In fact, they were so upset that certain of their leaders had Jeremiah imprisoned as a traitor (Jer 37).

When Jeremiah preached both Jerusalem's doom and Jerusalem's hope for the future, he was doing nothing more than obeying the commission given to him by God at the beginning of his prophetic ministry:

> See, today I appoint you over
>   nations and over kingdoms,
> to pluck up and to pull down
> to destroy and to overthrow,
> to build and to plant. (Jer 1:10)

In his book, *Hopeful Imagination: Prophetic Voices in Exile*, Walter Brueggemann assesses the roles played by three prophets — Jeremiah, Ezekiel, and Second Isaiah (prophet of the exile) — to help the Israelites experience hope during the preparation for and the period of the exile and the return to Palestine. Concerning Jeremiah, among other things, he remarks that Jeremiah's message of doom was bathed in his own tears, tears not unlike those of God. But the tears did not sap Jeremiah's vital hope. Rather they only made him stronger as he viewed the new things that God had prepared for Israel. Consider Walter Brueggemann's assessment in his own words:

> *Jeremiah is profoundly a poet of hope.* He remembered his full call, so he focused on the four verbs of 1:10, "to pluck up and tear down, to destroy and overthrow." He helped people relinquish a false world that is under threat from God . . . . [But Jeremiah] remembered that 1:10 also said a word about planting and building. Out of that commission of Jeremiah comes his resilient hope. He was able to speak a true word of hope at the point of genuine nullity.[5]

When we turn from Jeremiah to Ezekiel, we find a prophet who is as convinced as is Jeremiah that God will do a new thing for Israel following the exile. In the vision of the dry bones (Ezek 37:1-14), God explains to Ezekiel that the return to life of the dry bones is symbolic of the Israelite nation's return to Jerusalem. Whereas Jeremiah spoke of God's returning the Israelites to their homeland for their own sake, Ezekiel portrays God doing this as much — perhaps, more so — for the sake of God's good name. Also of interest is the declaration that it is to be through outward ritual cleansing and the gift of a new heart that the Israelites will come to covenantal obedience (Ezek 36–37).[6]

We noted above that Brueggemann credited caring Jeremiah and Jeremiah's caring God with the deep feelings (pathos) that enabled Jeremiah to offer the Israelites the hope they so desperately needed. To what extent Ezekiel understood the meaning of a caring prophet or a caring God, his emphasis was elsewhere: the holiness of God. Ezekiel proclaimed that a holy God would both punish unfaithful Israel and bring her back to Palestine. Or as Brueggemann chooses to put it, it is God's "work of hope":

> After the judgment, when the city [Jerusalem] has fallen, does it follow that God's holiness has finished its work and now withdrawn from the field with nothing left to do? . . . it is evident . . . that the holiness of God is also a constructive force making new life possible.[7]

Whereas Jeremiah had urged the Babylonian exiles to make Babylonia their home in every sense, some two generations later Second Isaiah had to urge the Israelites of his days to give up their houses in Babylonia to return to their true home, namely Palestine. While some of the exiled Israelites were too comfortable to leave Babylonia, others felt such hopelessness that they dared not even contemplate such a move. To the latter, the prophet appealed to their experiences with God as creator and the chief mover in their historical events. Concerning the creator God and their own feelings of hopelessness, he remarked:

> Why do you say, O Jacob,
> and speak, O Israel,
> "My way is hidden from the
>   LORD,
> and my right is disregarded by
>   my God"?

> Have you not known? Have you
>   not heard?
> The LORD is the everlasting God,
> the Creator of the ends of
>   the earth.
> He does not faint or grow weary;
> his understanding is
>   unsearchable.
> He gives power to the faint,
> and strengthens the powerless. (Isa 40:27-29)

As to God, known to them as the chief mover in their historical events, the prophet urged the Israelites to look to such ancestors as Abraham, Sarah, and David:

> Look to Abraham your father
> and to Sarah who bore you;
> for he was but one when I called
>   him,
> but I blessed him and made
>   him many. (Isa 51:2)

> Incline your ear, and come to me;
> listen, so that you may live.
> I will make with you an
>   everlasting covenant,
> my steadfast, sure love for
>   David. (Isa 55:3)

It was the duty of both Jeremiah and Ezekiel to help the people of their generation to accept their planting in Babylonia and, at the same time, promise them that in God's good time they would be replanted in Palestine (Jer 29ff, Ezek 1ff). It became Second Isaiah's duty to report to the people of his generation that God's good time had arrived. The prophet reports that God has commissioned him to do just that.[8]

> Comfort, O comfort my
>   people
> says your God.
> Speak tenderly to Jerusalem,

and cry to her
that she has served her term,
    that her penalty is paid,
that she has received from the
    LORD's hand
double for all her sins. (Isa 40:1-2)

At first there was reluctance on the part of the prophet, and even more reluctance on the part of the people, as we have seen above. It became the duty of the prophet to overcome their reluctance and to prepare them for going home. The prophet called on the people to find strength in their God by activating their memories of God's creative activities and great deeds of the past. This, then, according to Brueggemann, became Second Isaiah's primary contribution to Israel's hopes relative to the exile:

> One may have guessed the poet [Second Isaiah] had other more important things to do [than call on Israel to remember] . . . . [However], the memory makes available to Israel in exile models, paradigms, and concrete references about old impossibilities which linger with power. The tale of Sarah and Abraham thus is told as a memory which continues to be actualized and fulfilled in this time in Israel's life. The power of this memory of impossibility works its transformative, subversive effect in the imagination of the present generation. Clearly only this memory, powerfully and passionately made available, prevents [Israelites from succumbing to a spirit of hopelessness].[9]

Hope and the Day of the Lord

During a time of crisis such as that experienced in the Exile, the Israelites called on God to intervene on their behalf. Some spoke of this time of intervention as the "Day of the Lord (Yahweh)." Sometimes it was referred to as the "Day of the LORD's Wrath" or simply as "That Day." Not only did they pray for salvation and a return to Palestine, they called on God to bring terrible judgment on their enemies. Nowhere is the latter expressed more vividly than in the words of a psalmist in exile:

Remember, O LORD, against the
    Edomites
The day of Jerusalem's fall,
How they said, "Tear it down!

Tear it down!
Down to its foundations!
O daughter Babylon, you
    devastator!
Happy shall they be who pay
    you back
what you have done to us!
Happy shall they be who take
    your little ones
and dash them against the rock!" (Ps 137:7-8)

While prophets such as Amos (Amos 5) thought that on the Day of the LORD judgment would fall on both Israelites and Gentiles, the vast majority of Israelites preferred to believe that the day would bring judgment for Gentiles alone and salvation for themselves. Among the many glorious things that could happen to the Israelites on the Day of the LORD, the following are mentioned: restoration of health, enjoyment of agricultural products, friendly relationships with others, peace between humans and lower creatures, return of Israelites to Palestine, and special witness to the Gentiles:

On that day the deaf shall hear . . . .
The eyes of the blind shall see (Isa 29:18)

He will give rain for the seed with which you sow the ground . . . . On that day your cattle will graze in broad pastures. (Isa 30:23)

I will make for you a covenant on that day with the wild animals, the birds of the air, and the creeping things of the ground; and I will abolish the bow, the sword, and war from the land; and I will make you lie down in safety. (Hos 2:18)

On that day a great trumpet will be blown, and those [Israelites] who were lost in the land of Assyria...will come and worship the LORD on the holy mountain at Jerusalem. (Isa 27:13)

Then the nations that are left all around you shall know that I, the LORD, have rebuilt the ruined places, and replanted that which was desolate; I the LORD have spoken, and I will do it. (Ezek 36:36)

While the glorious things mentioned above might be near at hand, there developed among the Israelites the belief that such glorious things might best be thought of as part of a future golden age that would come at the end of time or maybe beyond time.

One thing of interest in terms of Israel's hope for the future — whether near at hand or far away — was how she viewed this future in terms of the best she knew from the past. James Muilenburg expresses this idea thusly:

> The new age is of course understood in relation to the old, to all the *magnalia* from the creation to David the king. In many contexts, the sacred writers seem to be thinking of a return or repetition of that seminal period of Israel's faith, the Mosaic age. But it is much more than return or repetition. It is magnified, deepened, and more glorious. It is the consummation of what Yahweh had intended in the initiation of his activity in history.[10]

Thus we may say that Israel looked upon the new age in light of the paradise stories of the opening chapters of Genesis and of her own former great days, namely the days of the exodus and the Davidic kingdom. While the future mirrored in these three experiences from the past can be found expressed in various parts of the Old Testament, especially the prophets, past and future are interlocked together in Isaiah 11 as in no other one place. The following selections illustrate how the prophet expresses the future in term of Eden, the exodus, and the David Kingdom:

> The wolf shall live with the lamb,
> the leopard shall lie down with
>   the kid, . . .
> and a little child shall lead them. (Isa 11:6)

> And the LORD will utterly destroy
> the tongue of the sea…
> so there shall be a highway from
>   Assyria
> for the remnant that is left of
>   his people,
> as there was for Israel
> when they came up from the
>   land of Egypt. (Isa 11:15-16)

> A shoot shall come out from
> > the stump of Jesse [David's father],
> and a branch shall grow out of
> > his roots . . .
> but with righteousness he shall
> > judge the poor,
> and decide with equity for the
> meek of the earth; . . . .
> On that day the root of Jesse shall stand as a signal to the peoples; the nations
> shall inquire of him, and his dwelling shall be glorious. (Isa 11:1, 4, 10)

One other feature of the New Age (Day of the Lord) needs to be considered: the matter of leadership and how this leadership relates to the later expressions concerning the concept of Messiah as set forth in post-Old Testament Jewish writings and the New Testament. There is a sense in which God will be the leader (See Isa 40:11; Jer 31:10). God proclaims in the book of Ezekiel:

> I myself will be the shepherd of my sheep, and I will make them lie down,
> . . . I will seek the lost, and I will bring back the strayed, and I will bind up
> the injured, and I will strengthen the weak, but the fat and the strong I will
> destroy. I will feed them with justice. (Ezek 34:15-16)

But later in the same passage we read:

> I will set up over them one shepherd, my servant David, and he shall feed
> them; he shall feed them and be their shepherd. And I, the LORD, will be
> their God, and my servant David shall be prince among them; I the LORD,
> have spoken. (Ezek 34:23-24)

Thus there arose and developed the idea of leadership in terms of an ideal Davidic king. Among the passages that express this idea are those contained in Isaiah 9 and 11 and in Jeremiah 23. Note the following words from the latter chapter:

> The days are surely coming, says the LORD, when I will raise up for David
> a righteous Branch, and he shall reign as king and deal wisely, and shall
> execute justice and righteousness in the land. (Jer 23:5)

However, the leader is not always said to be a Davidic leader. Either more than one type of leader was expected, or else the one leader was visualized in more than one way. For instance, Second Isaiah speaks of such a leader as "servant" (Isa 42:1-4; 49:1-6; 50:4-9; 52:13–53:12).

The evidence in the various passages concerning the identity of the servant — Israel, a remnant of Israel, or an individual — is not clear. For instance, Page H. Kelley, in his commentary on the book of Isaiah, remarks:

> In the first three Servant Songs (42:1-4; 49:1-6; 50:4-9), it is difficult to determine whether the servant is the nation itself or an individual within the nation. In the fourth song [52:13 to 53:12], he is unmistakably an individual, ministering to the nation but distinct from it.[11]

However the reader interprets the identity of the servant, one cannot help but marvel at the description of that great and glorious future for those involved with the servant. For instance, justice for both Israelites and Gentiles shall be established on the earth:

> Here is my servant, whom I
>   uphold,
> my chosen, in whom my soul
>   delights;
> I have put my spirit upon him;
> he will bring forth justice to the
>   nations. (Isa 42:1)

But such justice shall come at a heavy price because the servant shall suffer greatly on behalf of both Israelites and Gentiles:

> Surely he has borne our infirmities
>   and carried our disease;
> yet we accounted him stricken,
> struck down by God, and
>   afflicted.
> But he was wounded for our transgressions,
> crushed for our iniquities;
> upon him was the punishment that
>   made us whole,
> and by his bruises we are
>   healed.

All we like sheep have gone
    astray;
We have all turned to our
    own way,
and the LORD has laid on him
the iniquity of us all. (Isa 53:4-6)

One other "leader" needs to be considered, namely, one designated as "son of man" in the book of Daniel:

As I [Daniel] watched in the night visions,
I saw one like a human being [a son of man]
coming with clouds
    of heaven.
And he came to the Ancient One
and was presented before him.
To him was given dominion
and glory and kingship
that all peoples, nations, and
    languages
should serve him.
His dominion is an everlasting
    dominion
that shall not pass away,
and his kingship is one
that shall never be destroyed. (Dan 7:13-14)

Since the "person" addressed above is interpreted to Daniel by an "angel" as the "holy ones of the Most High" (Dan 7:18), the passage probably refers to the good Israelite remnant. However, since the description of the kingdom to be established in the Daniel passage is similar to the ones considered above in the Davidic and servant passages, ideas in the various passages lend themselves to a possible blending, especially as seen in the post-Old Testament Jewish writings and teachings and in the life and teachings of Jesus. See more below in the excursus dealing with "Jesus as Messiah."

With the following excurses, we find ourselves again, as we did in the paradigm passage of chapter 1, on a road leading westward out of Jerusalem. *Thus we have come full circle.* Both passages speak of Old Testament interpretation and application for the early church. In Acts 8 Philip interprets for a prominent member of the court of the queen of Ethiopia the meaning of the

Suffering Servant of Isaiah 53 and applies that teaching to Christ. Sometime earlier, the same Christ, on the day of his resurrection, "beginning with Moses and all the prophets . . . interpreted to them [two of his followers] the things about himself in all the scriptures" (Luke 24:27). The authors of this modest Old Testament theology hope its modern readers, like those ancient travelers, have found its instruction enlightening and rewarding.

The Old Testament and the Christian concept of Life after Death

Concerning the Old Testament and the Christian concept of life after death, two brief remarks will suffice. First, it is not improper to read the Old Testament through Christian spectacles. A case in point is the King James Version of Psalm 23, especially its closing section which reads:

> Surely goodness and mercy shall follow me all the days of my life: and I will dwell in the house of the LORD for ever. (Ps 23:6)

Concerning these words, Robert L. Cate remarks:

> Unfortunately, this is a mistranslation. The Hebrew literally says, "I shall dwell in the house of the Lord for length of days." All the psalmist was expressing was a confidence that he would be with God as long as he lived. (Note that the New Testament message has clearly given us a full picture of life after death. For the Christian to use this in stating his confidence that God will never abandon him in this life or the next is not incorrect). (232)

Second, in the New Testament the Christian comes to understand that Christians will not only experience a future resurrection through Jesus but that they will experience a spiritual fullness in the present life through Jesus who claims to be resurrection as he remarks to Martha:

> "I am the resurrection and the life. Those who believe in me, even though they die, will live, and everyone who lives and believes in me will never die." (John 11:25-26)

Note

Robert L. Cate, *Old Testament Roots for New Testament Faith* (Nashville: Broadman Press, 1982), 232.

Jesus as Messiah

On the Sunday following his crucifixion, the resurrected Jesus joined incognito the company of two of his distraught followers on the road that led from Jerusalem to Emmaus. Jesus sought to comfort them with selected Old Testament passages. The book of Luke records:

> Then he said to them, "O, how foolish you are, and how slow of heart to believe all the prophets have declared! Was it not necessary that the Messiah should suffer these things and then enter into his glory?" Then beginning with Moses and all the prophets, he interpreted to them the things about himself in all the scriptures. (Luke 24:25-27)

However, his presentation of the scriptural passages did not dispel their sorrow. That only came with his breaking and blessing bread. Luke continues his narrative as follows:

> Then their eyes were opened, and they recognized him; and he vanished from their sight. They said to each other, "Were not our hearts burning within us, while he was talking to us on the road, while he was opening the scriptures to us?" (Luke 24:31-32)

Jesus seems to be a bit hard on these two followers to speak of them as "slow of heart" concerning their failure to grasp the idea of a suffering messiah. However, he was no harder on them than he was earlier on Peter who berated Jesus for even intimating that Jesus, as messiah, must suffer. Jesus bluntly addressed Peter as Satan. (See Matt 16.)

How do we account for this "slowness of heart" on the part of Peter and the other followers of Jesus? For one thing, all of them probably thought of messiah in the sense of military deliverer, which left no room for the idea of suffering. In the Old Testament, the word messiah — which usually means an "anointed one" — generally refers to a king, especially David or one of his dynasty. With the passing of David's dynasty during Judah's exile to Babylonia, the Israelites began to think of God's raising up an ideal king somehow related to David. Moreover, even before this new use, the word had been used in something of a fluid way. For instance, it had been used to refer to the anointed Patriarchs (see Ps 105:15), to refer to an Israelite priest (Lev 4:3), even to refer to a Yahweh-anointed Gentile emperor, namely Cyrus (Isa 45:1). However, by New Testament times, the word messiah was being used mainly as a technical word to refer to an ideal deliverer in the lineage of David.

If the meaning of messiah took on the coloring of the various ideas that developed in Israel's long history, it took on new meaning as seen through the lens of the life and teachings of Jesus. Already early in his public ministry Jesus refused a Davidic-like leadership, with all its splendor, as offered to him by Satan in the wilderness. Jesus increasingly understood that he must forego a Davidic-like splendor while at the same time embracing suffering as seen in Second Isaiah's "Suffering Servant." Luke states:

Then he took the twelve aside and said to them, "See, we are going up to Jerusalem, and everything that is written about the Son of Man by the prophets will be accomplished. For he will be handed over to the Gentiles; and he will be mocked and insulted and spat upon. After they have flogged him, they will kill him, and on the third day he will rise again." But they understood nothing about all these things; in fact, what he said was hidden from them. And they did not grasp what he said. (Luke 18:31-34)

Malcolm Tolbert, commenting on the above passage, remarks:

There is no detailed account in the prophets of a death like the one described in vv. 32-33, nor is there a prediction that there will be a resurrection like the one described in v. 33. How can the experience of Jesus, therefore, be interpreted as a fulfillment of the things *written . . . . . . by the prophets*? The answer is that the prophets speak of two figures who will play a part in the drama of redemption. One is the Suffering Servant of Isaiah; the second is the Son of man of Daniel, along with the King—Messiah of the Psalms and elsewhere. In the experience of Jesus these two figures merge and become one Person. God's Servant is to suffer; this is equated with the cross. He is to rule in glory; this is equated with the resurrection, ascension, and Parousia. This is the way that Jesus fulfills what the prophets declared about the suffering and glory of God's Servant, the Son of Man. (145)

Note

Malcolm O. Tolbert, "Luke," *The Broadman Bible Commentary*, vol. 9 (Nashville: Broadman Press, 1970).

Notes

[1] Clinton McCann, "The Book of Psalms," *New Interpreters Bible*, vol. 4 (Nashville: Abingdon Press, 1996), 877.

[2] H. H. Rowley, *The Faith of Israel: Aspects of Old Testament Thought* (Philadelphia: The Westminster Press, 1956), 165.

[3] Ibid., 167.

[4] Walter Brueggemann, "Exodus," *New Interpreters Bible*, vol. 1 (Nashville: Abingdon Press, 1994), 675ff.

[5] Walter Brueggemann, *Hopeful Imagination: Prophetic Voices in Exile* (Philadelphia: Fortress Press, 1986), 29.

[6] Jeremiah also speaks of a new heart in Jeremiah 31.

[7] Brueggemann, *Hopeful Imagination*, 72.

[8] For this interpretation see Page H. Kelley, "Isaiah," *The Broadman Bible Commentary*, vol. 5 (Nashville: Broadman Press, 1971), 297.

[9] Brueggemann, *Hopeful Imagination*, 114-15.

[10] James Muilengburg, *The Way of Israel: Biblical Faith and Ethics* (New York: Harper Torchbooks, 1961) 135.

[11] Page H. Kelley, "Isaiah," *The Broadman Bible Commentary*, vol. 5 (Nashville: Broadman Press, 1971), 341.

Appendix

The Old Testament

Genesis
Exodus
Leviticus
Numbers
Deuteronomy

Joshua
Judges
Ruth
1 & 2 Samuel
1 & 2 Kings
1 & 2 Chronicles
Ezra
Nehemiah
Esther

Job
Psalms
Proverbs
Ecclesiastes
Song of Solomon

Isaiah	Jonah
Jeremiah	Micah
Ezekiel	Nahum
Lamentations	Habakkuk
Daniel	Zephaniah
Hosea	Haggai
Joel	Zechariah
Amos	Malachi
Obadiah	

The Hebrew Bible

Genesis
Exodus
Leviticus
Numbers
Deuteronomy

Joshua
Judges
Samuel
Kings

Isaiah
Jeremiah
Ezekiel
The Book of the Twelve:

Hosea	Nahum
Joel	Habakkuk
Amos	Zephaniah
Obadiah	Haggai
Jonah	Zechariah
Micah	Malachi

Psalms
Job
Proverbs
Ruth
Song of Solomon
Ecclesiastes
Lamentations
Esther
Daniel
Ezra/Nehemiah
Chronicles

The Apocrypha*

Tobit
Judith
Additions to Esther
Wisdom of Solomon
Ecclesiasticus (or Sirach)
Baruch
The Letter of Jeremiah
Additions to Daniel:
The Prayer of Azariah &
       the Song of the Jews
Susanna
Bel and the Dragon
1 & 2 Maccabees

* The apocryphal books listed are
books found in the Roman
Catholic, Greek, and Slavonic
Bibles.

Author / Subject Index

Scripture Index